Coaching the Spread Offense:
By the Experts

Edited by
Earl Browning

ISBN: 978-1-60679-088-5
Library of Congress Control Number: 2010922221
Cover design: Brenden Murphy
Text design: Brenden Murphy
Front cover photo: Ronald Martinez/Getty Images

Coaches Choice
P.O. Box 1828
Monterey, CA 93942
www.coacheschoice.com

Contents

1

Option Routes in the Spread Passing Game

Mike Bellotti
University of Oregon
2006

Thank you. It is great to be here and have a chance to talk football. When I get the chance to go out and represent the University of Oregon, I get excited.

I was very proud of the way we played this season. In the past, we had not done a good job of focusing and finishing. This year that became our motto. We put emphasis on every thing we did offensively, defensively, and special teams–wise.

We decided to make some changes. We have talked for two years about changing our offense. We decided to change the offense after watching a team on tape against Arizona State. The team was Northwestern. I watched the Arizona State– Northwestern game on tape because we played Arizona State. I knew Northwestern had done a good job in the Big Ten with lesser material than anyone in the league. Watching them move the ball against Arizona State really intrigued me.

This year, we had the fewest sacks allowed in this conference throwing the football. The year before we lead the conference with the most sacks. That really bothered me because the three years before we had been among the leaders in least sacks allowed.

We were number one in pass interceptions, number one in kickoff returns, and number two in turnover margin in the conference. That is the most important statistic.

If you win the turnover margin, you will win football games. We were number two in sacks and pass efficiency. We were number three in scoring defense, scoring offense, and pass offense. Statistics do not win games, but it tells you about achievement.

I started to talk about why we went to the spread offense. I had a quarterback who, in my mind, was a great player. He put up good numbers the year before, but we did not win. We had not put him in a situation to be successful. He was 6'2", 218 pounds, and cowboy-tough. He was strong and an accurate passer, but was not comfortable in the pocket.

We ran a pocket-style offense, with play-action passes and a dropback scheme. It did not do him justice. I felt like he would be better in the shotgun set with more space to operate. That was the main justification for going to the offense. We wanted to match our personnel.

What I will talk about today is option routes in the spread passing attack. Even if you do not run this offense, I think you can incorporate elements from what I am going to talk about into your offense. In the past, we ran option routes to our tight ends, but we ran out of room. Now we have spread out the offense and work into open throwing lanes.

I want to show you some advantages and disadvantages to running this offense. Some of these things may seem obvious. This year, we ran the spread/shotgun and 60 to 70 percent of the time we ran four wideouts. Our tight end could line up in a tight or spread position. That kept us from changing personnel to get into the sets. We had the personnel at tight end to either come inside to block or play in space. Defensive coaches like to match personnel packages and this kept them off balance.

If you spread the field, you force the defense to cover the width and depth of the field. That creates more one-on-one situations in the running game and passing game. The offense gets more RAC opportunities. Those initials stand for "run after catch" in the passing game or "run after contact" in the running game.

The spread/shotgun gives the quarterback a chance to see the blitz coming, or the defense must blitz from a distance. If they blitz from a distance, they cannot get to the quarterback. Otherwise, they have to tip their blitz and give the quarterback time to automatic or adjust the blocking scheme.

The defensive secondary has trouble disguising coverage against a spread offense. To get to their positions they have to move early and tip the coverage to the quarterback. That makes it easier for the quarterback to read the coverage and makes it difficult for the secondary to disguise.

In the shotgun set, the quarterback separates from the line of scrimmage. Immediate pressure takes longer to get to him. We do not have to worry about the A and B gaps, because the quarterback has a five-yard cushion. In that amount of time, he can get rid of the ball.

With this type of offense, there are also disadvantages. You lose your lead back in the power-running game. The lack of a power-running game was one thing that concerned our defensive staff. In spring ball and preseason practice, we ran a two-back power-running game for our defense. That helped our defense work on defending the power game, but also let us work on short yardage.

The eyes of the quarterback must be on the shotgun snap as the ball comes back. That means he loses his ability to read the coverage for a split second. When the quarterback is under center, he can concentrate on reading the defense all the time. The bad snap is a possibility with the long snap. That disrupts the running game as well as the passing game.

The offense leaves you with two openside offensive tackles with no help outside of them. That is a mismatch with a speed-rushing defensive end and an offensive tackle. The way we control that is with the option. That puts the defensive end in a two- or three-way bind. He has to respect the fact that the quarterback can run the ball and has threats inside and outside of him.

The defense can always outnumber the offense, which forces the offense to have answers for the blitz. We do it with the option, throwing hot, and using sight adjustments.

For this offense to be effective, the quarterback has to be a viable ballcarrier. That does not mean he has to be a 4.5 running back. All the quarterback has to do is take advantage of a defensive end that takes a wrong step. The bubble screen, to us, is a long handoff.

Let me cover the splits for our receivers in this set. If the ball is in the center of the field, we want to spread the field (Figure 1-1). The X-receiver takes a maximum split to the bottom of the numbers on one side of the set. The Z-receiver splits to the bottom of the numbers on the other side. The R-receiver splits the difference between the X-receiver and the offensive tackle. The Y-receiver splits six yards from the offensive tackle.

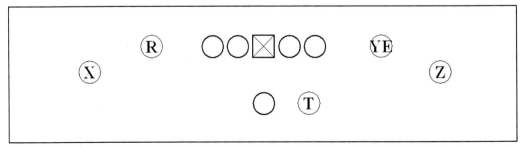

Figure 1-1. Splits double in the middle

In our formation set, the X- and R-receivers are on the same side of the formation in a double set. The Z- and Y-receivers are to the other side of the formation in a double set.

If we are on the hash marks (Figure 1-2), the X-receiver into the boundary side splits to the bottom of the numbers. The R-receiver splits the difference between the X-receiver and the offensive tackle. The Z-receiver splits eight yards outside the openside hash marks. The Y-receiver splits six yards from the offensive tackle.

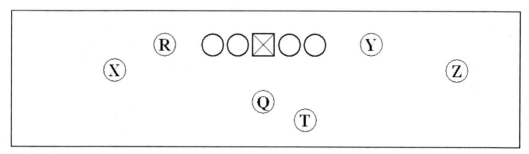

Figure 1-2. Splits double on the hash

You can choose any splits you want. There are factors to consider when you make your split rules. It depends on the arm strength of the quarterback and the distance the defense will split.

The split rules for the triple set with the ball in the middle of the field (Figure 1-3) are as follows. The split of the single receiver is a minimum split four yards from the top of the numbers. To the triple side, the Z-receiver takes a maximum split to the bottom of the numbers. The R-receiver splits four yards outside the wide side hash marks. The Y-receiver splits six yards from the offensive tackle.

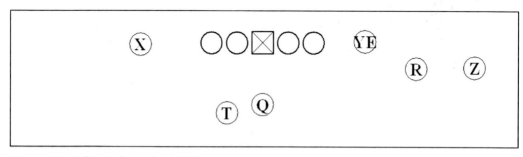

Figure 1-3. Splits triple in the middle

The split rules for the triple set on the hash marks start on the boundary (Figure 1-4). The X-receiver's regular split is two yards inside the top of the numbers. To the triple side, the Z-receiver splits to the top of the numbers. The R-receiver splits two yards outside the hash marks. The Y-receiver splits six yards outside the offensive tackle.

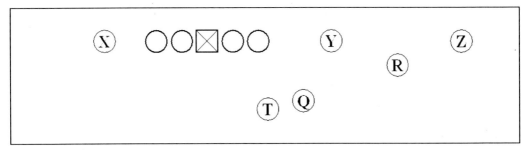

Figure 1-4. Splits triple on the hash

Our receiver coach would tell you our split rules are simple. He would say spread out, give the R-receiver space, and get the hell out of the way. However, the split rules are simple. Just create room for the option or choice runners to put the defender on an island. Give them room and clear the coverage.

Quarterback timing is important because we go from under the center as well as from the shotgun. I want to talk about this for a second because it changes. We practice every day taking snaps from under the center. You have to do both. From under the center, the quarterback takes a five-step drop with a hitch step when he reads zone coverage. The hitch gives the quarterback a gather step against a zone defense. There is no hitch step on a fast break against man coverage.

Obviously, the quarterback has to be aware of the object receiver on any particular play. In the shotgun, the quarterback takes a three-step drop and a hitch if he needs to let the receiver separate from any contact.

It is important to teach drops. Drops are like dance steps, the quarterback can practice at home in the mirror. The quarterback should never look at the feet or think about his drop. That has to be an automatic thought process so the eyes can stay on the defense.

An important part to any passing game is protection. We always assume we will get a six-man box. The five offensive linemen and a tailback make up our 600 protection series. The first diagram is our 620 protection against the over 4-3 defense (Figure 1-5). In the 600 protection, the offensive linemen take the four down defenders, plus the Will linebacker. The back in the backfield has a double read on the Mike and Sam linebackers. If both linebackers blitz, you must have an answer for the quarterback. It can be a hot receiver or a sight adjustment by a receiver.

In the over 4-3, the center and left guard have the shade tackle and Will linebacker. If the defense is an under 4-3, the down four are shifted to the other side. In that case, the center and right guard have the shade tackle and Will linebacker. The tailback double reads and blocks the Mike or Sam linebacker.

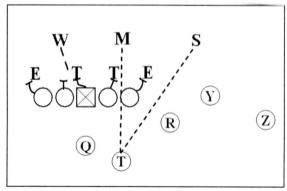

Figure 1-5. 620 protection against over 4-3

In the "3-4 look," we block the same rules. However, there are only three down linemen (Figure 1-6). In this case, we consider the Liz, left outside linebacker, as the fourth down linemen. The right guard and center take the noseguard and Will linebacker. The left guard and tackle take the left defensive end and outside linebacker. Nothing changes for the tailback in the scheme.

If the defense runs a split even front, the scheme is the same (Figure 1-7). The center sets to the left and keys the Will linebacker. The center, left guard, and tackle have those three defenders. They block them using the techniques for twisting stunts and blitzes.

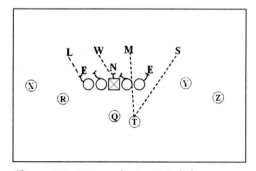

Figure 1-6. 620 against a 3-4 defense

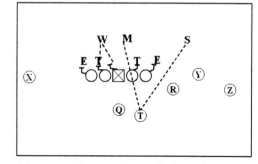

Figure 1-7. 620 against split (even)

Against the bear defense (Figure 1-8), we block five for five. All the offensive linemen are covered and they block the man on them. The tailback double reads the Mike and Sam linebackers and the quarterback is responsible for the Will linebacker. If the defense brings eight, there is a receiver running in the pattern uncovered.

I do not think that is asking anyone to do something they cannot do. The back is off the ball and takes the first blitz that shows from the inside going out. The quarterback, offensive line, and receivers must be on the same page. If the center steps the wrong way, the back misses an inside read, the receiver misses the hot read, or the quarterback misreads the coverage, you end up with a sack. Everyone has to do his job in the protection scheme.

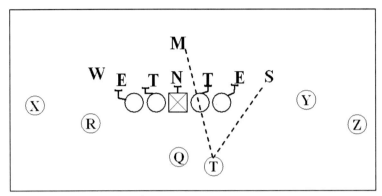

Figure 1-8. 620 against bear

We have a couple more adjustments I want to talk about in the protection game. This is 620 pro-Ralph (Figure 1-9). In this protection, we are gap sliding to the right and passing off stunts.

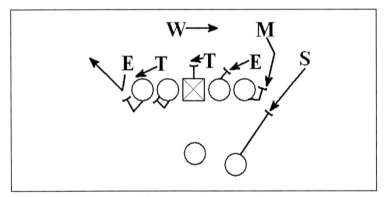

Figure 1-9. 620 pro-Ralph

The other pro protection is 620 pro-out (Figure 1-10). In this protection, we use the slide gap blocking to the left. The backside also blocks out. The tailback is responsible for the backside A gap. That allows us to get a full slide protection to the left without the center coming back for the slanting noseguard. If the back has to block a lineman coming through that gap, he cuts him.

I want to talk about the R-choice from the two-by-two or double set (Figure 1-11). The R-choice route is a play designed to give the R-receiver the option of running a route where he can turn inside or outside at eight to 10 yards against a zone defense. If the defense is man coverage, he stays on the move and runs away from the defender. We build all of the other routes around the R-receiver.

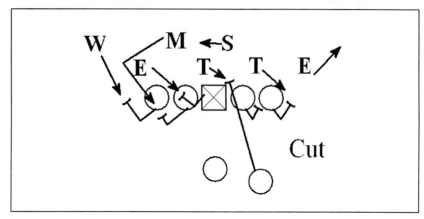

Figure 1-10. 620 pro-out

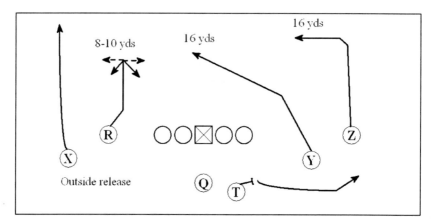

Figure 1-11. R-choice

The R-receiver is the focal point of the route. The quarterback takes his drop either five or three steps, depending on his position under the center or in the shotgun. He reads the object receiver. The tailback goes to his protection scheme and executes a swing pattern if neither linebacker blitzes. The Y-receiver has a close split. He takes the best release he can get and runs a crossing route to a depth of 16 to 18 yards. He is the primary receiver if the coverage squeezes off the choice route.

The X-receiver takes a max split. He outside releases and executes a go route. He looks for the ball in the hole against a cover 2. If the coverage is pressed-man, he has to win that match-up. You must have an X-receiver in this offense that can beat double coverage. The Z-receiver takes a regular split and executes an In route at 16 yards. He is the last resort on this play.

The R-receiver takes a divide split, loses the number 2 defender on the release, and runs a choice route. He runs the pattern at eight to 10 yards and runs away from the defender assigned to cover him.

The quarterback's thought process is to peek at the home run first. If the defense takes away the choice route, the crossing route is the next read. The quarterback has to think deep, choice, cross, and recovery. That means after he reads, he throws the ball away or scrambles. The goal is to get the ball back to the line of scrimmage and not take negative yards.

The next set is a three-by-one set, or triple. We might run the Y-choice with this set (Figure 1-12). The Y-choice is just like the R-choice. The Y-receiver is the object receiver to the three-receiver side. However, the quarterback can select a one-on-one route on the other side to the X-receiver. The quarterback bases his choice on the secondary roll.

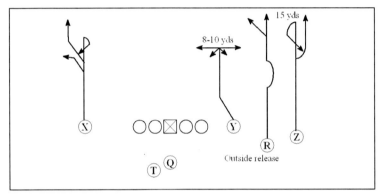

Figure 1-12. Triple-set Y-choice

The tailback sets away from the triple set. He takes his pass protection read and releases if no one comes. He releases at the outside linebacker and spots up inside or drifts to the flat. We call that a spat route. The Y-receiver runs his option route at eight to 10 yards.

The R-receiver has a plus-two split outside the hash mark. He takes an outside release and executes a hash read. The Z-receiver takes a max split and executes a stem route at 15 yards. On the stem, he plants at 15 yards, turns in to the quarterback, and works back outside. If he reads cover 2, he turns his pattern into a fade.

The X-receiver may become the primary receiver on this play. If we get single coverage, the quarterback throws to him. The X-receiver has to win. Our X-receiver this year was Demetrius Williams. He was a 6'4" and 230-pound wide receiver. He was a special receiver and will be the hardest player to replace next year in our entire offense. The X-receiver has a number of things he can do.

He can run the stem route. If he reads cover 2, he converts to a fade. We may have a signal built in for the receiver as to the pattern we want run. Otherwise, with no signal, he runs a stow route. The stow route is a stop-and-go route. We base the stow pattern on the depth of the corner or the retreat of the corner in his drop. If the receiver can beat the corner deep at 10 to 12 yards, he goes. If the corner gives a big cushion, he stops.

The quarterback's first read in the Y-option is the X-receiver. We base the pattern the receiver runs on game planning. He can run a quick hitch, stow, or out. If the defense doubles the X-receiver in any way, the quarterback looks at the Y-receiver with the R-receiver running an outside hash route. That creates room for the Y-receiver to get open.

If the defense doubles the Y-receiver in a cover 3 look, the quarterback shoots for the hash route by the R-receiver. If the defense plays a quarter scheme, the quarterback looks through the option route to the stow route on the outside.

I want to show you one more option route using the empty set. When we go to the empty set, the R-receiver is to the two-receiver side. The tailback becomes the third receiver to the triple side. He aligns wide with a maximum split. We can get to the empty set by aligning in it, motioning to it, or shifting to it. We do all three of those things.

We call this R-option (Figure 1-13). However, since it is run from an empty set, it is slightly different from the R-choice run from the double set. The inside receivers, Y and R, run choice routes at different depths. That gives the quarterback a chance to look at the receivers in the order they come open. The other three receivers run go routes. The quarterback looks for the advantage in match-ups based on the game plan.

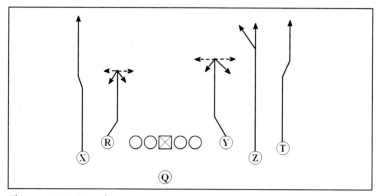

Figure 1-13. R-option empty

The option route receivers have to handle the bumps they get from the linebackers. They must be able to put their foot in the ground and redirect their pattern. They must be quick enough to run away from a strong safety.

The object of the pass is to clear the coverage with the vertical routes and give the choice routes a chance to operate in space. The quarterback reads from the R-option to the Y-option. He goes to R first because it is the shorter route and comes open more quickly.

The quarterback looks for any match-up he thinks is favorable. If all things are equal, the quarterback looks at the R-receiver and lets him work. If the inside linebacker doubles the R-receiver, he goes to the Y-option on the other side.

It is not rocket science. The spread offense is not a quick passing game. However, it allows the quarterback to make quick decisions so he can get rid of the ball. One of the things we talked about when I hired Gary Crowton was the quarterback holding the ball too long. He stood and waited too long. Part of the reason was getting receivers out from backfield alignments. The quarterbacks love this offense.

In addition to this offense improving our offensive production, it helped our defense. After working against this offense in practice, our secondary and linebackers are more comfortable working in space.

2

Quarterback Techniques in the Spread Offense

Mike Bellotti
University of Oregon
2008

I am going to talk about quarterbacks and fundamentals in the spread-option offense. However, before I get to that, I want to talk about teambuilding. I think teambuilding is very important. The togetherness and chemistry of players is a bigger factor than talent level in the success of your program. Everyone has talent; what you do with it is what is important. How that talent plays together makes for a successful team.

One of the things we have done over the years is create team play. Most of the stuff we do is recycled from someone else's ideas. You get your ideas from someone else and put your team mark on it. This positive part motivates gang mentality. The idea is "all for one, and one for all." Players have not changed. They still want structure, discipline, and a chance to compete, but they want to feel like everyone is in this together. One of the things we want our players to understand is what it means to have the opportunity to play football. Playing football is more than what happens on the field. This is the pledge we put before our players: we want them to play with extreme courage. Extreme is a big word today because it resonates with players.

We want them to take responsibility for all their actions and inactions on and off the field. All of us like to talk about the things we have accomplished. However, we do not want to talk about what we fail to do. To evaluate ourselves, we have to take responsibility for what we do or fail to do both on and off the field. The player's commitment to excellence does not stop when he leaves the football field. That applies for the coaches as well as the players.

We want them to play with great confidence and believe in themselves. I am amazed ever year. We get some of the best athletes in the world. They are big, strong, and fast, but they lack confidence. They do not believe they are ready to play. That is a standard rule for every freshman. They all want to know if we are going to "red-shirt" them. I tell them it is up to them as to how quickly they prepare themselves to play.

We want them to play with great intensity. We want to give it everything we have and finish every play in every game. We want no regrets and no excuses. Most of the things in life we regret are things we fail to do or try to do.

Our motto is to finish every play in every game. We want to be in the picture at the end of every play. If you are there, you are playing for your team. If we can outnumber our opponents in that picture, we will probably win the game. If we can get 11 players in the picture, it is an awesome deal. That is why we do pursuit drills every day. We want that pursuit as our defensive mentality.

Coaches and players have to accept each other and treat each other like family. Players have to accept coaching. Too many times, players hear things but they do not really listen. As soon as they feel criticism, they close the ears and do not listen. The coach has to teach communication, and it must go both ways. You must have communication from player to coach, coach to player, player to player, and coach to coach. The players notice coaches' feelings and attitudes.

You must continually push your players to be the best in their athletic and academic lives. You must be a positive role model for your family, university, and community. We want players to respect all races, creeds, and colors. We want them to be honest with others and themselves.

The last item is probably the most important. Enjoy something positive, and make football fun for everyone. When I took the job at Oregon, I said this was something we had to do. How do you make it fun? The way we do it is to practice less and compete more. Make sure you write that down. You have to do a certain amount of drills, but players do not like drills. They like to compete. Put a creative and competitive aspect to everything you do. That goes for everything you do, including conditioning. Reward the winners with prizes and the losers with push-ups. Make football fun for everyone.

Three years ago, we went to the spread offense. We did it for a couple of reasons. I looked at our personnel and decided we had to get better. I felt the type of personnel we had best fit that type of system.

In the PAC-10 this year, we were number one in total offense, scoring, rushing, first downs, and turnover margin. We were number two in red-zone offense and number three in third-down conversion. We lost our quarterback with three games to go in the season. We had to work with a fourth-string player at quarterback and finally with a fifth-team player.

When our first quarterback went down, he was leading the country in the Heisman Trophy competition. When he went down, it took the wind out of our sails. It was not the simple fact that he was a great athlete, but he was the team leader. We went to our #2 quarterback, but he was injured the next week. Our #3 quarterback was already out with an injury, which left us with the fourth-string quarterback.

Our fundamental teaching for the quarterback has never changed. That allowed us to survive the injuries. The fundamentals for the quarterback have not changed; however, we have added the read option to our package. That is what takes the time.

The advantages of the spread offense are to force the defense to cover the width and depth of the field. That is the vogue with things right now. It allows you to spread the defense and not allow them to outnumber you defensively. It keeps the defense from overloading the box. If they overload the box, you have the opportunity to throw the football.

The spread offense gives receivers 1-on-1 opportunities to run after they catch the ball. We refer to that as RAC, which means "run after catch." We run bubble screens and quick screens, which are nothing but long handoffs. We have players who can make the defense miss tackles in space. We create more of those opportunities by spreading the field.

The big concern I have is how to make the offensive line successful. They are the least athletic players on the field. Their match-up with the defensive line is the toughest match-up on the field. By spreading the defense, the defenders must show us where they are going to blitz or blitz from a distance. When they blitz from a distance, they cannot get to us. That becomes extremely important in pass protection.

In the spread offense, it is easier for the quarterback to read the coverage. It also makes it more difficult for the secondary to disguise the coverage because of the spacing of the receivers. Because of the spread, the defender has to declare earlier to get into position. Because the defense has to show their scheme, it gives the offense time to adjust their protection.

In the shotgun, the quarterback is off the line of scrimmage, and it takes immediate pressure longer to get to him. This is a huge advantage from our old offense. We were a pro-style, West Coast, I-formation type of offense. The problem we had in that offense was blitz protection. Blitzes in the A gap forced us to tighten down our splits and made offensive backs take on defensive ends in that protection scheme. The shotgun helps us with the inside gap pressure.

There are disadvantages when running the spread offense. You lose your power running game in short yardage and in the red zone.

The shotgun alignment of the quarterback forces him to keep his eyes on the snap. If he is under the center, he can continually look downfield at the defense. When the quarterback removes himself from under the center, he has to watch the snap. You have to focus hard on the football and soft focus on everything else.

Another disadvantage is the openside offensive tackle has no help on a speed-rushing defensive end. We give him help with the option. Running the option at that defender keeps him honest in his play. It slows the defensive end in his play. If the defender comes hard, it makes an easy read for the quarterback. Because of the threat of the option, it makes the defensive end play softer in his pass rush.

We have five offensive linemen and a running back in our protection scheme. On some occasions, we are empty in the backfield. The defense can always bring one more defender than you can block. You must have an answer for those types of situations. Our answers are option, screens, sight adjustments, and hot patterns. You must have that built into your system. The quarterback and receivers must be on the same page with all their reads.

The quarterback in the spread offense must be a viable ballcarrier. That does not mean he has to be a blazer or sprinter, but he must be agile.

When we look for a potential quarterback recruit, he needs to have some mental characteristics. He must be intelligent, and he must have common sense. He must have football sense. He must have good character, be responsible, and establish good work ethics. One additional point is the quarterback must be coachable.

The number-one thing we look for is intelligence. We want to know if he can listen and translate that into performance on the field. The quarterback has to be a leader. He has to be your coach on the field. He is the person you trust with the football every single play. His job is to make everyone else successful, and when things break down, he has to make a play.

In a quarterback, there are performance characteristics we look for. This player gets on the practice field before everyone else and stays out there until everyone else leaves. He has to be the leader on the field for your football team.

Vision is critical for quarterbacks. They have to focus hard and soft on specific areas. They have to keep their eyes down the field, but must feel the rush without looking at it. If you have a quarterback who looks at the rush, he will never make the plays for you. The quarterback must have repetitive accuracy. He has to throw the ball where the receiver can catch it.

The great quarterbacks are not the ones who have the most talent. They are the ones in the huddle who show leadership and confidence. They get the players on their team to play better than they are.

The release of the football is important. It is a hard thing to teach. Generally, when I get them in college, I cannot change their mechanics. High school coaches have a chance to develop the release, if you start working with them early enough. We still teach the drops, but they are different in the shotgun. We have a one-step, three-step, and a quick five-step drop in the shotgun set.

We have physical characteristics we look for in a quarterback recruit. We look for overall athletic ability. We look for quickness and acceleration. We want to know if he has speed on change of direction. We want our quarterbacks to be 6'3" or taller. We want them to have agility and foot skill. We want arm strength, and we want them to be able to throw the ball with velocity. We want quarterbacks that can run a 4.6 or better 40-yard sprint. We are looking for the quarterback who has good body strength.

The next thing in quarterback fundamentals is the stance. In the stance, it does not matter whether we are in the shotgun or under the center. We want a balanced stance. The feet are about shoulder-width apart with the weight on the inside balls of the feet. We want to bend at the knees with a slight bend at the waist. We want the back erect with the head up. The hands frame the target in both the shotgun and center snap.

The arms should hang down at less than a 45-degree angle to the body with a slight bend in the elbows to allow the quarterback's hands to ride the center. The bend in the arms allows the hands to act as a shock absorber. The eyes are up going from the clock to the keys to hot reads in the coverage. With the quarterback under the center, he has to get his hands in position, keep pressure on the center, and ride the center as the ball is coming up.

In the shotgun stance, we do not change much. The thing that does change is the depth of the quarterback. We still want the balanced comfortable stance. The arms extend with the hands open to give the center a target. We have a hard focus on the ball through the center's legs. The toes of the quarterback are at five, five-and-a-half, or six yards, depending on the play. We want him to scan the secondary into the front. He signals the center that he is ready and brings his eyes back to the hard focus on the ball.

Our pre-practice routine is very important. Every day, we start practice with the quarterbacks under the centers. We have five centers and quarterbacks taking direct snaps. They take the snap going both ways with the centers snapping the ball and moving both ways. After the direct snaps, we go to the shotgun snaps and do the same thing. The center snaps the shotgun snap moving both ways in his stance. We want consistency on the snap whether we are under the center or in the shotgun.

We use a drop step as part of our footwork. The drop step is a cheat step the quarterback can use. He aligns in a balanced stance. If he drop-steps to his right, he drops his left foot four to six inches. He points the toe of his right foot in the direction he is going and pushes off the left foot. That allows the quarterback to turn his hips and get out of the way so an offensive lineman does not step on him. If he pivots off his right foot and leaves his left foot in the ground, the odds of him being stepped on are good. If he goes the other way, he reverses the action. This step allows the quarterback to turn his knee, hip, and lower body in the direction he wants to go. It also eliminates the possibility of a false step toward the line of scrimmage.

This method is a timing sequence for quarterback's drops and the teaching of those drops.

Drops

- One-step drop, shift weight, align shoulders (0.8 set-up) (1.0 to 1.2 delivery)
- Three-step (1 medium, 1 brake, 1 plant = 3 yards depth) (1.0 to 1.2 set-up) (1.5 to 1.8 delivery)
- Five-step (1 medium, 2 long, 1 brake, 1 plant = 7 yards depth) (1.4 to 1.6 set-up) (2.0 to 2.4 delivery)
- Seven-step (1 medium, 2 long, 2 gather, 1 brake, 1 plant = 9 yards depth) (1.8 to 2.0 set-up) (3.0 to 3.4 delivery)
- Sprint (1 medium, 2 depth, 2 turn, 2 attack = 6 yards depth at tackle) (2.0 to 2.2 set-up) (3.0 to 3.4 delivery)
- Screens
- Play-action

You must time your quarterbacks and match that timing up with the type of passing game you have. You actually have to time your quarterback to see how fast they can get to the launch point. You have to time the receivers to see how fast they can get down the field. You have to figure out how to time up the quarterback and receivers to have a timed passing game. In the chart, the medium, brake, and plant are steps in the pass drop. Medium means we take a medium step as opposed to a long step. The brake step keeps the quarterback from falling backwards on the plant step. He has to drop his hips on the next to last step so he can come to balance on the plant step and is ready to throw.

The front shoulder of the quarterback in the drop has to be down. We practice the fundamentals in all our drops. The throwing motion of the quarterback is tremendously important. On the grip of the football, the thumb and longest finger should be opposite each other on the ball. The angle of the ball and the forearm should be a right angle. If the nose of the ball is down, the ball will drop and the quarterback will have trouble with the deep pass and the ball will be tough to catch.

If the nose of the ball is up, the quarterback has a weak grip and the ball will float on him. That is great if he throws the fade, but it is bad to throw curls and most other patterns. We want a right angle between the forearm and ball as the quarterback releases the football.

The second thing is the quarterback alignment and weight transfer to the target. If we throw the ball to a target, we turn our hips to the target and open them into the power position. As we throw the ball, we overframe the target. That means his left foot is outside the target line. His belly button points toward the target. It is easier for a right-handed quarterback to throw the ball to his left than his right. That is why quarterbacks have to work harder throwing the ball to their right.

The platform of power in the throw comes from the lower body and not the arm. You do not create the strength from the arms. It comes from the hips and feet. The feet lead the hips, the hips lead the shoulder, and we release the football. We want the same throwing motion every time we get the chance.

The next fundamental skill is the handoff. It does not matter whether he is under the center or in the shotgun. The first thing he does is seat the ball. He pulls the ball into the pouch or third hand, as we call it, so no one can knock the ball out of his hands. By doing that, the lead back, lineman, or ballcarrier cannot knock the ball out of his hands accidentally.

When we extend the ball to hand it off or fake, we do it in different ways. When you coach this skill, you should do it from the defensive side of the ball. You have to see what the defense sees and whether he is hiding the ball from them. We show the ball with one hand and slide it back, or we keep the ball in the pouch and use the hand in the fake. Make up a contest with the quarterback to see who hides the ball the best. There are many schools of thought about faking. It is what works best for you.

The individual drills we use with the quarterback emphasize quick hips and feet. I always want to be moving and never static or lock the knees. You do not throw the ball with locked knees. The only time the quarterback should be standing straight is when he releases the football. That is why I want maximum height as he throws the ball. Before that, I want a slight bend in the knees and hips because I want the quarterback moving. Whichever way the quarterback throws, he wants to transfer the weight and create the power with the lower body.

We use drills to promote the throwing motion. I am sure most of you have used these drills at one time or another.

Throwing Drills

- One knee/other knee
- Dart (short arm motion)

- Opposite foot forward
- Facing sideways
- Long arm motion
- Movement
- Goalpost
- Garbage cans in the end zone 35 to 45 yards downfield at the sidelines
- Net drills/stationary movement

Let me go over the goalpost drill. I put the receiver on the 17-yard line. The quarterback stands on the other side of the goalpost and must throw the ball over the crossbar on the goalpost to the receiver. I want to get him as close to the crossbar as he can. This helps the quarterback to raise his release point so the ball will turn over as it comes down. This helps the quarterback make the seam throw when we want to catch the ball 18 to 20 yards down the field. The quarterback ends up seven to nine yards behind the goalpost, and the throw is 23 to 25 yards down the field, which takes into account the drop of the quarterback.

I want the ball as close the crossbar as possible. This is a great drill to get the quarterback to elevate his release point and get the trajectory of the ball to turn over. That allows him to throw the four vertical routes to the inside.

The drill of throwing the ball into garbage cans help the quarterback with his touch on fade patterns. We put garbage cans in the corners of the end zone. The quarterback stands on the five-yard line and throws the ball into the cans. That allows the quarterback to practice the time he uses on the fade route into the end zone.

We also place the garbage cans 35 to 45 yards down the field on the outside of the numbers and let him throw the ball into them. That gives the quarterback a three-to five-yard cushion against the sideline to throw the ball. We want the quarterback to use his five-step drop and throw the ball so it lands 35 to 45 yards down the field. You can pick the depth to suit your quarterback's arm strength. We throw many of these types of passes as a timing pattern. The quarterback throws the ball to a spot and the receiver runs to that spot. He does not wait for the receiver to get open. He delivers the ball on time.

When we use the net drill, we have two nets. The nets are 10 feet by 10 feet and have three holes in them. One of the nets has the holes in the high right position, middle, and low left position. The other net is just the opposite. We want the quarterback to catch the ball and release it quickly. We watch all the mechanics of the throw as the quarterback works to the targets in the net. He works on transferring his weight and releasing the ball. The quarterbacks compete to find out which one can release the ball the fastest and who is the most accurate. We work on the quarterback getting rid of the football.

We do the drill as a stationary drill with the quarterback throwing into the holes. We start out with the quarterback throwing to the holes on his own, and later the coach will call the target for him to hit.

We can use a play-action or sprint-out scheme to put the quarterback on the move throwing into the net. There are numerous drills to utilize the net as a teaching tool.

We also use a defender in the middle of the net and make the quarterback react off his movement. He throws to the target opposite the movement of the defender. This helps with the quick passing game and many times is the answer to a blitz. This is a combination drill that trains vision, footwork, ball skills, and decision-making.

We use individual drills to teach the drop. These are drills where the quarterback works on his individual techniques in the drop and not necessarily the throw. In these drills, we teach ball carriage, delivery, depth of drops, and speed drops. In the drills, we can let the quarterback throw the ball or not throw the ball. All the drills require the quarterback to move in his drop and work on his footwork.

When the quarterback does his drop drills, I want him to maintain a passing posture. That means I want to keep the quarterback's hips perpendicular to the line of scrimmage. That allows him to keep his eyes downfield, attack the line, but still throw the ball.

In practice, we use combination drills with the receiver against air and defenders. When we work against air or no defenders, we strive for a 95-percent completion rate. If we cannot complete 95 percent of our passes against air, we have to get a different route, quarterback, or receiver. I mentioned different routes first because you have the talent you have. If the quarterback is not successful at throwing a particular pattern, let him throw the passes he can complete. You must find a way to make the quarterback successful. Sometimes, you cannot replace the quarterback you have.

In the "routes-versus-air drill," we have five quarterbacks and five receivers (Figure 2-1). On the snap of the ball, the receivers run the pattern. The quarterbacks throw the ball to a particular receiver in the route. The quarterbacks rotate, and we run the pattern again. Each time we run the pattern, the quarterback is throwing to a different receiver in the progression in his read. The quarterback with the first read should deliver his ball first. The quarterback with the second read throws second, and each quarterback works through his progression throwing to all five receivers as he rotates his position.

In the drill, each receiver has an opportunity to catch a ball on each play. Each quarterback is working his reads and throwing a ball on each play. There are no defenders in the drill, but you may chose to place stand up dummies in the positions of defenders. This allows you to see zones that may occur in a particular defense. The quarterback simulates the reads on the route, even though he knows to which receiver he throws the ball.

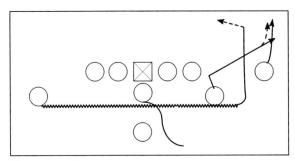

Figure 2-1. Routes on air

The 3-on-2 drill is probably our best drill. In the drill, we have a linebacker, corner, and safety against two receivers. It can be any combination of receivers. It can be tight end and wide receiver or two wide receivers. We do this drill repeatedly because we feel it is a realistic drill. This should be a highly competitive drill. The defense knows the offense is only working one side of the field. That makes the offense work harder to get open. Once we can become successful in that drill, we feel like we can defeat most coverage.

This next statement is tremendously important. Team passing drill is more important than any other drill. When you throw the ball, you can develop a false sense of security in 1-on-1, 3-on-2, half-skeleton, and 7-on-7 drills. You have to be able to throw the ball in the 11-on-11 or team drill. That is the real determining factor. That tells you what type of passing attack you have.

We have specific exercises for the quarterback in addition to basic core strength program. The quarterbacks do what everyone else does in the program plus specific exercises designed for their development.

Specific Exercises

- Triceps extension (above head)
- Bent arm pullovers (bench)
- Straight arm pullovers (ground)
- Wrist rolls and reverse forearm curls
- Wall pulley machines
- Sit-up with full twist (glute-ham developer / Roman Chair)
- Russian twist (glute-ham developer / Roman Chair)
- Medial shoulder rotation (bench)
- Medicine-ball routine

In our practice organization, we devote Tuesday through Thursday to more individual work early in the week and early in the season. We do more teamwork later in the week and later in the season. The first four weeks of practice is pre-season camp.

We have double day practice and an unlimited amount of time spent in practice. For the first four games of the season, we spend two-and-a-half hours maximum time on the practice field. The next four games, our practice time drops to two hours and 15 minutes. The last four games of the season we spend only two hours on the practice field. If we play in a bowl game, we treat it like fall practice and do whatever we need to do.

In practice we warm-up in a 5 to 10 minutes pre-practice period. During that time, we throw, snap, and do individual stretches. We go to team stretch for the next 10 minutes. We follow that period with agilities and drill work for five minutes. Somewhere in those first three periods, we do our Fuji drill. Fuji is our no huddle. Fuji is a great drill, but I cannot tell you what it is. If I told you, I would have to kill you. If you come to our practices, you will find out.

We place the ball on our 23-yard line on the left hash mark. It is our first defense versus the first offense. The coordinators and substitutes are on different sides of the field and they are hooting and yelling. We snap the ball and run a play against the defense. Whatever happens on that play, we move the ball 10 yards. I yell, "Right hash!" Regardless of where the ball ends up, the manager spots the ball at the position. Everyone has to run to the ball and get ready for the next play. We run seven plays down the field.

When we get to the other end of the field, we turn the ball around and put the second teams on the field. We do this for five minutes. In that time, we get 15 plays. We go up and down the field with the fastest tempo we can possibly use. The first time we do this drill, the offensive and defensive lines cannot get down in a stance because they are dying out there on the field. After awhile, they love the drill because it is so competitive. As a head coach, I love it because I get to watch us compete.

In our week of practice, we cover in team drill the specific situations we encounter in the game. In a 20- to 25-minute team period, we cover these situations.

Game Situations

- Normal downs
- Red zone
- Backed up/coming out
- Clutch
- Specials/shots
- Four-minute offense
- Goal line
- Two-point plays
- Short yardage

- Long yardage
- Third downs
- Second-and-long

We try to finish every day with a competitive drill. We do it as a semi-live drill. We do not tackle anyone. We use what we call a reaction tempo, which means we go live but do not tackle the ballcarrier. If we do a second-and-long situation, the first units get two plays, the second units get two plays, and third units get two downs. If anyone gets a first down, the team gets a point. At the end, we want someone doing push-ups for losing the drill. We have them do the number of push-ups I determine.

The key is what we learn from the drill. In a second-and-long situation, we learn two things. It teaches the quarterback decision making. He may have to decide to throw the ball away or scramble to get into a manageable third-down situation. This allows us to get into a two-down strategy of how to avoid the third-and-long situation.

The first video clip is two quarterbacks doing an off-season workout using a 10- to 12-pound medicine ball. In the first scene, they are passing the ball over their heads. In the second shot, they are standing back to back, passing the ball around their bodies. This requires them to twist their torsos to receive the ball and pass it off. This promotes the type of twisting that benefits the hip turn and transfer of weight in the throwing motion.

We practice the option play daily (Figure 2-2). We have a center or manager snapping the ball every time. We have the quarterback and one or two backs in the drill. We practice the snap, ride, and pitch of the option play. We use a two-ball drill for the quarterback. He takes the snap and reads the mesh to give or keep the ball. If the read tells him to give the ball, he gives the ball and continues to run the option. He receives the second ball from the manager as he runs and performs the pitch on the option.

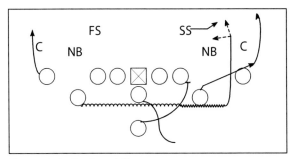

Figure 2-2. Option drill

The quarterback works the handoff, the pitch, and the timing of the play. We may bring one of the backs in motion on the play. The back is responsible for the mesh of the handoff. The quarterback has the read and the pitch. We spend 15 minutes working the option and handoff drill.

We want to protect our quarterbacks. We tell them to think touchdown, first down, out of bounds, or get down. Those are their thoughts on protecting the football.

In addition to the backs, we have our quarterbacks and receivers work the handoff drill because anyone in this offense can be a ballcarrier, blocker, or receiver.

The first clips are of the running game. The first play is an option read play (Figure 2-3). The quarterback keys the end man on the line of scrimmage opposite the zone play. If the defender steps up the field, the quarterback gives the ball to the running back, and we run the zone play. In the read option, the quarterback has to handle one of the down linemen on the front. The five offensive linemen are responsible for the next three defenders or combinations of linebackers and down linemen. They block the next five defenders with a zone-blocking scheme.

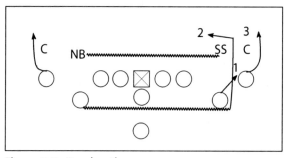

Figure 2-3. Read option

We have worked for two years on what the quarterback should read in this option. We used to read shoulders and the inside knee; now, we read eyes of the defensive end. We do not care what his shoulders do because his eyes will go to the person he is assigned. If he has the dive, his eyes will go to the dive back. If he has the quarterback, his eyes will be on him. We found that was the best way for the quarterback to read the defensive end. We do not get confused as much with this read.

During the season, we wore 12 uniform combinations. We have three helmets, four jerseys, four pants, three colors of socks, and three shoes. I have no clue sometimes which team we are. I let our captains decide what we wear, and they have a lot of fun with it.

I am out of time. I want to thank Nike and the Coach of the Year Clinics for this opportunity. Thank you.

3

Keys to the Spread Offense

Joe Casamento
Christian Brothers Academy (New York)
2005

It is a pleasure to be here. I am going to talk about the spread offense. Before I get started, I want to ask a couple of questions. How man coaches in the audience run the spread offense? How many coaches are thinking about installing the spread offense? How many coaches are trying to figure out how to stop the spread offense?

I have been the head football coach at Christian Brothers for six years. Before that, I was at an inner city school, Henninger High School, which had a great program. We were an I-formation team with great tailbacks. When I got to Christian Brothers Academy, I found out that my backs were slow and my big players were fat and rather un-athletic. I had a great quarterback and a couple of receivers. We tried the Iformation, but it did not work out. As a result, we went to the spread out of desperation.

The spread formation is in vogue now, and everyone seems to be running it. If you think X's and O's are going to do it for you, you had better think again. The big thing is to make sure your players believe in themselves. It is about their attitude, work ethic, and intensity. Do not let them think just because you run the spread offense, you are going to win. If you do, you will eventually find a situation where their X's are stopping your O's, and it will be all over.

ADVANTAGES OF THE SPREAD

Every offense has advantages and disadvantages. We have a winning private school program, and players want to come to our school to play for us. My wide receiver this year had offers from Southern Cal, Miami, Syracuse, and a number of other schools. The kid who played inside of him went to Syracuse last year and caught 103 passes, for 1457 yards, and scored 28 touchdowns. We have athletes now, but when we started in the spread offense, that was not the case. We were slow, but we were smart and very coachable. If you have smart kids, the spread can be a great offense for you.

The spread offense stretches the field both horizontally and vertically. We want the defense to cover the whole field. This offense allows our athletes to play in space. I am going to give you one illustration to which I think you can relate. Put two tackling dummies on the ground, three steps apart. If you make my receiver run through that space and elude your linebacker, the linebacker will make the tackle every time. However, if you put those dummies 15 yards apart, my receiver will win eight out of ten times. In fact, my receiver makes a big play 70 percent of the time. If you have a well-disciplined receiver who can run good routes, he can make plays for you.

The spread offense allows you to run the football without having a great back. We still have not had a great back, but we have one coming. In this offense, you have six defenders in the box. If the quarterback has the ability to run, this offense is very difficult to stop.

The offense allows you to play less athletic offensive linemen effectively. I have a great athlete playing for me. He is 6-2, 310-pounds, squats 600-pounds, and has a 26-inch vertical jump. However, he is polite and nice. He will not knock your head off although we work at it. He is a good pass blocker, because he is a big body. All he has to do is get in the defense's way in order to be effective.

The protection schemes with the spread offense are very simple. We went the entire season one year with only a slide protection. Probably the biggest advantage of running the spread offense is what it does to the defense. This offense will not allow the defense to play their normal scheme. It will not allow them to play the defense they practice all year round.

We give the defense an abnormal look with our sets and motion. They do not see that week in and week out. The quarterbacks and receivers the defense needs to give them a realistic look generally play on the defense. Therefore, the defense never sees a true picture of what they will face.

This offense puts defensive players on all three levels on an island. We can put the defensive end on an island and attack him. We have the ability to chose individuals on the defense and put them on an island.

The spread offense is similar to the two-minute offense. You are never out of the game. We scored 28 points in two minutes and 11 seconds in the state quarterfinals. Our team never thinks they are out of the ball game.

Penalties are easier to overcome from the spread offense. If you got a penalty on a third down and four yards to go in an I formation, the drive was over. I do not think we get as many penalties playing the spread offense.

The type of offense we run tires the defensive front. We have three different tempos to run our offense. We played a great New Rochelle team in the state finals. They had six Division 1 players on their team. At the beginning of the third quarter, you could see that the rush from their defensive line slowed down.

We have an advantage in attitude with this offense. Our players believe they can score on anyone. We have gotten good at what we do. We averaged 49 points a game last year. Our quarterback this year was the first player in America to make All-American in football and to be a McDonald's All-American in basketball. He was the Gatorade Player of the year in football and is up for the Gatorade Player of the Year in basketball. He is a great athlete. I would like to think it was my coaching, but he is tremendously talented.

My players believe they can score on anyone. If I told our team I arranged a scrimmage with Syracuse University, it would not matter to them. They know they can score on them, but would not know how to stop them. They honestly believe they can do that. If we ever get ahead by more than one score, we should never lose the game. We played five playoff games to win the state championship and punted once. I want to attack on offense.

Our defense plays hard, even if we are behind. Our defense knows we can score and are never out of the game. They know we can score and score fast.

DISADVANTAGES OF THE SPREAD

Although the offense is a great offense, there are some concerns. For example, when you do pass drills all the time, the offensive linemen lose their aggressiveness. The difference in this year's team and others I have had, was our ability to run the ball. We spent 20 minutes a day working on the inside run game. Our offensive linemen do not put their hands on the ground. We run block from a two-point stance. We have to get low, come off, and get after people. We have a drill we call "nasty session." We put 14 defenders on defense against 11 on offense in our inside-run period. This is where we teach aggressiveness. Twice a week is not enough for this type of drill. You have to do it every day.

When we are in the spread offense, we never know what type of defense we will face. There are not many spread teams in our area. Therefore, you have no other teams to compare and give us clues as to what the opponent is going to do defensively. We more or less do our scouting on game day. I assign one assistant to watch the defensive ends to see what they do. The coaches in the press box can see the stunts, fronts, and coverages. The offense is so spread out you can see the coverages well. We played a team this year that ran seven different coverages in the first 10 plays. I did not know there were seven different coverages.

The spread offense is less effective as a two-back offense. We have a two-back offense, but we do not have enough time to practice it. We are not as good in that offense as we should be. The scout films we look at are not helpful, because most of the offenses are two-back offenses. The only thing we can tell from scout films is what type of athletes our opponents have playing for them.

With the type of offense we run, it puts our defense on the field too much. I had a defensive coordinator ask me in a game to quit scoring so fast. His defense did not get time to rest between series. This year when we got up in the score, we threw short passes and ran the ball more to let the defense get their legs back under them.

To run this offense, you need a smart quarterback. I have been blessed with great quarterbacks. For six years in a row, I have had the all-state quarterback.

I would like to think that some of the reasons for this string of success is we have a good program that nurtures that type of player. You have to find the right player. My quarterback this year probably could not bench 150 pounds. However, he was a genius on the field. You have to get on the blackboard with him every day. We talk defenses, audibles, progressions, and situations. That is the key. We are a small school and only have 275 boys.

In reality, it is a lot easier to find three quarterbacks and work with them, than it is to find five stud linemen, a great fullback, and tailback every year. If you do not have many athletes, the spread is a great offense.

PROTECTION SCHEMES

In our protection schemes, we are simple. We block big-on-big as the first element of the protection (Figure 3-1). We put our big offensive linemen on their big defensive linemen. On whichever side the back is set, he has responsibility for the linebacker to that side. The center has the linebacker away from the back.

One of the exercises we do to emphasize the time factor in protection involves putting a cone seven yards off the line of scrimmage to mark the spot of the quarterback's drop. I then put a defensive end in his alignment, give him an audible cadence, and see how long it takes him to get to the cone. When we time it, it usually takes about 1.8 - 1.9 seconds. We do the same thing, only this time we make him charge off movement. When we do that, it takes him about 2.1 seconds to get to the quarterback. We put a stopwatch on all our throws in practice. For most of our passes, we deliver the ball in 2.8 seconds.

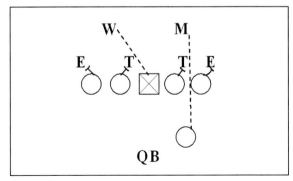

Figure 3-1. Big-on-big protection

I tell our quarterbacks if they do not throw the ball in 2.8 seconds, they deserved to be sacked. How hard is it for an offensive lineman to block a defender for one second? I tell our linemen they have to hold the defense off for four seconds.

I tell the quarterback if he does not throw the ball in 2.8 seconds, it is a sack. In a game, you would be surprised. We make about half our throws in 2.4 seconds. Literally, it is a pitch-and-catch exercise for the passer and receiver.

The protection is a critical part of the attack, but it is not that complicated or difficult. In our slide protection (Figure 3-2), we slide the linemen into a gap-protection scheme and the tailback blocks the 5-technique opposite of the call.

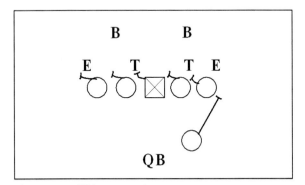

Figure 3-2. Slide protection

This is something that spread coaches need to know. If we want to play-action pass, we give a special call, "Deke." Our numbering system puts our odd numbers to the left and the even numbers to the right. If we call "Deke-26," the line hears "Deke," and automatically slides away from the call. On the 26-play, the line slides to the left.

The last protection scheme is called "Trio" (Figure 3-3). We take our best offensive blocker and single him up on the defensive end. He blocks by himself, and the rest of the offensive line slides away from him. The running back takes the remaining linebacker to that side.

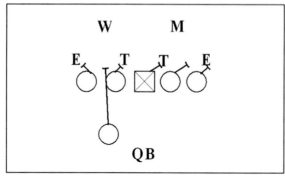

Figure 3-3. Trio protection

The reason we came up with this protection was the 3-3 defense. We ran into it about six years ago. The defense came with two fast defenders off the edge with only the tailback to block them. Our quarterback was running for his life all night.

PLAY CALLING

We have a passing tree we use to call our plays. Table 1 illustrates our tree, which runs from 90 to 99.

90 hitch
91 stop
92 slant
93 out
94 in
95 comeback
96 skinny post
97 post/corner
98 quick fade vs. cover 2
99 fade or go

Table 3-1. Passing tree

We use the terms "inside" and "outside" to determine the order of the patterns. One receiver runs the tree pattern, and the other receiver runs the go pattern. If we call, "inside-93," the inside receiver runs an out pattern, and the outside receiver runs a go route. If we call outside, the pattern reverses. This is our three-step game.

Anytime the quarterback sees a defender out of place in the defense, he can automatic the call. If the defender cheats off the wide slot to get back inside into the box, we audible. When the quarterback calls his cadence, he calls a word and a number. If he calls "Ohio-93," that is an outside pattern. The outside receiver runs an out pattern, and the inside receiver runs a go pattern. If he calls "Indiana-93," the pattern is an inside pattern, and the routes reverse.

We do all this from a no-huddle offense. All the words mean something to the offense. If we call "Rutgers," we run the football. If we call "Loyola," the offense freezes and the defense jumps offside. You must have a freeze play from a rapid tempo and a no-huddle game. The letter "L" is not the only one designated as the freeze call. At times, we call the freeze play and the defense does not jump offside. In that case, the quarterback goes back to the original cadence and calls his play. Because we are no-huddle, the quarterback has time to look to the coach and get the play.

We have some coverage principles that guide our audible and play calling. The first rule is the cover-down principle. Do not let the linebacker align inside your slot receiver and cheat into the box. If the defenders do not align on the receivers, throw to that receiver. The defense must cover all our receivers and be within five yards of him, or we throw the ball to that receiver. The receiver or the quarterback can call "Purple" or "Black," as the automatic throw.

We do not throw hot routes anymore. When teams blitz us, we block the blitzes and try to hit for the home run. When you install this offense, never allow a receiver to go uncovered, and not make a call to his quarterback. Never let the quarterback snap the ball until he checks all four receivers. If there is no cover on the receiver, throw him the ball. The quarterback always keys the safety. If the safety starts to move, he knows someone is coming off the edge.

If the defense has a two-deep look, we do not run up the field on a go route. We run a bubble screen. The slot receiver is usually our best athlete.

PASSING GAME

Our base pass pattern is the four-vertical route (Figure 3-4). We want to throw the four-vertical pattern seven to eight times a game, even if we cannot complete it. It turns the opposing coaches white with fear when we throw vertical. They want to make sure no one gets behind them deep. We run the pattern against any coverage. The quarterback reads inside-out, and moves the safety with his eyes and throws behind him. If the outside receivers read cover 3, they convert their patterns to comebacks at eight yards. The inside receivers widen into the middle. The quarterback looks the safety off and drills the ball to the opposite side.

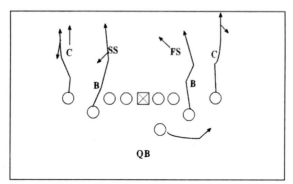

Figure 3-4. Base four verticals

We begin our pass session every day with the base vertical route. We want to make sure we are very proficient with the pass. That is the first thing our opponents work on in practice. If we read cover 2, we run a skinny post by the slot receiver. We run the pattern to both sides, but do not ask our quarterback to read the entire field. I had a great quarterback, but I did not ask him to read the entire field and throw the ball in 2.4 seconds. He picks a side before he snaps the ball.

If the safety jumps the skinny post, the quarterback goes behind him to the tube route of the outside receiver. If the safety's first steps are back or to the outside, the quarterback goes inside to the slot receiver. If the safety freezes, we go behind him to the outside receiver.

You noticed in the diagram, I flared the running back. We block big-on-big and flare the running back to the outside. In most cases, there is no one within 15 yards of him. It is like a hand-off to him. After we repeatedly slide protect, the middle linebacker forgets the back and begins to look for receivers getting behind him in the middle of the field. We get the running back a lot on this play.

There are some things that you can do to make these plays work. Our first 26 pass combinations are state calls. The four-man routes are the names of states. This pattern is "Arizona" (Figure 3-5). The left slot receiver runs a crossing pattern, and the other three receivers run the base route. If I want the other right slot to run the cross, I call "West Arizona." The slot receiver goes up the field five yards and comes across. All he looks for is the hole in the defense.

We do not designate a depth for him because I coach in high school. I do not have a clue where the linebackers are going. You can coach the linebackers all day on their drops, but they seem to drop where they want. The receiver is keying the linebacker wherever he is and runs to the open spot in the coverage. We work high-to-low in the quarterback progressions. The first read is to go on top with the ball if the corners do not bail out in their coverage. If we have three receivers on two-deep, we want to throw deep. Why take a five-yard completion when you can get a 50-yard touchdown?

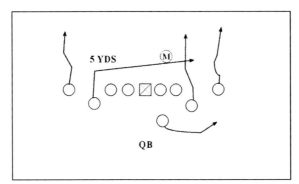

Figure 3-5. Arizona

The second read is the right inside linebacker. If he jumps the tailback running the flare, we have the crossing route by the slot in a big hole in the defense. If the linebacker takes the crossing route, dump the ball to the running back in space. If the quarterback reads man-to-man coverage, he wants to go to the crossing route. The crossing route is the man-beater route in the pattern. We probably run this play seven or eight times a game.

PACKAGING PLAYS

We like to package our plays and love to run motion. If we run motion and do not call a route for anyone, the receivers automatically run the bubble screen. We package our counter trey play with the bubble screen. The team is running "26-counter trey" (Figure 3-6). The quarterback is watching to see how the defense is reacting to the motion. If they are not reacting to the motion, he runs the bubble screen. Too many times, the linebacker covering the slot in motion does not go with the motion or the linebackers do not bump over with the motion. Do not run the counter into an extra defender; throw the bubble screen. You have them outnumbered at the point of attack. We have our best athlete in the slot, so we throw him the ball.

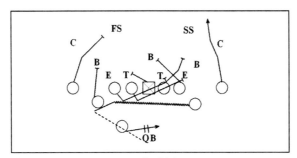

Figure 3-6. Counter trey/bubble screen

The quarterback did not change the play; he goes to another read. The line and back ran the "26-counter trey." That gives a great play action to the screen.

From the same set with the back to the other side, we package the "58-option" with the bubble screen (Figure 3-7). The read for the quarterback is the same. If the linebacker goes with the motion or they bump over, we run the option. If they do not go, we run the bubble screen.

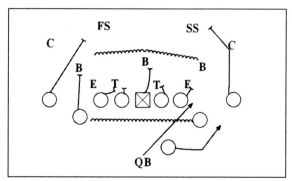

Figure 3-7. Option/bubble screen

We package the bubble screen with five or six plays. People do not realize we read the motion and throw accordingly. They wonder why we keep running the same play

We have many plays. We name them after states, cars, and outlaws. This comes from our outlaw series. We call this play, "Josey Wales." When we started running this, I was convinced it would be a touchdown every time we ran the play (Figure 3-8).

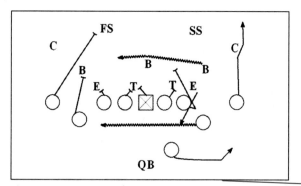

Figure 3-8. Josey Wales

I do a lot of yelling and screaming during practice. My line coach came over and said, "You're a hard man, Josey Wales." That is a line from the Clint Eastwood movie "The Outlaw Josey Wales." The player thought that would be a good name for this play. On the play, the tackle takes one quick step and pins the inside linebacker. The defensive end is on the island. Normally, the defensive end attacks the quarterback and we throw the ball to the flaring running back. We pin the linebacker inside, and the tailback is running in space.

We ran this play in the first game of our regional play, and it went for 40 yards. If the defensive end goes with the flare back, the quarterback runs the ball into the huge gap created by the end leaving. If the outside linebacker does not move with the motion, throw the bubble screen. This is triple option football.

From the same concept, we run "Jessie James" (Figure 3-9). If the defensive end is a great player, we can work on the inside linebacker. We do the same thing we did on Josey Wales, except we let the tackle turn out on the defensive end instead of blocking the linebacker. The quarterback reads the inside linebacker. If he runs with the flare back, the quarterback runs the ball into the B gap. If he does not take the tailback, the quarterback throws the ball to the back.

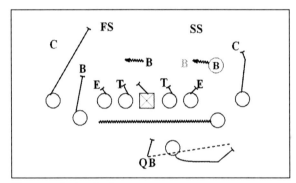

Figure 3-9. Jessie James

We do not have enough highly talented athletes to play at all 11 positions. However, we move them around into all the positions. Our great wide receiver could end up in the tailback position on this play. That draws attention right away by having him in the backfield. It makes people move and cheat to take him away. That makes these plays good runs for the quarterback. We did not run this play as many times as I wanted, because I did not want the quarterback running the ball that much.

ISOLATING PLAYERS

We can isolate the other defensive end and linebacker by running the play the other way. We obviously can isolate any of the secondary defenders. That means the only two defenders we haven't talked about are the inside tackles. I want to beat a team by going against their average players. If they play their best players on one side, I want to go to the other side. Find the player the other team is trying to hide and go at him.

If we play against a team with three stud linebackers, we play sissy ball. We do not take the ball into those linebackers and butt heads with them. We dink the ball around and make them chase it all over the field. More often than not, the coaches will replace those stud run stoppers and put in some smaller defensive-back types to cover the pass. Create the match-up you want and attack them repeatedly.

We have another play we package with the bubble screen and a quick hitch to the one-receiver side. The play is "703-Jail-90." The defense cannot fool around in their secondary and bring a defensive back up into the box. We will not let the defense do that. The "703" is the inside isolation play. If the linebacker moves into the box instead of going with the motion, we run the bubble screen. If they bring the linebacker into the box and rotate the secondary to balance up to the bubble screen, we throw the hitch to the single receiver. If the defense plays honest, we run the isolation.

If we want to go after an inside tackle, we can do it a couple of ways. We call this "Q.B.-Tide" (Figure 3-10). We run this play toward the 3-technique defensive tackle. The right guard makes a call to the left tackle. He tells him where the defensive tackle is playing. If the tackle aligns in a 3-technique on him, he calls 3-technique. The left tackle knows he pulls into the 2-gap. If there is a 1-technique to that side, the guard calls 1-technique and blocks him inside. The center and left guard combo block on the 1-technique. The right tackle sets in a soft pass set on the defensive end to influence him upfield. After the end goes upfield, the tackle releases up on the inside linebacker to his side. The right guard pass sets on the 3-technique and blocks him.

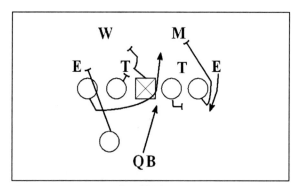

Figure 3-10. Quarterback tide

The left tackle pulls and reads the 3-technique tackle. If the 3-technique charges outside the right guard, the tackle pulls through the hole and cleans up on any linebacker. If both of the linebackers are blocked, he goes for the safety. The tailback back-blocks the left defensive end.

The quarterback gets on the rear end of the tackle and follows him. I tell the tackle to run for a touchdown. I do not want him to try to block the safety. If he runs, the safety will not get around him to tackle the quarterback. If the safety goes one way, the quarterback goes the other. If my tackle can block your safety, you need a new safety, or I should throw the ball at him every time.

While I am showing you how we isolate players, let me show you something else you can do. We can isolate the defensive back on a wide receiver by going to a three-by-one or motioning into a trips set. We give the receiver a choice route. The route we favor is the 95/99 route. That is the comeback-and-go route. The quarterback takes a three-step drop from his shotgun position and reads the hips of the wide receiver. At 14-yards, if the receiver's hips settle, the quarterback throws the ball back to the sideline at 12 yards. If the hips do not settle, the receiver is going deep, and he lets the ball go. We also like to throw the 2/9 and 6/9 combinations.

If we want to isolate the slot receivers in single coverage, we use a technique called "flex" (Figure 3-11). When we call "Flex," the outside receivers align off the ball. The slot receivers move up and align on the line of scrimmage. We bring the outside receiver in motion to the trips side and isolate the slot with the choice route.

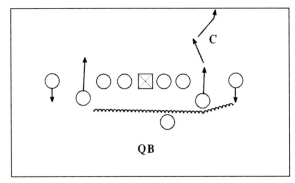

Figure 3-11. Flex

You can isolate the outside and inside receivers. You can isolate all the linebackers. You can isolate any of the defensive ends and tackles. Find the player you want to isolate and make the defensive coaches go crazy.

JO-JO PASS

I promised some of the coaches in this room that I would show this pass. We have never failed to complete it. It matters not what the coverage is, but this is especially effective against cover 2. We coach the quarterback where to throw against cover 3, cover 2, or man coverage. The quarterback is the nerve center of the offense. You have to trust him as much as he trusts you. You cannot get after the quarterback if he makes a bad read. The play is called "Jo-Jo" (Figure 3-12). You can do this with a back in the backfield or run it out of the empty set. I like it with a back in the backfield. If you keep the back in, the defense will go with the defense they called. If you empty the backfield, they may automatically blitz.

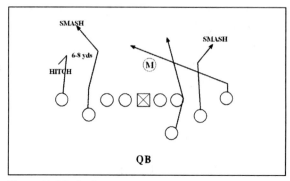

Figure 3-12. Jo-Jo

The inside receivers run a smash route. That is the short corner run at 10-yards, breaking to 20-yards deep. The outside receiver to the right takes one hard step upfield and runs a crossing route. By driving at the corner with the hard step, he should be able to get inside him. The tailback comes out of the backfield and goes down the middle of the field. The stud linebacker who will rip your head off is playing in the middle over the ball. He is the worst pass defender and the one we read. When the inside receivers run the smash routes, the safeties have to take them. That leaves the Mike linebacker to take the tailback running deep down the middle of the field.

As the Mike linebacker vacates the middle, the crossing pattern is coming into the area. If the coverage is man-to-man, the crossing pattern is great because of all the room ahead of the cross. We number our receivers in a right-to-left direction. The number-4 receiver is the left outside receiver. He runs the hitch pattern between six- to- eight yards deep, breaking it back to six-to-four yards in depth. If the receiver reads cover 3, he takes his pattern to eight yards and back to six yards. If he reads cover 2, the pattern is a six-yard back to four-yards pattern.

If the quarterback reads cover 3, he goes to the hitch pattern immediately. Take what the defense gives you. If the secondary is cover 2, the quarterback looks for the vertical routes. The Mike linebacker, in his effort to cover the tailback, turns his back to the quarterback and is oblivious to the crossing pattern in the middle. If the coverage is cover 2, the number-1 receiver can throttle down in the middle and be wide open. In cover 2 man, the quarterback throws to the number-1 receiver coming across. If the coverage is cover 4, he looks for the hitch or the cross.

MIDDLE SCREEN

We have a middle screen we throw (Figure 3-13). We align in the wide double slot and motion the slot back. If the defender does not come with the motion, we throw the bubble screen. If the defender follows the motion back, or they bump the linebacker across, the motion back or number-3 receiver comes up the field and blocks that defender. We try to snap the ball when the motion back gets to the position of a tight-end alignment.

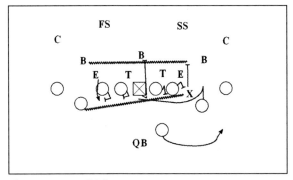

Figure 3-13. Middle screen

The number-2 receiver takes one step back and comes inside behind the center. The left tackle and guard are pass blocking to the outside. The center short-sets and goes up on the backside linebacker. The right guard and right tackle soft set and influence the defender upfield and release on the linebackers. The tailback flares to the right. The quarterback sells the pass and drops the screen inside.

This is a good pass to throw inside the 10-yard line. Inside the 10-yard line, the defense is probably in man coverage. You can run the play either way. After you do it to the defense a couple of times, everyone wants to stop the middle screen. They forget about their responsibility and let the tailback run free.

When you call plays, give your quarterback an option. That gets you into the best play possible. We did not run the middle screen once this year because last year we ran it three times in every game. We put it on the shelf last year, but we will bring it out again after some of our opponent's coaches retire.

25 SEVILLE SLIP

I want to show you one more thing before I stop. We align in the double slot and motion across into the trips set. From that part of our passing game, we can run our three-man game to the trips side of the formation. The protection is a Deke protection, which brings the tailback to the backside to block because the line is sliding right. The things we want to do are tag the play and get the tailback out into the flat. Our huddle call is "space right, Deke-Seville 25 slip" (Figure 3-14). The space is the motion call run to the right. The Deke is the protection sliding away from the 25 call. The Seville is a three-man pattern and the slip is the tailback slipping into the flat. The tailback hits the end and slips into the flat naked. There will not be a defender within 15 yards of him.

The Seville pattern is a 14-yard comeback by the number-1 receiver. The number-2 receiver runs the smash to the short corner, and the number-3 receiver runs the go pattern. The quarterback looks at the Seville, before he comes back to the flat pattern. If he finds an open receiver, he goes to that receiver. The quarterback reads the corner.

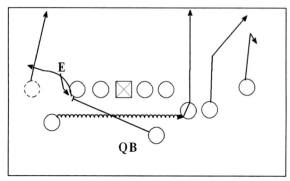

Figure 3-14. 25 Seville slip

The comeback is into the sideline. No linebacker or strong safety can get under the sideline cut. It is a long throw, but our quarterback can make that throw.

In our bubble screen blocking, we want to block the most dangerous man. In our bubble screen, we do block the outside defender. When we come inside to crack on the inside defender, we call that a "Yale-Block." The reason we do not block the outside defender is to set up our "North Call." Anytime we tag any pattern with a "North Call," the receivers all go vertical after they run the route. We call our curl/slide pattern to the two-man side "Kentucky." If we call "North Kentucky," the patterns become a slide-and-up and a curl-and-go.

NORTH YALE

When we run the crack back block on the inside defender from the outside position we call "North Yale" (Figure 3-15). The outside receiver starts in on the crack-back block. The defender reads what he thinks is the bubble screen. He attacks toward the line of scrimmage, and the outside receiver goes north and is wide open down the field. The quarterback fakes the bubble screen and hits the number-1 receiver down the field.

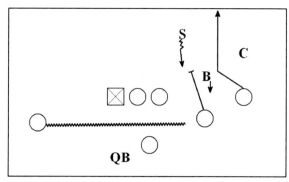

Figure 3-15. North Yale

If the defender is in a press position on the outside receiver, we must block him. We could cross block with the two outside receivers, but we have to block him.

We use formation, motion, shifts, and tags to help confuse the alignment of the defense. When we add these things to the set, it becomes a handful for the defense. We have a bunch set we call "snug." Our trips formation is Rip and Liz. Our double slot formation is a spread look. We also line up within two and three players in the backfield. We have a wishbone set. We use the term "scatter" to shift from one formation to the other. The call is "scatter, snug/spread Arizona." On the cadence, we shift from a bunch set to a spread set and run the Arizona play.

If we add a tag to the call, it means something else. An example of a tag is the name Bower. He is one of our wide receivers. If we call "Bower, scatter/Liz Arizona," we shift from snug to Liz, except the "Bower" call puts that player in the halfback set in the backfield. The tag creates a difference to what the defense expects to see.

If we get into a wishbone set with two wide receivers, we call that "explode." We call "explode to Rip, 8 Seville." That shifts us from the wishbone set to a trips right. The eight is a sprint-out right and the Seville is the pass route. The next time you call "explode-45." We come to the line of scrimmage and run power football up inside, while the defense is waiting for the shift. The assistant coaches come down the sideline and tell me there are five defenders in the box. I keep trying to think of a pass to call, and they tell me, "Just run the damn ball." I always want to throw it.

As I said before, it is a pleasure to be here.

4

The Shotgun Spread Offense

Greg Critchett
Cherry Creek High School (Colorado)
2007

I want to thank the Nike clinic for allowing me to speak here today. A lot goes on in games, and I like to talk with the kids about those things. There are things that are good and things that are bad that happen in a game. How we handle those things is what makes the difference for us.

I want to give a brief history on where I came from. I was at New Mexico Highlands University for 10 years. Then I migrated to Colorado. I have been the head coach, and I have been a coach at a Division II level.

When I was at Highlands, it was a mixture of the good, the bad, and the ugly. I experienced a lot of things in those 10 years. I saw the first back-to-back winning seasons in 25 years. We were co-champs in the RMAC in 1999. The school had some tough times financially and they had to cut funds. They cut out recruiting budgets, coaches' salaries, and finally they cut scholarships by 50 percent.

While at Highlands, I saw the good times before the cuts and I saw the bad times shortly after the cuts. We went through an 0–10 season. I learned a great deal from that experience. I wrote down everything that I did and that reinforced what I had been doing to win in the game of football.

While I was at Highlands, I worked for four different athletic directors, three presidents, and four head coaches. I was the fifth head coach. When I took over, I was the third head coach in three years. Since I have been gone, they have gone through three more athletic directors and two presidents. Everything just keeps cycling over and over. In 1999, we decided to buy a house because we wanted to be there for the long term. They needed some stability, and we were assured we would be allowed to ride out the growing pains for the program. In 2003, I decided I needed to move on and decided to look for a job in Colorado.

For those of you who have interviewed for a head coach, or if it is your goal to be a head coach, there are one or two points that you need to consider. I interviewed twice for the job at Highlands. The problem I have with the interview process arises when you are moving up at a school. You face problems which I call "they problems:"

- The people interviewing you think they know who you are.
- They think they have a clue as to what you are going to do.
- They think they know what they are getting and that there is no honeymoon period.

The plus side of interviewing is the positive side of the process:

- You know the situation.
- You know the personnel.
- You know the way things work or do not work.

When I interviewed for the job at Cherry Creek, it was a different story. They did not know me. I had a booster-club member come up to me and tell me he wanted to write a check for 15 grand. "What do you need to get the program going?" I had never seen that type of response. The process there was very neat. There definitely was a honeymoon at Cherry Creek. They did not know what they were getting. The administration had an idea, but some of the other people did not have a clue.

I interviewed at eight high schools in Colorado before I took the job at Cherry Creek. In some cases, the schools I interviewed with already had their coach picked out. I was interviewed only to validate the situation. They wanted to be able to say we interviewed a person from the college ranks, but we want to go another way.

To be successful, you need a "shot blocker" in the chain of command who will back you and allow you to have a chance at success. It could be the athletic director or the principal. We have parents that will go over the coach's head and call the board of education on issues without going through the proper chain of command. I expect the president or principal to "block shots" for me. Also, I expect the same from the athletic director. I "block shots" for my assistant coaches, and they "block shots" for our players.

```
┌─────────────────────────────────────────┐
│          President / Principal            │
│                   ↓                       │
│            Athletic Director              │
│                   ↓                       │
│               Head Coach                  │
│                   ↓                       │
│         Coach 1, Coach 2, Coach 3         │
│                   ↓                       │
│    Player 1, Player 2, Player 3, Player 4 │
└─────────────────────────────────────────┘
```

The question that must be asked of the administration is this: Are you going to give me a chance to be successful?

In the five years I have been at Cherry Creek High School, we have had only one athletic director and one principal, and we have had three head coaches the last 19 years. The school has only had five head coaches in 52 years.

After about three years, I sat down with the athletic director and he asked me some questions about our program. Then he hit me with this question: "What are your plans for the next year, and three or four years from now?" I had not thought much about that question at the time. Like most coaches, I was trying to survive the next day, the next week, and the next month. I had not thought much beyond that time frame. It made me take a look at the total picture and gave me a better feeling of where I wanted to be at each stage of our program.

One of my weak points is that I have a tendency to try to please people. I try to make things work for everyone. I had to realize that at times we are not going to please everyone, and at times we are not going to please anyone. Even when we went 12–1 and won the state championship, I still had people complaining. "Hey, coach, you changed the uniforms a little." "Hey, coach, you did not play the seniors long enough." People are always going to find something to complain about. Another point is this: Now that we are in the shotgun offense, we have had great success. People complain that we are not under center in the offense, but people who want to find something to complain about will—winning or losing.

I believe in making our kids accountable in terms of what they do outside of the football field. Here are some of the things we have done away from the football field.

One of the first things we did was to put on a Cancer Camp Field Day. We selected special activities they could do. We got great publicity for this. We did not ask the press to be there, but they were. We did get some great publicity as a result of that event. I just wanted the kids to get a feeling of doing something for someone else instead of for themselves.

We have kids from a lot of different backgrounds in our school. We have players whose parents have money, and we have kids that have very little money. This gives us a chance to work with kids in developing leadership.

We have incorporated some special-needs kids to get them involved in our program in some capacity. We have setup a soup kitchen where they can raise money for the team.

We are trying to get our athletes to think beyond themselves. Our managers make a big difference in our program. This brings the kids in contact with people they normally do not connect with.

Let me talk about the football aspects in our program. One of the things we try to do if we are ahead is to slow the game down. We are 33-14 in four years. We have had eight losses with one touchdown or less. We have seven wins when we were behind in the fourth quarter.

We do things in the game that we concentrate on to slow the game down. We want our players to be aware of the clock-management situations. If you are looking for information on clock management, I suggest reaing Homer Smith's book entitled *The Complete Book of Clock Management (3rd edition)*. He has a lot of great ideas concerning how to possibly slow the clock, including

- Use the entire game clock.
- Take as much time as possible disengaging from the previous play.
- Avoid going out-of-bounds.

We can do all of those things to slow the game down. This is something that is painful on our own defensive coordinator. Our goal is to get 16 points on special teams.

Our philosophy on offense is to stretch the field. We like to throw the hitch routes and get the ball to the perimeter. I am going to cover a few plays that we use to accomplish this aspect of our offense. We want to stretch the field from sideline to sideline with the hitch-and-out routes. We want to use the screens, bubble pass, and options to get the ball on the perimeter. We want to stretch the field deep with the fade, corner, and post routes.

We are going to attack the middle of the field with runs based on zone and gap principles. We use the shotgun option plays. The blitz-beaters have been a good thing for us. We will do anything to beat the blitz. We will align for the maximum, we use motion, we throw hot routes, and we sprint away from the blitz. We try to isolate to get a one-on-one situation.

Our opponents think of us as a team that always makes the big play. We have been a team that consumes the clock in 15 or 16 play drives. We can wear on the opponents. We have been a good fourth-quarter team.

WHY THE SHOTGUN

- Type of kids we have
- Haven't had to go toe-to-toe with our kids
- Easier option read (no down-the-line collisions)
- We can see the blitz better.
- It allows more big-on-big concepts in our protection schemes.
- We can adjust to the different types of athletes we get.
- Perimeter throws downhill

The things we see that are changing in football are the following: The old five- and six-man rules do not hold true today. We see a lot of different defenses. We see seven in the box, and then we see them drop out of the box. The thing we have decided is that we must be able to run the ball regardless of the defense. If they have five in the box (or eight in the box), we must be able to run our offense. We see a lot of pressure defenses with the heat coming from the outside edge. These are problems for us.

We like to run four plays that give us a chance to be successful regardless of the defense we face. This is the main focus of the lecture today. We call this our smoke where we run the outside receiver on a hitch route (Figure 4-1). The tailback runs the screen route. The inside receiver is going to block inside for the back getting the screen.

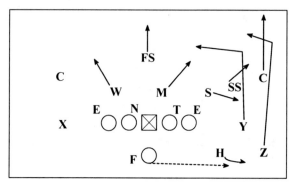

Figure 4-1. Smoke pass routes

This is a very easy play to install into your offense. At first I thought it as a lot of junk, but when you put the play in the offense and work with it, you will see it can be a great play. This is a play that gains three or four yards each time and it is very consistent. At times the play breaks for 10 to 15 yards gained. This is a play we are completing behind the line of scrimmage.

I am not going to cover a lot on the bubble screen, but I will show you a couple of things we do off the bubble screen. You have to hold the block for a long time on the bubble screen. For us, the hitch screen is a lot easier to block for. It is a better percentage play on completions (Figure 4-2). We tell our receiver on the play that we want him to run three quick steps up the field, plant the outside foot, and come back down the stem against the man coverage. He must come back for the ball.

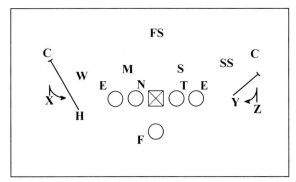

Figure 4-2. Wide receiver screen

If the wide receiver is pressed with man coverage by the corner up tight, he really has to work those first three steps to get the defender to back up a few steps. Then he comes back down the stem for the ball. This has been a big key for our players. If the receiver is lazy coming off the ball, the defender will jump them right away.

The receiver may have to adjust to the ball on the pass. They may have to drift inside, or drop off more if the ball is behind the line of scrimmage. He must gauge his move on the release of the quarterback.

On the block on the inside receiver (or the Y receiver in this case), the closer the corner is on the Z back, the sooner Y has to go to block him. We want him to look at the corner as he comes off the ball. If the corner bails out and drops back, then he can turn back and pick up the most dangerous man inside (Figure 4-3). It could be an outside safety or a linebacker, depending on the defense. This has been a very good play for us.

What we see is the fact that the linemen do not have to hold their blocks for a long time. Some teams pull the onside tackle outside to block on the play. We still block the tackle down inside. We may tag the play sometimes where we have the screen pass on one side and a route on the other side. We have not been called for pass interference on the play as of this year. I think it is a legal play because the ball is behind the line of scrimmage most of the time.

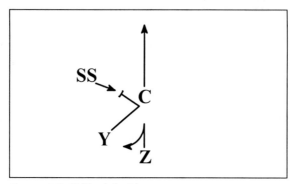

Figure 4-3. Y Block inside

The play we like off the smoke is our fire play. We have the outside receiver run the hitch routes. The inside man, the Y receiver, runs his normal route to block at the point of attack. Just as he gets to the point where he would make contact with the corner, he breaks up the field vertically (Figure 4-4). This has been a great combination route for us. When we see they are biting on the hitch route, we take a shot on the fire.

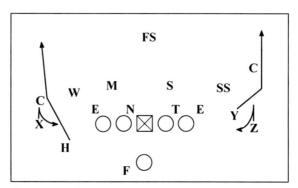

Figure 4-4. Fire route

We have two routes that look like the bubble-screen pass. We run what we call spin, or a speed-in (Figure 4-5). It is a 10- to 12-yard spin move by the two outside receivers toward the middle of the field. We want the outside receiver to break his spin down like he is running a curl route and then he trickles behind the Y receiver. We want to create separation on the route.

The quarterback looks for the first speed-in to open over the line of scrimmage, behind the linebackers. If the linebackers or strong safety wall the first receiver, then the outside speed-in should be open. The bubble route is the dump-off man.

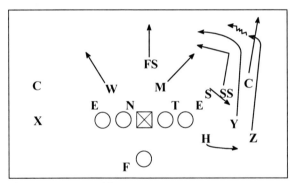

Figure 4-5. Speed-in

We always get a defender jumping the flat receiver. It is usually the outside backer. The receiver who is threatening the flat area should get some movement toward that area. Typically, we get linebackers who are getting a wider split and walling off the receivers. The quarterback is reading the first receiver inside and the second receiver outside. If the defense does a good job and reroutes the first spin by the inside man, we know there is a window between the first receiver and the second receiver.

The only thing we must be careful with is for the quarterback to throw the ball with some zip on it so he does not get it intercepted. He cannot put a lot of air under the ball on the pass.

The other route that we have out of this set is our double post route. We run the double post with the bubble action (Figure 4-6). We threaten the flat and try to get a jump on the defense. The first inside receiver is the Y. He runs the inside post to keep the strong safety occupied. We are trying to open an alley to throw deep to the outside receiver. It is a skinny post route similar to an inside fade route. The quarterback must get the ball to the open receiver. The quarterback looks the safety off toward the inside receiver. Again, the bubble is the dump-off man.

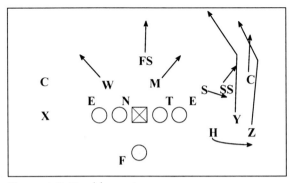

Figure 4-6. Double post

I have some film of these routes that I want to go over with you. If you have questions, feel free to ask.

We did not have time to cover the bubble package, but showing the spin, speed-inside routes have helped us on the bubble plays. We have been able to force the defense to back off to defend the deeper routes on the speed-inside routes.

If you are looking for plays to complement the bubble screen, we have some good plays to set up the bubble screen. We are going to try to get the speed into the middle of the field. As long as it is not a high pass that gets tipped, we feel good about the play.

If we think we are going to get heavy pressure from the defense (or if they are going to blitz on the corners), we can protect with the running backs or the receivers. On the double post, we want to make sure the inside receiver runs toward the middle enough to keep the free safety occupied. It becomes an inside fade route for the outside receiver. That is the shot we really want.

We can tag the backside receiver on a speed-in across the middle. or we can run him on something shallow underneath the deep defenders. With what we like to run screen-wise, these plays complement each other. This gives us more options on the pass from this formation.

We are changing our system to fit the talent we have coming into our program. We look at our talent and try to figure out how we can get the ball to the key players to get the most out of the talent we have. Our definition of a spread offense is one with four wide receivers. You can run three wide receivers with two backs, but it is still the spread concept. We are still running the hitch route, the corner route, and the vertical routes on the outside. Even when we have a double-tight-end set, we can run the double post with a single wide receiver and the tight end. Lately when you hear the spread offense, you think of the shotgun option-type plays.

If you have any other questions, I would be willing to spend time with you. Again, I want to thank Nike for having me at the clinic. I hope you got something out of the lecture.

5

Spread Offense Running Game

Scott Deuschle
Webster-Thomas High School (New York)
2006

Thank you very much for being here today. I appreciate the opportunity to speak with you. I hope you can pick up some techniques that will help your program down the road. Webster High School was a large public school. The school system split the school into two schools, and I had the opportunity to take over the program at Webster-Thomas. It has been an exciting experience.

When I got to the school, I did not know what I was getting into, but it worked out well. My hat is off to my staff sitting in the back of the room. They go beyond what I expect of an assistant coach.

We have had success over the last four years, but we have not gotten over the hump yet. We played in the state finals this year and the state semi-finals last year. In both cases, we lost to the team that won the New York state championship.

I am going to talk about the running game in the spread offense. We installed the spread offense, because in our early years we did not have the offensive linemen we needed to be successful in a conventional offense. We played our first season with sophomores and juniors.

We went to the spread initially to get all of our athletes on the field and it fit our personnel. It has worked out for us. I am a big proponent of running the football. I wanted to run the ball effectively from the spread offense. We use the ground game to set up our passing game. Most coaches think it is the other way around. This past year, we ran the ball 60 percent of the time.

We primarily ran out of the shotgun set. We had an athletic quarterback. With the quarterback as a run threat, it stretched defenses more.

Running the football is a mindset which we developed from day one in our program. We had four receivers on the field, and selling stalk blocking to them was difficult at first. Everyone in your program must be committed to the run for it to be successful.

I want to give you an overview and philosophy of our team before I get into the nuts and bolts of our running game. If you have any questions, just shout them out.

Our receivers are the key to our running game. They have to block, especially the slot receivers. We treat them as offensive linemen. They have an extensive period every day on takeoff and positioning in the stalk block. They come over into the seven-on-seven drills and our air raid drills. Sometimes they take a beating blocking in the running game.

We have to sell the takeoff, getting their hands inside on the chest of the defender. Every time we run the ball, our mindset is to break the play for a touchdown.

In the running game, you want to stretch the field vertically as well as horizontally. By using the spread formation and motion, we create a numbers advantage in the running game.

We use the no-huddle offense as part of the package to control the tempo of the game. If we get up on a team, we want to keep the tempo at a fast pace. We use the armband system of signaling our plays into the game.

We run the shotgun set to use the extra blocker. A large part of the offense is the quarterback reads on the 5 technique or defensive end.

As we break the huddle, the quarterback is reading the safety to see whether the middle of the field is open or closed. We played with a junior quarterback this year. We threw a lot of offense and reads at him and he did a great job. The next thing we read is the number of defenders in the box. If we have a free safety in the middle and six in the box, we can run the ball inside or on the perimeter.

If there are two safeties on the hash, more than likely there will be five in the box. We definitely want to run in that situation. If there is no safety in the middle, we see some kind of blitz. We have designed plays in the game plan that goes with that situation.

We consider the box to be an area two to three yards outside the offensive tackles with a six- to seven-yard depth. That of course depends on where we think the opponent might line up.

The backbone of the perimeter run game is the stalk block of the receivers. Watching the game films from two years ago to last year, we are going in the right direction. However, we are not there yet. I tell our wide receivers that stalk blocking is 80 percent effort and 20 percent technique.

An important part of the stalk block is knowledge. The receiver has to know who to block. We ran into those problems this year. Our slot receiver got confused in some of the defensive looks he faced.

We strive for no penalties in our stalk-blocking scheme. Since the position is so exposed to the referee, it is hard to block defenders in the open field without grabbing them. Holding is the big penalty usually called on offensive receivers. We do not want them to block behind the ball and we do not want them to clip. To avoid penalties it is important for the blocker to be in proper position that aids his techniques.

The wide receiver must have great takeoff. We want his chest over his knees and his knees over his toes. We must take off with a violent hand movement that causes the defensive back to bail out of his coverage. We have to sell the takeoff deep.

The receiver has to read the alignment of the defensive backs. If the defensive back is off the receiver by five yards or more, the receiver pushes the defensive back until the cushion becomes four yards. At that time the receiver breaks down and moves his body into the stalk block.

If the defensive back is less than five yards, the receiver uses a two-yard rule in the execution of the stalk block. If the defensive back plays press coverage, we run him off until he looks back.

Our inside zone play is 11-12 and 13-14. On 11-12, the aiming point of the running back is the inside hip of the offensive guard. The 13-14 play has an aiming point of the inside hip of the offensive tackle. In our play calling, we assign the even-numbered play as plays to the right. The odd-numbered plays go to the left side of the line.

Our offensive line this year was the best by far in the history of our school. They were all two- and three-year starters and made running the football somewhat easier.

The first play is the 12 play run to the right (Figure 5-1). Our double-wide slot is our cat formation. Each offensive line player zone steps together with his right foot. We refer to the zone step as a bucket step. As they step, they lose ground slightly. That puts them on the proper angle with the defender. We work combo blocks for the linebackers in the front. The defense is a 4-2 look inside with all the wide receiver covered with a safety in the middle.

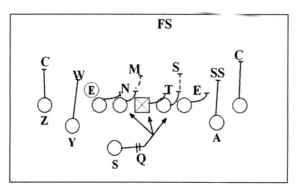

Figure 5-1. Inside zone at 12

The offensive line runs the inside zone-blocking scheme. We combination block the backside stack with the backside offensive guard and tackle. We block the playside stack with the center and playside guard. The playside offensive tackle zone steps to the outside of the defensive end. The backside defensive end is not blocked. The quarterback has to control him. The K-, A-, Y-, and Z-receivers stalk block the men covering them.

The quarterback in the shotgun set drops his back foot to the side of the running back. His eyes go directly to the 5-technique end on the backside. If the end crashes inside down the line, he pulls the ball and goes out the back door. If he gives the ball to the S-back, he carries out his fake to the outside.

The S-back takes an open and a crossover step before he hits downhill at the aiming point. The mesh occurs on the second step and the quarterback pulls the ball or gives it to him on the third step.

He has to be patient and not force the play. The longer the linemen stay on the combo blocks, the better the play works. He reads the defensive linemen. We tell him to cut back one hole for every defender that crosses his face. We want the linebackers to step up and fill the line of scrimmage. That is when the cut-back lanes occur.

We work on our shotgun snaps and steps every day. The quarterback and running back work on the mesh point and we have the quarterback read a defender on every play.

Let me go over the outside zone or stretch play (Figure 5-2). The linemen run their zone-step scheme. The playside is right. The formation is a three-wide-receiver set. The twin receivers are to the backside of the run.

The aiming point for the S-back is the outside hip of the tight end or offensive tackle, depending on the formation. The offensive line has to take care of level one first with each member keeping his eyes up to look for linebacker blitzes. The running back stretches the play toward the boundary looking to get vertical. If the flow by the linebacker is over the top, the back cuts the play back.

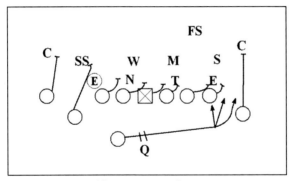

Figure 5-2. Outside Zone Stretch

The quarterback from the shotgun has the same assignment on the 5-technique read. If he is under the center, he hands the ball off and fakes the bootleg.

We ran the option game with our quarterback as the alternative to get on the perimeter. We probably ran this play more than the stretch play.

There are a number of different ways to block this play. We can load the scheme and block the defensive end or read him. Game planning or alignment of the defense will make the decision. We like the option against an aggressive defensive end. We use a man-blocking scheme. In the past, we were fortunate to have fast athletic tackles. That gave us the opportunity to reach the defensive end and option the flat defender.

The option play is 18-19 (Figure 5-3). We can run the play either way or from under the center. If you run the play under the center, the play hits quicker. When you run it from the shotgun, you have the built-in space between the quarterback and the defensive end. When you run option, you hold your breath every time the quarterback runs the ball.

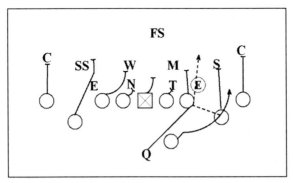

Figure 5-3. Option 18-19

The quarterback secures the snap in the shotgun and gets his eyes on the defensive end. The quarterback has two hands on the ball and makes the defender make a decision. He has to take the quarterback or cover the pitch. The pitch relationship must be good so the defensive end cannot force the quarterback to pitch and tackle the pitchman before he turns the corner.

As the quarterback delivers the ball, he steps at the pitchman. He makes the pitch by extending his arm, rotating the palm of his hand out, and then turning the thumb down. He follows the flight of the ball with his back hip and knee. We want velocity on the ball at the same time. If the pitch is bad or the running back fumbles the ball, the quarterback's momentum is in the direction of the ball. It is possible for him to recover the fumble.

As a change-up, we put the S-back to the other side and ran the option away from his alignment. That kept the defense guessing. They cannot key the alignment of the back as to the flow of the option.

The off-tackle play is 35-36 (Figure 5-4). On this play, we kick-out the defensive end with the backside guard. Defensive ends like to wrong arm on trap blocks. In that case, the guard logs the defensive end and the play goes outside. The backside tackle pulls and reads the block of the offensive guard. If the guard kicks out, he turns inside and blocks the first opposite jersey. If the guard logs, he takes it outside.

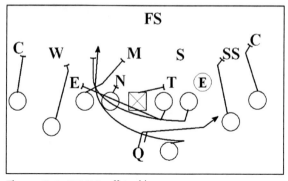

Figure 5-4. 35-36 off tackle

The playside guard, tackle, and center are sealing to the backside. They use combination blocking if there is a stack to that side. As I said before, our tackles were athletic types who pulled extremely well. We could run the play equally to both sides. In some occasions, we do not pull the tackle when we run the off-tackle play. If we got a hard inside charge by a defender aligned over the tackle, we left him in to block that technique.

The S-back takes a counter step away from the hole to let the tackle clear. He gets on the hip of the tackle and reads the block. If the tackle turns inside, he follows him into the hole. If the tackle goes outside, he stays on his hip. The quarterback keys the backside defensive end. If he runs flat down the line, he disconnects and runs out the backside.

We have a quarterback counter. We call the play 4-5 (Figure 5-5). It comes off the inside zone fake to the S-back. It is a tackle trap. The tackle pulls and kicks out the defensive end. If the end attacks the pulling tackle with a wrong-arm technique, the tackle logs him inside and the quarterback takes the play outside.

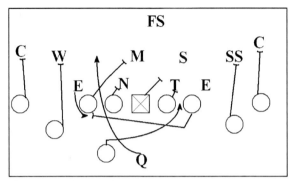

Figure 5-5. Quarterback counter 4-5

We run the play off the inside-zone play and we try to make it look that way with our backside blocking. The S-back runs the inside-zone fake aiming at the outside hip of the guard. If we are effective at running the inside zone, the linebackers will fly across the top with the S-back. If the defensive end closes inside with the offensive tackle pull, the S-back picks him off.

We also run a quarterback draw called 21-22 (Figure 5-6). The S-back is responsible for the playside linebacker. The right guard and tackle invite their blocking assignment to take an outside rush. If they go outside, we push them up the field. If we get an inside move, we take the defender inside and the backs adjust their path. The center and backside guard are responsible for the down lineman to the backside linebacker. The backside tackle kicks out and pass blocks the backside pass rusher.

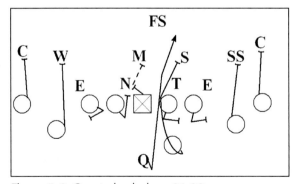

Figure 5-6. Quarterback draw 21-22

We run this play because our quarterback is highly mobile. If we want to run the draw to the S-back, we call 23-24. It is basically the same blocking.

Off the inside-zone play, we run a simple play-action pass to the slot receiver (Figure 5-7). When we find the Mike linebacker flying over the top and trying to get upfield, we run the slot receiver behind him. We tell the receiver he has to get inside the flat defender and watch for the safety dropping down to the inside. He comes inside to a position over the Mike linebacker and looks for the ball. It is a short pass, but if you catch the free safety out of position, it can be a big play.

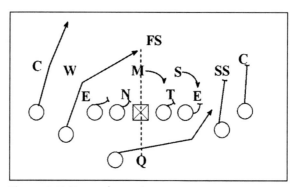

Figure 5-7. Zone play-action pass

Gentlemen, that is all the time I have. If you have any question, I am going to the breakout room and I will answer them there. It was a pleasure for me to address this group. Thank you for the opportunity.

6

Spread Offense:
Three- and Five-Step Timing

Larry Fedora
University of Southern Mississippi
2009

I want to tell you my background so you will know where I am coming from. I was born and raised in College Station, Texas. I played high school and college football in Texas. I started coaching at the high school level just outside of Dallas. From there, I became a G.A. at Baylor University in Waco, Texas, under Grant Teaff. I spent two years there and Coach Teaff retired. When he retired, Chuck Reedy, who was the offensive coordinator, became the head coach. He hired me and I worked there for the next four years.

From there, I had the opportunity to go to the United States Air Force Academy with Fisher DeBerry. Fisher was a tremendous coach, and I learned a lot of football there. We were teaching and coaching great players at the Air Force Academy. It was a great opportunity and I spent two years there.

I got a call from Middle Tennessee State University wanting me to become their offensive coordinator. That was a big move for me. I had a lot of things in my head that I wanted to see work. While I was at Air Force, Coach DeBerry let us travel around and visit with other coaches and programs to get ideas about coaching. To my knowledge, there was only one program in the country at that time running a no-huddle offense. That is what I wanted to do, so I took the job at Middle Tennessee.

I felt that type of offense put the most stress on a defense. When I went to football games in the early 70s with my father, I started to think about this type of offense. Teams would play all afternoon going three yards and a cloud of dust. They played like that until they got desperate or at the end of the half. In those situations, they opened up the offense and made some big plays. I wondered why they did not do that the whole game.

I was told early on that I could not run an offense like that. As I started to build my philosophy, I visited with Rich Rodriguez who was at Tulane University. They were the only team in the country doing it. They were also the only team running a multiple-tempo offense.

When I went to Middle Tennessee, we needed an edge. They were a 1-AA school that was getting ready to make the jump into the 1-A division. We were going to play 1-A competition with 1-AA players. I had to figure out what type of offense to run. The first thought was to run the option like we had at Air Force. At Air Force, we ran every type of option there was. In the two years I was there we won 23 games. We averaged over 40 points a game and were very successful.

Going to Middle Tennessee, I felt we had to run the option or spread it out and throw the ball. We needed some type of edge. We needed something to be different. We did not have the same talent as the people we were going to play. We were going to get our butts beat if we tried to do what everybody else was doing.

When we got there, we did not have a quarterback to run the option. We decided to spread the field and throw the football. The first year we threw the ball, but we could not run the ball. That was probably my fault because I was not sold on running the ball. We won three games and ended up 32nd in the country in offense. That was when I decided that to be successful you have to run the ball out of the spread offense.

In the spread offense, you have to be balanced and be able to run the ball as well as throw it. From Middle Tennessee, I went with Ron Zook at Florida. After that, I went to Oklahoma State with Mike Gundy for three years and, finally, to Southern Miss as head coach.

The reason I am telling you all this background is I want you to understand that this offense is time-tested. This offense has been at four different schools in four different conferences. Over that 10-year period we have averaged about 200 yards rushing and 240 yards passing. It did not matter what school or conference we played in, the offense was successful. It has not been the same offense the entire time. You have to adjust to the personnel you have at each school.

BALANCED OFFENSE

In 2005, I went to Oklahoma State. The first year was terrible. We tried to do exactly the same things we had done at Florida without their personnel. It was a bad year. They wanted to run me out of town. Mike Gundy was a two-back coach and wanted to run the ball. He brought me into OSU to run the spread, and the way we played that first year was terrible. We stuck with what we were doing and adjusted to the personnel we had at Oklahoma State.

If you look at what we did at Middle Tennessee the first year and what we did at Southern Miss last year, you will see the same system. However, there are some changes in the offense. The offense changes with personnel.

In this offense, we want to take what the defense gives. I believe if you can run and throw, the defense cannot stop it all. The defense will tell you they are going to stop the run first. They will put eight or nine defenders in the box if the offense allows them to do it.

I cannot allow them to do that. First of all, I am not smart enough to block all those bodies. We spread the field horizontally and create vertical seams in the defense—that is the key to our success. If the running back gets the ball, there is never going to be more than six defenders in the box. We have five offensive linemen to block five defenders. The quarterback handles one of the defenders and the running back has a chance to move the ball.

If the defense puts more defenders in the box, we are going to throw the ball. I am not the kind of coach who goes into any game with a determination to run the ball for 200 yards. If the defense loads the box, we will throw every down. I go into a football game and take what the defense gives me. If they allow me to rush the football, I will run it.

Balance to me does not mean we go into a game and run the ball 40 times and throw it 40 times. One week, we may rush the ball for 100 yards and throw for 300 yards. The following week, we may rush it for 300 yards and throw it for 100 yards. I do not care how we move the ball, but I want to be able to do both. I do not believe a defense can take both the pass and the run away from you. If they do, they are that much better than you are.

Our base running game consists of the inside zone, outside zone, power, counter, and option. We will always run the inside zone in every game. We may not run all five of those running plays in a game. We may go two games and not run all five of them. However, we have the ability to run them in a game. We work on them every week. These are the plays we hang our hat on. However, the inside zone play has to go for us to be successful. It is the most important run in our offense.

We have to get the ball outside with the outside zone and option. We run the power so we have that smashmouth mentality. Do not get me wrong—we spread it out, but we are going to hammer the football. If you can average 200 yards a game running the football, you are doing something right. You always need some kind of counter. On the play we run, we pull only one blocker.

I am going to talk about one running play before we get into the passes. We run the zone option and it is one of the staples in our running game. This play will be in every game plan we have. The quarterback does not have to be a burner to run this play. We ran this play about four times a game. I like to run this play on first or second downs and third-and-medium. Last year, this play averaged 10 yards a carry. We have used this play over time, and we feel we have answers for anything the defense does. This play is also good against the zone blitz, which we are seeing a lot.

When I talk about the play, I talk about the middle of the field being open or closed (Figure 6-1). If the defense has two safeties, we talk about the middle of the field being open. If there is a single safety, the middle of the field is closed. The middle of the field is the quarterback's first read. The first defense is an *over 4-3 alignment*.

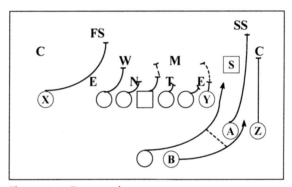

Figure 6-1. Zone option vs. over

ZONE OPTION BLOCKING RULES

- TE: Full zone work with PST to second level
- PST: Covered reach; uncovered trail; overtake DE or climb
- PSG: Covered reach; uncovered trail; overtake DL or climb
- Center: Reach A gap; uncovered trail; overtake DT or climb
- BSG: Scoop
- BST: Scoop; B-gap threat; possible shift

The blocking rule for the *tight end* is a full zone scheme with the playside tackle. He is working with the tackle and getting up to the second level of the defense. The tight end is at the point of attack and has to set the edge. He has the most critical block. He has to handle the C-gap defender up to the playside linebacker. He works with the playside tackle depending on the technique of the defender playing on him.

He steps with his near foot. If he has a 9 technique on his outside shoulder, he has to step wide. If he has a 6 technique head-up on him, he steps to the outside shoulder and tries to get his head outside the shoulder using his inside arm. We do not have to get both hands on the defender because we have help from the tackle coming from the inside. He must have his eyes on the linebacker. He comes off the block when the linebacker makes him come off. He stays on the combination block until the linebacker threatens the line of scrimmage. If the linebacker never shows up, he stays on the defensive end.

The blocking scheme on this play is the exact blocking scheme for the outside zone. If the *playside tackle* is covered, he reaches the defender. If he is uncovered, he is going to trail and overtake the defensive end block from the tight end. He is working with the tight end and is responsible for the C-gap defender. The ideal situation is the tackle taking over the defensive end and the tight end getting off on the linebacker coming over the top.

The tackle and tight end's eyes are on the linebacker. We have two sets of eyes on the linebacker. If the linebacker does not move, the tackle and tight end double-team the C-gap defender as long as they have to. If the linebacker tries to run underneath the play, the tackle comes off on the linebacker and the tight end blocks the defensive end. We work on this block because it is the block we use on the inside zone, outside zone, and option.

The *guard* has the same rule as the tackle. If he is covered, he reaches the defender. If he is uncovered, he trails the next defender outside or climbs to the second level. I want defenders on the ground. We cut them as much as we can. A defender cannot make a tackle if he is on the ground.

If the *center* is covered, he reaches the playside A gap. If he is uncovered, he is trailing the guard and overtaking the defensive tackle or climbing to the second-level linebacker.

The backside guard is scooping to the center. The backside tackle scoops his B gap for any threat into that gap. He checks for a possible shift by the linebacker. If the defense brings the safety down to the line of scrimmage, the tackle will shift up and cut him off like he did on the linebacker. If there is a tight end on the backside, he runs a scoop scheme.

The second defense is an *under 4-3* with the middle of the field open (Figure 6-2). Nothing has changed for the tight end and playside tackle. They are working a zone scheme on the defensive end coming off for the inside linebacker.

The guard does not run through the nose to get up on the linebacker. He is zone stepping as the center is coming hard into the A gap. We do not feel like we have to get up on the backside linebacker. We want to get the A-gap defender blocked.

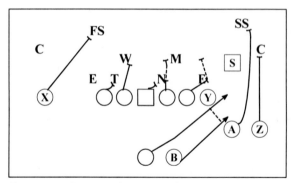
Figure 6-2. Zone option vs. under

We keep track of knockdown blocks. We take pride in that. We keep a chart of that for the players. We talk about it every day and they have a goal of how many knockdowns we are shooting for. We have goals within the separate units and team goals.

If we do not get many knockdowns, we are looking for "loafs." We chart loafs and knockdowns. If we have a lot of knockdowns, we probably do not have many loafs. However, if we do not have a lot of knockdowns, we are probably loafing in the offensive line. A loaf for us is a lineman not busting his butt all the way to the end of the play. It does not matter if he is on the playside or backside. If he is not going full speed from the beginning to the end, that is a loaf.

After the games, we have Sunday practices. After practice on Sunday, we handle the loafs from Saturday's game. At the end of practice, the team circles up. We call it the "Eagle circle." The coach is in the middle. He calls out a player's name. The player sprints his butt to the middle of the circle. The coach tells him how many loafs he had in the game. If he had three loafs, he yells his name and announces, "My name is John Smith and I let the team down three times." The whole team does three up-downs. The player sprints back to his position and the next player's name is called. We handle all loafs this way. I have been in situations in spring football where we have done 150 up-downs. However, we have done as few as 12 for a game. Everyone on the team is graded including the quarterback. If he does not carry out his fakes all the way to the line of scrimmage, he gets a loaf.

The first thing the quarterback has to do is identify the pitch key. He has to make sure the receiver to that side and the back know who the pitch key is. We have used a thousand different ways to identify him. It does not matter how you do it but everyone has to be on the same page. One thing I would not do is call out the jersey number of the key defender.

The way we do it now is to point at the pitch key. The receiver points to him also. That is the simplest way to do it. It is not a giveaway because we point out blitzes, linebackers, and many other things. In this diagram, the pitch key is the Sam linebacker.

After the quarterback points out the pitch key, his next big job is to secure the snap. That is something we never take for granted. We work with our centers and quarterbacks every day on the snap. The centers snap and move on every play in practice. You cannot take the snap for granted. It does not matter who the pitch key is if the quarterback puts the ball on the ground.

The quarterback secures the snap and attacks the outside cheek of the pitch key. We do not run at the inside shoulder or hip. I never want the quarterback in a situation where he has to run the ball and not pitch it. If he attacks the inside shoulder of the pitch key, the defender can cut off the pitch and make the quarterback run the ball.

We do not want to pitch the ball backward. When I was at Air Force, the pitches were downhill. We did that this year in our pitch scheme. This year, we had a bad pitch that was called an incomplete pass. That is the type of pitch I am looking for. I want the back to catch the ball going downhill. I do not want the back catching the ball on the pitch and have to run five yards to get to the line of scrimmage.

In practice, every day we do a five-minute option and screen drill. We run two huddles is this drill. The first huddle calls the play and runs it. As they are coming back, the second huddle is running their play. In that five-minute drill, we are running 16 to 18 repetitions. We are going hard and fast for the entire five minutes. The players do not like the drill because we are going so fast.

It is hard for the scout team to get lined up because we are going so fast. The coaches are yelling at everyone because they are not getting to coach their players. If you want to make a correction, it has to be done on the run. We do not stop the drill for correction or coaching. It is as rapid as we can go. The players that are going to get the work are the slot receiver, the running back, and the quarterback. The defense is doing something different every time. The quarterback has to be thinking all the time.

I want the quarterback to pitch the ball every time. It does not happen that way. Defenses will design their coverage to make the quarterback carry the ball. That is one reason we do not run it more than four times a game. I do not want the quarterback running a lot. He has to run the ball enough with the normal things that happen in a game. He has to pull the ball down on a pass and run on occasion. On a busted play, he sometimes gets stuck with the ball and has to run. We do not like him to run that much. I will run the quarterback as much as we need to.

When we pitch the ball, the quarterback delivers it with a thumb motion. We have tried others, but the best pitch for us is made with the thumb snapped down.

The quarterback has to identify the D-gap player. He looks for the first defender outside the tight end. That is the pitch key. He could be on the line of scrimmage, on the second level, or in the secondary. If the defense has disguised the alignment and moved, that is fine. Once we identify the pitch key, we run the play.

ZONE OPTION RECEIVER RULES

- TB: Open crossover footwork; run and gain; maintain pitch phase 4 X 2
- Z-back: Block man on
- A-back: Block next defender beyond the point
- X-end: Block man on

The Z-back's rule is to block the man that aligns on him. It does not matter what the coverage may be. If he recognizes the defense as man coverage, he can run off the defender. The only thing I do not want him to do is cut the defender. You cannot cut a defender at the point of attack on an option. If they cut the defender, he will get off the ground and make the tackle because it takes some time for the ball to get to him.

The A-receiver is the slot receiver. He has to know who the pitch key is and block the next defender. The X-receiver is backside and he cuts off. If he was on the playside, he blocks the man on him.

If we are going to spread the field and be in a one-back set, our receivers must be great blockers. They are the reason we run for 200 yards a game. Our receivers understand that fact. They may not understand it when they arrive on campus, but they do before they play. I do not believe in the *prima donna* receiver that thinks he is just a pass catcher. I want our receivers to have a linebacker mentality. That is the way we coach them. We work them hard and challenge them. If one of them backs down, we challenge his heart. We call them out in front of everyone and challenge their pride. We get after them and expect them to block.

The frontside blocks are basic stalk blocks. My two years at the Air Force Academy, I coached the wide receivers. With as much option as we ran at Air Force, we did a lot of stalk blocking. In our stalk block, we attack the outside number of the defender unless he is within five yards of the receiver.

If he is within five yards of the receiver, he is in the "danger zone." In the danger zone, we must protect the inside first. That keeps the rolled-up corner from hitting the tailback before he gets the ball. If the defender is within the danger zone, the receiver comes off and attacks his inside number. If the defender squats, the receiver works to his outside numbers. The reason we work the outside number is to get the ball pitched and on the sideline away from all the defenders.

The pursuit drills that the defense runs in practice is exactly what I want the play to do. I want to be on the sideline with everyone chasing from the inside. I want the backside corner to have to make the tackle. By using a multiple tempo offense, the defense does not get to rest as they usually do. This type of offense fatigues the defense.

I do not want to show the defense whether it is run or pass by the release of the receivers. If the defender can read run in the first two or three steps, the receiver is giving him the advantage. We want to push hard off the ball and sell the pass. As he gets into the danger zone, he begins to break down. At that point, the receiver becomes an offensive lineman. We take short, choppy steps so we can be balanced. We want to drop our tail, get in a good football position, and climb up the defender.

We want to close the distance, get the hands inside, and grab cloth. When he gets in that position, he takes him wherever he wants to go. If the receiver can get his hands on the defender, it is over with. If the defender widens to keep outside leverage, the receiver drives him out-of-bounds. He tries to take him over the water cooler and the cheerleaders.

We take the defender wherever he wants to go and the back cuts off his block. If the defender gets off the block, the receiver has to let go of the jersey. If we pull the jersey, the referee will call holding. However, most defensive backs cannot make a tackle if the wide receiver is pressing on them. The thing we cannot do is let the defensive back control us and make the tackle. We have to move him somewhere. You cannot let him hold his position.

We are in the shotgun and the quarterback is five yards from the line of scrimmage. The tailback's toes are aligned on the heels of the quarterback. That puts the tailback at five-and-a-half yards from the line of scrimmage. I am not as concerned with his depth as I am his width. We want him splitting the playside tackle's inside leg. If he can widen a little more and not give the play away, that is great. We want to outflank the pitch key as quickly as possible. The tailback works to get four yards in front of the quarterback and no deeper than two yards. If the quarterback has to adjust, the tailback adjusts with him.

I told you, I want the quarterback to attack the outside cheek of the pitch key. However, I do not want him to hold the ball until the last minute before he pitches it. I do not want the quarterback taking a hit because he is trying to pitch at the last second. We pitch the ball when the tailback outflanks the key.

On the backside, we expect the tackle to cut off the 3-technique tackle. We expect the backside guard to get the Will linebacker cutoff. If he does not, the frontside guard or center will cut off the Will linebacker. In that case, the backside guard keeps working up the levels trying to get to the free safety.

The next defense is a 3-4 look with seven defenders in the box (Figure 6-3). The Sam linebacker is on the line of scrimmage in a 9 technique on the tight end. The defensive end is aligned in a 5 technique with the nose shaded to the tight end. We are still going to pitch off the D-gap player. That is the Sam linebacker because he is the first man outside the tight end.

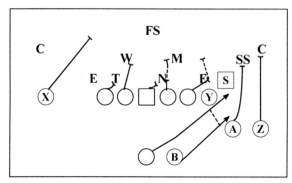

Figure 6-3. Zone option vs. 3-4

The slot receiver knows he has the next man who is the strong safety. The difference is the tight end. He still handles the C-gap player with the tackle. However, the defensive end is now a 5 technique. I do not want the tight end to step down on the defensive end. If he does, the linebacker will be over-the-top before he can get up the field. We want the tight end to come off the ball and get his inside hand on the 5 technique with his eyes on the Mike linebacker.

He steps with his inside foot up the field. He has his hands on the defensive end, but he watches the linebacker. As soon as the linebacker starts to come over the top, the tight end comes off and blocks him. The tackle zone steps for the defensive end, but he is aware of the linebacker. He knows if the linebacker is running fast, he has no help from the tight end. He has to block the defensive end by himself. Everything else is the same on this play.

The next diagram shows the option against the *3-3 stack* defense (Figure 6-4). We identify the pitch key as the rover in this diagram. The tight end and tackle have the C-gap defender up to the playside linebacker. The playside linebacker is stacked right over the C gap. The tackle knows he has almost no help on the defensive end.

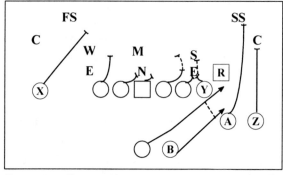

Figure 6-4. Zone option vs. 3-3

On occasion, the Sam linebacker will widen from his stack position. The tight end and tackle know they still have to get their blocks. If the tight end gets to the backside hip of the linebacker, we can still block him. The tight end drives the backside hip as far as he can. The quarterback can always cut the ball up inside.

If the defensive end jumps outside into a 9 technique, the tight end does the same thing. He knows if the end is on his outside shoulder, the linebacker will be inside. The tackle can block the linebacker and the tight end reaches the defensive end. If he cannot get him reached, he stays on him and pushes him outside. If the quarterback cannot get the edge, he runs it inside. It is just like the outside zone play except the quarterback is carrying the ball.

In the passing game, I am always looking for a simple pass. I want the type of pass where the offensive line does not have to block anybody and the quarterback knows where to throw the ball. I went with my wife on a vacation to Pawleys Island, South Carolina. I went to the golf course to play some golf and saw Tom Moore, the offensive coordinator for the Indianapolis Colts, on the practice tee. I introduced myself and asked if he was going to play. He was and I asked him if I could ride the round with him. I rode 18 holes with Tom Moore.

The only thing I asked him that day about football was his best play in a situation where you had to make the yardage needed for a first down. He told me the play was so simple that I would not believe him. He said this was Peyton Manning's favorite play (Figure 6-5). The formation was a tight end trips set with a split end to the backside. The split end runs a 10-yard hook and the back flares to that side. The tight end expands outside for two yards, drives upfield for 15 yards, and comes across the middle. The slot receiver and outside receiver push up the field five yards and run hard to the inside.

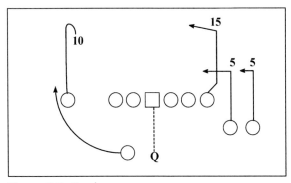

Figure 6-5. Cowboy

We tell the quarterback to throw the ball to one of the two receivers coming inside. We tell the quarterback to look at the inside linebacker. If he runs with the tight end, throw to the slot receiver. If the linebacker does not run with the tight end, throw to the outside receiver. They never throw the ball to the tight end, backside receiver, or the swing back.

We put that play in at Florida and it became a great play for us. It is still in our arsenal and we use it. We call it "cowboy." It is simple. In the passing game, you can make the plays as complicated as you want or as simple as you want. The Colts have the best quarterback in the game and they throw this simple pass. Being simple and executing what you do is what the passing game is all about.

We run a five-step drop with three-step timing. I believe a sack is the quarterback's fault. I can show you on film where the defensive end is turned loose on the quarterback and he still gets the ball off for a completion. That is the type of passing game I want.

The play I want to talk about is *double scat*. We have run this play for a long time. The success rate of this pass is 83 percent. We average 7.7 yards per completion. Thirty-three percent of the time, we throw this pass on third down. If you play against me, you will see this play. It is a blind call. When you get into a game and do not know what to call, this is the play. It does not matter what the defense or coverage is. It is a time-tested pattern.

I like to run this in some type of 3x1 formation (Figure 6-6). The double scat takes the slot receiver to the trips side and the single receiver to the backside.

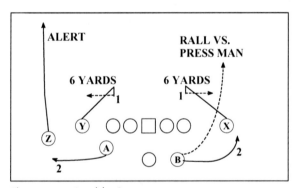

Figure 6-6. Double Scat

People know I am going to run this play, so we put some window dressing on it. We use some motion and set adjustments, but it does not really matter. Our players believe in it and it works. Our players do not care if the defenders know it is coming because they believe they can execute the play.

I do not want the scat receiver to be more than six yards from the offensive tackles. If the ball is on the hash marks, the receiver into the boundary is one yard from the top of the numbers. Landmarks on the field are critical in the passing game. One yard from the top of the numbers is a critical distance. They can be closer than six yards from the tackle, but no wider.

DOUBLE SCAT RULES

- Scat X-end and Y-end: Stem inside to a depth of six yards; sit versus zone, bounce out versus man; if blitz, look for the ball (hot read)
- Fade Z-end: Run fade; get over top of defender; work to catch ball over outside shoulder
- Bubble A-back: Run a bubble route; settle at numbers
- Swing route B-back: Free release; run swing route; settle at numbers; versus press man, run a rail route

The scat receiver to the single receiver side takes his alignment six yards from the tackle and locates the playside linebacker. I want the linebacker that is aligned in the box on the single receiver side. He wants to look at his inside foot. That is his aiming point. He runs directly to that spot at six-yards deep. If the linebacker drops to zone, the receiver sticks his foot in the ground, turns around, and catches the football.

We tell the receiver to take a picture as he runs to the spot. If the linebacker drops wide, the quarterback throws the ball on his inside number. If he drops straight back, the ball comes on the outside number. Where the quarterback delivers the ball tells the receiver which way to turn and get upfield. The quarterback takes the receiver away from the defender.

If the receiver goes to the inside and the linebacker sits and walls the receiver off, the receiver bounces off the linebacker and takes the pattern to the outside. We want to keep the pattern flat and not up the field. If you push up the field, the linebacker undercuts the pattern.

The next situation is the linebacker running a blitz. When the receiver sees the blitz, his eyes go straight to the quarterback. He is the hot read for the quarterback. If the quarterback throws the ball, he catches it and goes up the field. If the quarterback does not throw the ball he continues to the spot, sticks the foot in the ground, and bounces back outside.

The last situation is the pressed corner. As the receiver runs inside to get to the spot, the linebacker is running at him. The linebacker has the running back man-to-man or is running over-the-top of the coverage. The receiver gets to his spot, sticks his foot in the ground, opens his shoulders, and gets back to the outside.

The Z-receiver to the trips side runs a fade route. This is not a dummy route. We throw the ball to the fade receiver. If the defense comes up on the receiver and we feel we have the right match-up, we throw this pattern. We do not throw the ball to see if we can catch it. We throw the ball expecting to catch it. The quarterback throws the ball 18 to 22 yards down the field, five yards from the sideline. That is where we want the receiver. We drill those patterns five minutes every day. We want the ball caught over the outside shoulder.

The A-back is the inside slot receiver. He runs his pattern for width and not depth. The B-back has a free release with no blocking assignment. He runs a swing route to his side. When the bubble and swing routes get into the numbers they begin to settle. If we throw the ball to the back, I want him to catch it no deeper than two yards from the line of scrimmage. I do not want him catching it five-yards deep in the backfield.

The only thing the B-back looks for is press coverage on the split end. If he sees press coverage on the split end, his swing becomes a rail route. He is going to beat the linebacker in man coverage down the field. If he cannot get open, the quarterback knows he has the scat route coming back outside.

The quarterback reads the middle of the field. If he reads middle of the field closed, he is throwing the scat/swing into the weakside of the formation. If he reads the middle of the field open, he throws the scat/swing to the strongside of the formation. If he reads man coverage, he throws the ball to the scat/wheel to the weakside.

We run five-man protection with this pattern. If we get press-man coverage, the back will run a rail route. With the quarterback I have now, he can read the Mike Linebacker. If he works weak, we throw strong, and if he works strong, we throw weak. He can handle that because he understands the pattern.

I have enjoyed this. If you have questions about anything, give us a call. You can come by and talk ball anytime you like. Thank you very much.

7

Essentials in Installing the Spread Offense

Bob Gaddis
Columbus East High School (Indiana)
2009

Thank you. It is a pleasure to be here. I want to talk about how we implement our spread offense, and then finish by showing you some cutup action of what we do. As we go along, if you have any questions, I will be happy to tell you the way we do it.

THE WAY WE DO IT

Our spread offense emphasizes the pass. People who play us would say that they have to stop the pass first. So, when we train in the off-season, a lot of the things we do just emphasize throwing the ball, catching the ball, and all of the things that go along with it. We will start with our kids in March, one morning a week. They come into our open facilities, and they start throwing the ball around and catching it.

They will throw it and catch it all summer. We go to 7-on-7 competitions, and we go to camps that emphasize pass offense and pass defense. Kids like it and because that is what we want to do.

We want to throw the football, but there's another thing about the spread offense that I think is important. We learned this when we installed the offense. We want to run the ball when we need to and when we want to. We learned a lot of that by trial and error.

When we switched to the spread offense from the I formation, we were a power team that really wanted to run the ball. We had to change the way we thought. We had a lot to learn, but one thing we learned quickly was that you cannot be too soft when you run the spread. You still have to be able to run the football. Getting the ball downhill, by running the ball hard, and hitting up in there, north and south, is an important factor that I think has made us better in the last two or three years in the spread.

CONCEPTS

I am going to give you some concepts and ideas that we used in getting to the things we think we have to do to be successful. Then, I am going to show you our best pass and our best running play.

First, you have to stretch the field vertically and horizontally. Your kids need to understand what that means. We can throw the ball coming out of our opponent's red zone. In practice during team time, we want to put our kids in those positions. We go from the 20-yard line in our own red zone, we will go middle of the field, and then we will work coming out of the opponent's red zone. We will do that every time we practice offense. We want to spread it vertically and horizontally.

The first concept we teach in the summertime is four-vertical. You have to make four-vertical a threat, but it does not mean that you have to throw it every down. You may not throw it more than one or two times a game, but it has to be a threat.

What that means is that you want to see if they are going to commit four defensive backs to defend the four deep quarters of the field. Are they going to put four guys back there, or are they going to put three guys back there? If they put four back there, which we see most of the time, then that dictates how many they can put in the box and how many guys they can put in the flats. It is all dictated by you being willing to throw the football down the field on four-vertical.

In our offense, we can run a four-vertical play from a dropback, or it can be out of play-action. The concept is the same either way.

We decided to go to the no-huddle offense most of the time. We really like it. We can huddle, and we do, but not very often. We work on the no-huddle in practice, and then we run it in on game night. We can yell out plays to the quarterback. We have very few plays on the quarterback's armband. On some of them, we disguise with words. Sometimes, we might not do a good job of disguising them. We tell our guys we want to make sure we know what we are doing when we try to communicate in the no-huddle. We are not too much concerned what our opponents are doing.

The other thing I think that happens with the no-huddle is that you make the defense show their hand early. Defensive coordinators have gotten a lot better. They will have their kids just stand and watch us get the plays from the sideline. If they see spread, they have three choices. They can change their defenses. However, if you are really going fast, then they have to get lined up to play. A lot of times, they may give you a vanilla look, especially at crunch time. You might get them into a vanilla look, and you know where you are going to be able to attack them to be successful.

The other important thing is giving your quarterback the ability to change the play and live with it. We probably change the play 50 percent of the time. You have to coach him on why you are doing it and what you are trying to do. However, if he makes a mistake, I do not think you can jump his tail end for it when he comes off the field. If he makes a mistake, I might just ask him what he saw. If he has a good answer, we would move on to the next time, and that would be it.

COMMUNICATION

Communication is important in any spread offense. How are you going to communicate? How are you going to identify defenses? Everybody has to be on the same page, including your whole staff and all of your kids. We want to know if a linebacker is a flat player or a hang backer. Is he a middle backer, a Mike backer, a Sam backer, or a Will backer? What are you going to call him?

Is he a corner? Is the corner hard, or is he soft? Is the safety on the hash, or is he in the middle of the field? Are you going to call it middle open or middle closed? Those are the points you have to figure out. You must decide on how you are going to communicate, and how you are going to identify defenses. The thing I think you find out when you run the spread is that defenses have some choices, but they do not have many choices. You are either going to see five or maybe six guys in the box, and then the secondary comes off of that.

We teach our guys to read from the secondary down. If there are two safeties, they probably cannot get six guys in the box, and so on. You have to figure out how you are going to identify defenses, what you are going to call a front, what you are going to call a stunt, and what you are going to call the coverages.

We do not have many players who go both ways. We do not have that many who practice both ways. We try to make our offensive terminology the same thing we are hearing on defense. If we call it a 5 alignment on defense, we call it a 5 alignment on offense. We want to be able to communicate where players line up.

Players need to talk and communicate on the field. When we are in no-huddle, we want them to talk. We tell them what we want them to communicate. It does not really matter to me how they get it done. On the running play I am going to talk about, they have to be able to tell each other if the guy is in a 3 or a 1 technique, and if they are in an even or an odd front. They need to say that, but they might have different words to do it. It does not matter, as long as they can figure that out. We want them to talk on every single play.

SPEND TIME

As I said before, we spend a lot of time throwing and catching the football. In Indiana, there are no rules in the summertime, and we could practice every day if we wanted to. We throw once a week in the springtime and once a week in the summer, and then we go to all the 7-on-7s, but they need to throw and catch the football and get good at it.

I think it is important to pick a protection that you can teach. We do not want a protection that we can draw up on the board, but one that we can teach. Pick a protection that works for you, and rep it up. For example, our protection will not work with the quarterback under center. It will not work because we pick up the A-gap blitzes with a back most of the time, and the quarterback would get sacked if he was under center.

You have to be able to draw up every blitz imaginable and have a chance to pick it up. I am sure you understand that no matter what formation you are in, they can always bring one more guy than you can block. They can always do it. It does not matter what you are in. So use the protection that works for you against every front and blitz.

Here is how we do it. When we go to skelly in practice, our linemen are doing pass protection the whole time. We set it up with five offensive linemen and one back against every front imaginable. In the pre-season, we show them every front, and then we bring out the fronts and blitzes we will see from week to week. Then, we prepare specifically for them. They need to identify them, call out the blitzes, and then protect against them. We start out being able to protect three on each side but we can kick four one way and two the other, just as everyone running the spread offense does.

The thing is, you need to have an answer. What is your answer going to be if they do bring one more guy than you can block? You have to have an answer, and you need to do that in practice. We man up in practice and bring one more guy than we can protect. We see what our quarterback is going to do with it. I hope that he is going to change the play and get the ball out quick, or check to some kind of screen. That would be our answer.

We spend a lot of time teaching routes. We do not have a lot of routes, but we want to be able to get good at them. We spend a lot of time just teaching kids how to cut. We want them to get their foot down, get their nose over their toes, push off that foot, and make cuts.

We want to teach them how to shake guys. Sometimes, when we get on the board, we draw routes with just straight lines. Then, we tell them straight lines do not get open. You have to learn how to shake a guy, attack his technique, and flip his hips. We spend a lot of time on this, and we teach adjustments they can make in their routes.

We do a lot of sight adjustments. We call routes on each play. If we have a deep route on against a guy we know is playing us very deep, we will not go deep if we want to get him the football. He changes his route at the line of scrimmage. In addition, our quarterback can change it. It does not matter how they change it. Sometimes it is visual, sometimes it is with words, and sometimes they just look and nod to each other, and they know they are going to change it.

SPREAD FORMATION

Here is our formation. We are in a spread formation with two wideouts and two slots. The X and Z are the wideouts, and L and R are the slots. L and R are for left and right. Our tailback just has to know where to line up. It takes too much verbiage to tell him. When we teach alignment, we just teach alignment to the play.

Cover 3

For us, this would be a cover 3 (Figure 7-1). If the safety is in the middle of the field, two things can happen. It can be either cover 3 or cover 1. We tell our guys, the man in the middle is going to tip off if it is man or not. If he is deep, it is probably a cover-3 look.

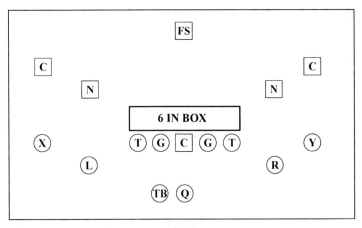

Figure 7-1. Spread vs. cover-3 look

We do not see a cover 3 very much. If we get it, we are throwing the ball down the field. I guarantee you, if our quarterback sees cover 3, he is jacking it deep. He is going to try to get the football out because they have six in the box and we can get 4-on-3 now.

We call the guy in the flat a nickel defender. It does not matter if he is a Sam linebacker or a strong safety. If he is in the flat, we call him a nickel defender. If he is over a wideout, he is a corner. If he is in the middle of the field, he is either a free safety or a half safety.

Cover 2

This is a cover-2 look (Figure 7-2). How do we identify a cover-2 look? If the two safeties are on the hash marks, it is a cover-2 look for us.

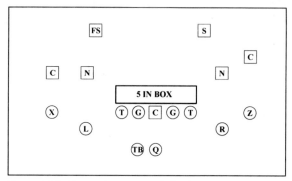

Figure 7-2. Spread vs. cover-2 look

The corner can be a hard cover-2 player, or he can be soft cover player. If he becomes soft, that would be a cover-4 look for us. The inside guy is still a nickel for us. They can only have five guys in the box. We think we have them outnumbered there, and we should run the football.

If the nickel starts walking down and he is going to blitz off the edge, we call that a storm. When he moves inside, our slot will yell inside to "Watch storm; watch storm!" Our linemen are in a two-point stance, and they stand up and look at the defense. Our quarterback will look at the defense as well looking for the storm blitz. They are all pointing at it and identifying it.

If one backer in the box comes, it is a blitz, and if two of them come, it is a Hawk. If a backer and a nickel are coming on the same side, to us that is a combo, and we will turn our protection to the side it is coming from.

PICK YOUR BEST

These are the things we have been able to do the best out of our spread offense. Our best run is the dash play. I will tell you why we like it. The play most everybody is running is the zone play, and we run that play, too. However, if we see the 4-1 front, we will probably run the zone play. If we think we can knock guys off the ball, get them covered up, and let our tailback just be a player, then we will the run zone. However, we cannot always do that.

Dash is back to the old isolation concept. The spread offense is viewed as a pass-first offense. Because of that, those 5 techniques are going to really get their tails upfield. They want to make the line of scrimmage come at the offense. We have to get the football going north and south right now.

We have to create a horizontal seam and get vertical. We do not want to take a long time reading zone and then going. The dash play gets the ball up the field right now. It is a power back play away from the play, and it is a zone-type play to the play. It is as simple as that.

Our best pass is four-vertical. We run several routes off it. As I said earlier, we want the defense to have to commit four guys deep. We will run some routes to take advantage of the areas that they give us.

DASH BLOCKING

The playside guard will recognize the defense and call out the technique in his area. If he calls out a 3 technique, then he and the tackle on that side will take a zone step, and they are blocking zone. Everybody else is picking back like the old isolation play. You are going to get a double-team back on the nose with a step off on the backside linebacker. The backside lineman who is uncovered pulls to the 1 technique area. On a 3 call, he pulls inside the 3 and leads the tailback just like on isolation.

Finally, the quarterback is still running an option read on that backside end. You can also take the play and let the quarterback fake it to the tailback, who would go block that end, and then let the quarterback run the same play. That is our best running play, and I will show it to you on the tape.

To finish up on dash blocking, we pull the uncovered lineman on the backside. If the playside guard calls 3, he comes to 1. If the playside guard calls 1, he comes to 3. It is not real hard. If the backside tackle is not the puller, he takes an inside zone step and looks for the run-through backer on the backside. He is not worried about the 5 technique. He will punch him and look for the backer running through.

Our receivers block alley to support. If we get a storm call to the frontside, it means we will also get a slant to the inside gaps. The quarterback will change the play. It is no good into that defense, so the quarterback may run the toss sweep outside of it. He may change it to a different direction and keep it himself, but he has to understand what that means.

Here is the dash versus the 4-1 (Figure 7-3). We have a 3 call on the right. The guard and tackle are zoning out. The center and guard are doubling, and the backside tackle pulls. The quarterback just puts the ball in the tailback's belly and reads that defensive end.

Here is the same play with the quarterback carrying the ball (Figure 7-4). If we want to have the quarterback keep it, everything looks the same. Nothing changes with the blocking scheme, but the tailback has to take care of the defensive end. If they run some kind of twist, the tailback has to keep his eyes up and get a piece of the edge player.

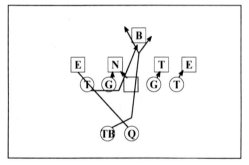

Figure 7-3. Dash vs. 4-1

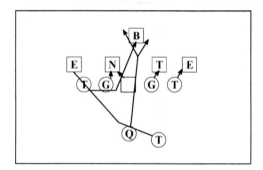

Figure 7-4. Quarterback dash vs. 4-1

If the defensive end is any good and is coached up, he may try to run the track and get down inside. If he does that, our quarterback can still pull the ball. If our tailback can beat him and get a piece of the end, we can still get the ball north and south.

At times, they turn the defensive end loose, sit back, and play the quarterback with the nickel. That is why four-vertical is such a great play off this look. They cannot get any collision on the slot, and he can run free right down the field.

We see a lot of 3-2 and 3-3 fronts. Here is dash versus 3-2 (Figure 7-5). This is what it should look like. The guard has called an odd front, so he gets to pick back and double with the center. If they get some kind of twist with the backside backer, they pick that up. The backside tackle should step up and take any kind of a run-through. The frontside tackle will zone out. We pull the guard around and get right up in the backer's face, and the tailback follows him. The quarterback still makes the decide read on the end.

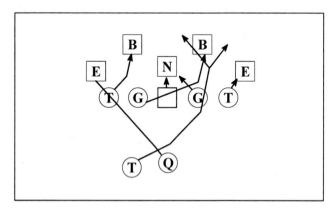

Figure 7-5. Dash vs. 3-2

When they play cover with a nickel player on one side in the flat, to control that nickel we run a bubble on it. If we want to run a bubble, we put a tag on the play. For us, the dash play is simply a 4 call. If we call 4 bubble, the slot runs the bubble, and we have a triple option.

The quarterback can give it, keep it, or throw it to the slot. If the nickel is jacking around inside, the quarterback puts the ball in the tailback's belly and then throws the bubble.

We do not block the nickel. We do not crack block. We just take our X-receiver and block the corner. The only time we throw the bubble is when we think our slot can outrun the nickel.

Here is the dash versus the 3-3 stack (Figure 7-6). This is the hardest one to block. They have six guys in the box. Theoretically, we should not be running the ball in there, but we need to have a way to run it on this front.

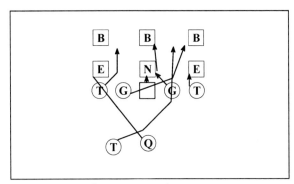

Figure 7-6. Dash vs. 3-3 stack

If we tried to run outside zone on this, our offensive line would have some disadvantages. At least, when we run the dash, we get a chance to double the nose. In other words, you are not asking the center to catch that backer. We will go ahead with the same blocks with our tackles. The quarterback still has his decide read on the end. However, our playside tackle will not take his zone step against that 4 technique. He steps with his inside foot and does battle with anybody who comes inside. The other thing we do on this play is take big splits. We split them way out.

FOUR-VERTICAL

I am going to go through four-vertical and the other routes quickly. As I said earlier, we want to stretch the field, and present the threat of four-verticals on every snap we are in spread. We throw it off dropback or play-action, and then come back to our variations. When we make the defense think we are running four-verticals, we can throw it somewhere else. If they are going to play man on us, and blitz us, then we have to do something else.

This is our four-vertical against cover 3 (Figure 7-7). It is run like everybody else in America runs it. We tell the guys to the field that they are not coming off the hash. If the ball is in the middle of the field, then our R would be on the hash. We are just going to stretch them with 4-on-3. That is easy.

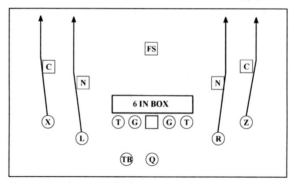

Figure 7-7. Four-vertical vs. cover 3

If we get cover 2, here is how we do it (Figure 7-8). If the ball is in the middle of the field, then R stays on the hash and works vertically up the field. Our L receiver then becomes the reader. He will read the free safety and try to get to that soft spot in the middle. If they line him up 18 yards deep and just bail him, then we cut our L receiver off right there at 17 or 18 yards and let him try to work to the hole.

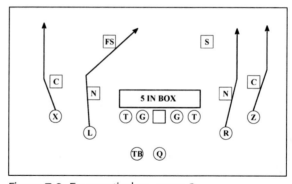

Figure 7-8. Four-vertical vs. cover 2

VARIATIONS OFF FOUR-VERTICAL

One of our best plays off four-vertical is what we call hitch (Figure 7-9). We are running the same four-vertical plays. The inside men are running their vertical routes. The outside guys make it look like verticals, and then they sit the hitch down.

We tell the outside guys to get six yards on the hitch. The nickel is the guy who can stop the route, so we keep the thing away from the nickel.

Here is the hitch versus cover 2 (Figure 7-10). If we see cover 2, we are not running the hitch. We convert it and go back down the field. It is now just like four-vertical again. If the safety gets too deep, our R receiver may set down at 17 or 18 yards.

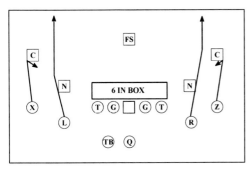

Figure 7-9. Hitch vs. cover 3

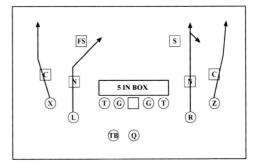

Figure 7-10. Hitch vs. cover 2

Smash is an excellent route off four-vertical (Figure 7-11). When we teach smash, L is our first read. He has been our reader a lot of times. He comes inside, looking at the quarterback. He is trying to get that safety thinking he is coming to the middle of the field. Then, he plants his foot and takes it back to the corner. We want to make it look like we are adjusting four-vertical.

We tell the outside receiver to get open at eight yards, plant his foot, find the nickel, and stay away from him. If it is man coverage, he just plants his foot and runs.

All of our routes are mirror routes. If we do not want to mirror them, and work the backside, we call left or right (Figure 7-12). If the ball is in the middle of the field and we run smash, we might call a smash right. We get a double post on the other side. The safety cannot be right. It is good against cover 2, and it is like stealing against cover 3, because the post will be wide open.

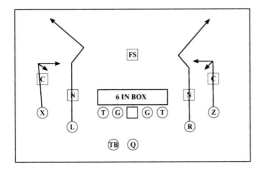

Figure 7-11. Smash Vs. Cover 3

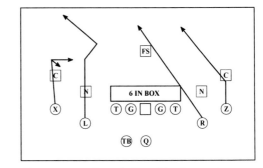

Figure 7-12. Smash Post Vs. Cover 3

We read the smash, look at the smash, and find the free safety. If the free safety runs with R—and Z flips that corner's hips as I mentioned earlier, and shakes him a little bit and takes it to the post—if that happens, the quarterback has an excellent alley to throw the football.

Another route we really like that comes off of four-vertical is choice. We do not make it any harder than it is. When we run choice, our inside guys get open. They simply attack the nickel's technique and run away from him. If he is inside, run outside. If he is outside, run inside. If he is right on you, get him off you as if you are running vertical and squirrel it down.

Against cover 3, our outside guys run out and up routes. Against cover 2, they run fades. That is it. We are going to work those choice routes off of those nickels.

One of our best routes is our squirrel play. On squirrel, all four receivers run a base route of 12 yards and back to 10 yards, coming back to the outside. It is a great route to run on third-and-five. Just get past the sticks, get open, and get the ball out on time. If they think you are running vertical, it is a good route.

I want to thank you for being here today. Thank you very much.

8

Pass Protection and the Spread Offense

Chan Gailey
Georgia Tech
2002

I hope you can see the overhead, because I'll be using that a lot this morning. The title of my talk this morning is "The Georgia Tech Offense." We haven't even had a spring practice yet. So, we don't know exactly what a Georgia Tech offense is. It should be an interesting time down there. For those who have followed Georgia Tech, you know they used Ralph Friedgen's offense. They have been successful using all the multiple looks he has with the option and the passing game.

I have been an offensive coach for the last 20 years. The first 10 years of my career I was on the defensive side of the ball. I was the defensive coordinator at the Air Force Academy and moved on to special-teams coach for the Denver Broncos.

The question has already been asked if I am going to change the offense at Georgia Tech and run the things that I have always run. I'm not the smartest sucker that has ever rolled down the pike. But, they have been averaging 31 points a game, and I'm not going to change a thing right now. We are going to keep on doing what they were doing. Billy O'Bryan is a great young offensive mind. He will continue to run things on the offensive side of the ball.

What I want to talk to you about this morning is where we are headed with our four and five wide receiver package. I am going to talk about our protection scheme that goes with the four and five receiver package and our best passes off those sets. I want to make sure we get to answer your questions. I do not want to be so formal that I can't get your questions answered.

You have unique situations at every one of your schools. We have unique problems and things that come up at Georgia Tech. Your job is to take the talent you have and move the football with it. Very few of us are fortunate enough to have a system that we can force people to play 100 percent within that system. If you have been able to do that through the years, you are a very fortunate person.

In high school, your talent changes on a yearly basis. In our situation and at the pro level, it happens to us. Even though we can recruit in college and draft in the NFL for certain needs, we recruit or draft the best athlete and find a way to use him. That is what we are doing with our four- and five-wide receiver package. We are trying to get our four or five best athletes on the field and use them. If your best athlete is a tight end, you need to find a way to incorporate him into the offense so you can use him.

Any offensive passing game has to start out with the protection scheme. I'll start with our four wide-out protection. We call the number of down linemen and linebackers in the game. When we call 41, we are talking about four down linemen and one linebacker in the game. When we talk about this situation, we are talking about personnel not alignment. I'll talk about 42, 32, and 33. If there is something else you want to see, just ask.

I'll talk about a slide, a five down, and a pack protection. I'll talk about what all three of those terms mean. I'll go through all those protections in our four-wide receivers scheme.

In our shotgun set with four wide receivers, we usually see one linebacker with a nickel and dime back in the game. This protection is a slide protection. Our tackles are in a two-point stance, and the guards are in a three-point stance. Our back is set in the weak halfback position, and the center is sliding away from him. The center does not always slide away from the back, but in base-slide protection, he does. If he played the protection the same way every time, the guys playing defense would figure that out. At times, he will slide toward the back, run him across to the other side, and protect from there. The center, guard, and tackle to the right are sliding to the right.

We use what we call a sort technique to the slide side. We block the first rusher who comes to that side. It doesn't matter if it is a lineman, linebacker, or secondary player. We block the first rusher coming from that side. We don't man up. We block whoever comes on the rush. If defensive brings the nickel back, they could bring him from the outside or inside in a stunt with the defensive end. The offensive tackle sorts the first man coming from the outside as his man.

The thing the offensive line assumes is the defense is going to rush in lanes. If the defense screws up and has two rushers in the same lane, you have to block that. We assume if the nickel comes from the outside, the end and tackle will be slanting one gap inside. If the nickel rushed in the B-Gap, we assume the defensive end is coming outside. We assume the defense is going to be sound in their techniques.

On the backside, we are locked up man-to-man with our guard and tackle. The tailback is double reading from the inside to the outside. He is checking the linebacker afor a blitz first and then checking the dime back for a blitz.

Our quarterback is in the shotgun set. I believe that is the best way to go to keep the rush from getting to the quarterback too quickly. We tell the quarterback if he gets two defenders blitzing from either side, he has to throw hot to one of the receiver on that side. The receivers are reading the defense. If they see two blitzers coming from their side, they break to their hot routes. We call our slide protection toward or away from the back in the huddle.

One of the problems the defense can create for the slide protection is to walk the linebacker up on the line of scrimmage over the center. The defense wants to draw the block from the center. They like to bail the linebacker out into coverage and bring a blitz from the outside. The back is responsible for the linebacker if he comes. The center is going to slide his protection, and the back will block the linebacker if he comes. If the quarterback is under the center, this protection will not work. The quarterback can't get away from the center without being tackled by the linebacker. The back can block the linebacker if the quarterback is in the shotgun.

We have a call that we can go to if we see an overload blitz coming. We can call ringo and get the center and back to the same side

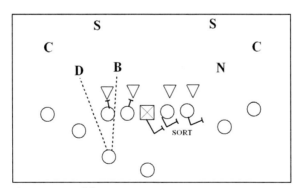

Figure 8-1. Slide away

The next protection is called five-man-down. I'll give you the same defensive alignment to start with, and then we will go to something different. This is a catch-all protection. If there is a lot of confusion on the defensive side, this is the protection you want to be in. Let's say the linebacker's jersey number is 51. The quarterback comes to the line of scrimmage and calls; "five-down/51." If there are two linebackers in the middle, we call the number of the linebacker who blitzes the most. That means the center is taking the number 51 if he blitzes. The running back is on a search technique. The left side of the line is blocking a sort technique. If the linebacker walked outside and blitzed, the line would slide to the left, and the tackle would end up blocking the blitzing linebacker. The center and guard block their area gaps.

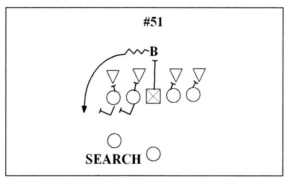

Figure 8-2. Five down

The beauty of this protection is we slide the protection to the side that number 51 aligns. If they stack the right defensive end and the linebacker walked up on the right side, the protection would slide right. If the defense is trying to confuse the offense as to where they are going to bring the fifth rusher, there is no gray area with this protection.

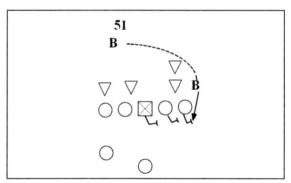

Figure 8-3. Five down shift

The running back is using the search technique. He is watching middle first, left, and right. If anyone other than the number 51 linebacker blitzes up the middle, that is the man he is taking. If the defense only brings one blitzer from the left other than number 51, the running back blocks him. If the defense brings one from the right other than number 51, the running back blocks him. He searches out the blitz other than the linebacker. He checks middle, left, and right, because of the hot reads. We tell our receivers on the five-down protection if there is a safety in the middle of the field, there are no hot routes.

As long as there is a safety in the middle of the field, the defense can only rush six defenders and still cover all the receivers. If that happens, we can block all six defenders. If the linebacker blitzes, the line blocks him. If one of the safeties blitzes, the running back blocks him. That accounts for all defenders. Those are easy reads for the quarterback and receivers. The receivers don't have to worry about how many blitzes came from their side. We are sound in that protection.

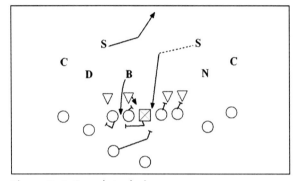

Figure 8-4. Search technique

The defense can spoil this protection if they know what they are doing. There are entirely too many defensive coaches in this meeting. I'll show you what they can do, and let them try it.

The defense can rush your quarterback by using a zone blitz. They take both defensive ends and rush under the tackles into the B gaps. The nickel and dime backs both come outside from the secondary. The corners squat in the outside zones, the linebacker sinks into the middle hole, and the defensive tackles run for the curl area. That is how the defense gets to the quarterback.

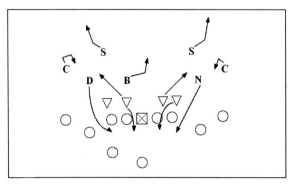

Figure 8-5. Down five breaker

But, remember one thing defensive coaches: This only works if we are in our five-down protection scheme. If we have called a slide protection, the defense loses because a slide protection will pick up that stunt. If the defense brings two from a side and we are in down-five protection, the offense wins. If we are in slide protection, the defense wins, and the offense has to throw hot. The two protections compliment each other. If you can slide and use five-down, you've got the defense guessing about which one you are using. We try to use one of these protections a week.

The reason for that is to stay ahead of the defense. If the defense has prepared to attack your five-down scheme and you use slide protection, it keeps you ahead. If they can't get to your quarterback, they will quit running the blitz. That is the fun part about this game. When we call a protection in the huddle, that is what we run when we come to the line. We feel like the responsibility of playing the guessing game should be on the shoulders of the coach not the player.

Let's go to what we call pack protection. The defense I am drawing up is what we see most of the time. If you want to see something different, I'll show you that in a minute. For the example, let's use the term five-pack. That means that everyone is stepping into their right gap and away from the five- hole. The back is taking the first defender that comes off the outside from the left.

We are assuming that the defense is going to rush people in gaps. If they do that, the protection is okay. If you are playing against a good sound defense, this protection is fine. If the defense is unsound and runs two guys outside the tackle, the protection could be in a bind. There are two reasons to run this protection. In our other protections, we are in a man-on-man situation away from the linebacker. If the defense has a man-beater stunt called to your man side, this protection eliminates that stunt.

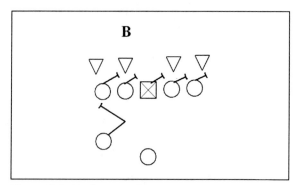
Figure 8-6. Pack protection

The problem this protection has is the back blocking the first threat to the backside. Coaches don't like to match a back up on a defensive end. Well, I'll tell you something fellows: That running back doesn't like the match-up either. The key to this protection is the technique of the defensive end. When a defensive end is coached, he is told if the tackle blocks down, there are a number of things he has to play. If the tackle blocks down, the first thing the end is thinking is trap, off tackle, or shovel pass. He is not thinking pass rush. All those other situations will slow down the defensive end, so he isn't coming off the corner like a runaway freight train.

If the defensive end is ignoring the down block of the tackle and attacking on the pass rush, run the trap at him. If the nickel and dime backs blitz, this protection should hold up. If the dime comes off the back's side, the defensive end's charge should be inside the offensive tackle to stay sound on defense. That means the right tackle takes the nickel coming from one side, and the back takes the dime coming the other way.

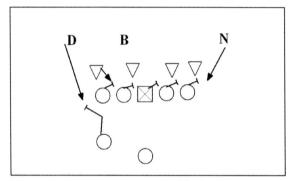

Figure 8-7. Pack vs. dime and nickel

That is the thought process of using the three protections. The slide, 5-man, and pack protections all tie together to give us a very workable pass-protection scheme. Defenses will figure out that we are only packing away from the back. That is why we are toying with the idea of cheating his alignment and letting him come to the other side and running the pass protection toward him. That doesn't give the defense much credit about catching the adjusted position of the running back to get him across to the other side. They will pick that adjustment up, but we will do something else to disguise it.

The second thing that fits into the protection is the running game. You can't do the pass protection and never run off tackle or throw the shovel pass. You can't think the defense will respect the down block of the tackle if all you do is pass block off of it. You have to threaten the defensive end to make him respect the down block. If you don't, you will get exactly what you were afraid of. You'll get the complete mismatch of that defensive end on your running back.

Let me quickly go through our protection versus the 42 defense. The first thing the defense has to figure out is how they are going to play your four-wide receiver set and keep four down linemen and two linebackers in the game. The first thing the defense is telling you is they have a great deal of respect for your running game. That means you have a quarterback who is also a running threat in your offense. That is an advantage for the offense because that means the defense is one-on-one with your receivers. The defense has a hard time rolling up in coverage from the four-two if they are going to keep two linebackers in the box.

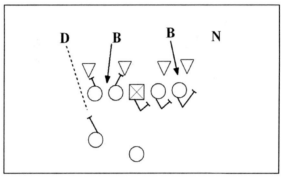

Figure 8-8. Slides vs. 42

If the defense backs the dime back up into the safety spot and moves the linebacker out to the position of the dime back, that is just like the four-one defense we just talked about. The slide protection works just fine against that scheme. If they bring one from the outside, we block him. If they bring two from the outside, we throw hot. It is hard to disguise anything in the secondary with one safety back there. The quarterback can watch his movement and figure out where the blitz is coming from. If the safety is moving right, the quarterback knows he has to be alert to his right. The safety is moving over to pick up the blitzing man's coverage.

The quarterback can tell who is in the box. We have gone to great lengths to define the box. It is 2.3 yards outside the tackles. Don't get carried away with that it is not hard to see. There are players who are going to align in what we call the gray area. The gray area is not in the box or not on the receiver. It is a player that is in the box one moment and out of it the next. He is on the receiver one second and somewhere inside of him the next. It is the coach's job to figure out the gray areas.

If the quarterback is under the center and the one-back is behind him, that is an advantage for the offense because the defense doesn't know which way the protection is sliding. Also, with the quarterback under the center, the running game is a little better. Those are two advantages to being under the center. In the shotgun with the back offset, the defense has a better idea which way the line will slide. However, the reason we are in four wideouts is to throw the football, not run it.

If we go to our five-down protection, we designate one of the linebackers to be blocked. If the linebacker's jersey numbers are 51 and 53, we call the one who blitzes the most. That means the center is on number 51 if he blitzes up the middle. If the linebacker wearing number 53 blitzes, he is blocked by the running back. The running back is searching middle first on any blitz besides number 51. From that point, he goes left and finally across to the right. If the middle linebacker comes inside the offensive tackles, that is a middle blitz for the running back. If the linebacker doesn't come, he looks at the dime back and then the nickel. Both the four-one and the four-two have the same reads for the search by the running back.

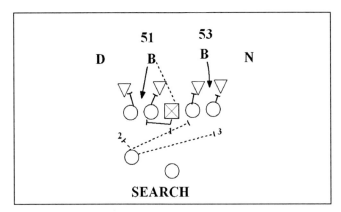

Figure 8-9. Down vs. 42

The receivers know there is a safety in the middle of the field, so there are no hot routes. If the safety moves over toward the right-slot receiver, the quarterback should begin to think he is going to have to throw hot. The safety is moving over to take the slot, so the nickel can blitz. If he moves the other way, the quarterback can easily see that and be ready for the blitz from that side. The defense could easily bring linebackers and either the nickel or dime. If they bring the nickel or dime, the safety has to take one of the receivers. The quarterback should be ready to throw hot on movement by the safety. Anytime there is no safety in the middle of the field, both slots run hot routes.

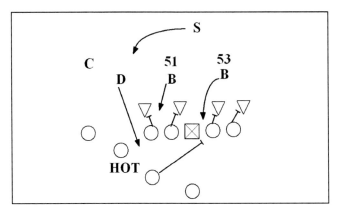

Figure 8-10. Down hot read

On our pass protection, nothing has changed. Running this protection allows us to pick up four defenders to one side. But, there is basically no change for this protection.

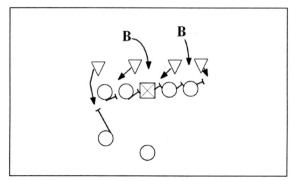

Figure 8-11. Pack vs. four-man side

Let's move on and talk about three-man fronts. When we go to slide protection in a three-man front, the backside guard blocks over the center. We have an extra guy to the slide side. The back reads linebacker to dime back. On a three-man front, the defense cannot make you hot to the slide side without going to great lengths. When the quarterback calls the three-man front, the receivers know there are no hot routes to the slide side. Away from the slide, it takes two blitzes to make us throw hot. That keeps it consistent for the receivers. They are breaking hot on any two-man blitz to their side in a four- or three-man front.

We don't throw the hot slant anymore. Too many teams are using the zone blitz and dropping the defensive lineman into the slant route. When we throw hot, it is the quick out, hitch, or fade. To the dual-receiver side, we change up our hot routes each week. One week, we will run a fade-and-out pattern, the next week, we may run double hitches. It changes from week to week. If there are some gray areas in the coverage, we may tell the outside receiver to run his route, and the inside receiver will handle the hot route.

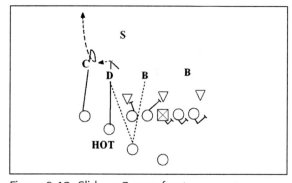

Figure 8-12. Slide vs.3-man front

In the three-man front we designate the three down linemen and the linebackers as the responsibility of the five interior linemen. We are not blocking man-on-man. We never block man-on-man when we have people off the line of scrimmage. We pass the linebacker-line stunt off from one man to another. We will lock up man-to-man with men on the line of scrimmage, but never with men off the line of scrimmage. If you get a team that does a lot of line and linebacker cross stunts, the five-down scheme handles it all. The search back stays the same. He is checking middle, left, and right.

The five-down protection is the same for every front. As soon as you designate the five guys the offense line is responsible for, nothing else changes. If there is a safety in the middle of the field, no one breaks hot. If there are two safeties in the middle, the only one who breaks hot is the receiver away from the back.

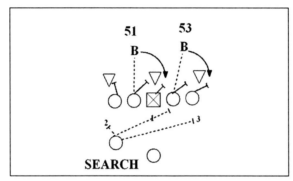

Figure 8-13. Five down vs 3-man

The pack scheme versus the three-man front is the same as it was earlier. Everyone is blocking away from the back. The back is picking up the first threat outside of the offensive tackle. The left tackle picks up air sometimes. But, we don't want him to ever turn back and block. If the defense ran a crossing stunt involving the nose guard, both linebackers, and the backside tackle, everyone would block their gaps. The back would take the linebacker as he came around to the outside. If the defensive end slanted across the offensive tackle's face, he blocks him down.

We can't run the pass protection every down in a football game, but it will take care of a stunting football team. Teams like Mississippi State that align in a three-three type defense and stunt like crazy is what the pack scheme was designed to handle.

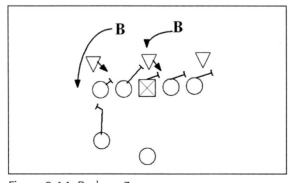

Figure 8-14. Pack vs. 3-man

You can't go into a football game with one protection. The guys on the other side of the ball are too good. We feel like we need three protections. We may only use two of them in a game, but for the course of the year, we need three protections. The pass protection is easy. The decision you have to make is which of the other two you want to keep in the offense. In some cases, having three is the way to go. That is a decision for you to make based on your personnel. The pass protection is designed to handle all the junk a defense can throw at you. There has to be a reason that you are doing these things. If you have a team that takes the linebacker, walks him to the end, and shifts everyone down, the five-down protection can handle that. If the defense plays base defense, the slide handles it.

Let's talk about the 33 defense. This is a defense people play when they think they have a better chance by putting linebackers in the game instead of defensive backs. If the defense moves the outside linebacker down over the tackle, and moves the defensive end inside, it gives them a 42 defensive spacing look. That is the way we treat it. The alignment of their personnel looks likes a four-two defense even though they have three-three personnel in the game. We designate one of the three linebackers as a down lineman. After we do that, we apply our rules like it was a 42-defense. The protection rules hold up for the slide, five down, and pass protection against the three-three. If the linebacker's jersey numbers were 51, 53, and 56, we would designate 56 as a defensive lineman. He is the linebacker they like to align on the end of the line or stack him in the middle to run stunts.

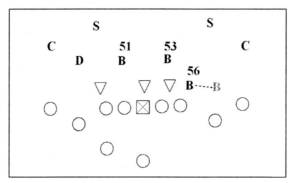

Figure 8-15. Three-three

When you are in a spread offense, you have to have a protection for a five-wideout scheme. The five-wide receiver set is commonly called the empty set. When we get into this formation, we have a three-by-two wide receiver formation. I believe the defense would put the dime and nickel together on your slot receivers in the trips set. The running back would be the slot receiver to the other side with the split end. I believe the linebacker will adjust toward the running back in the slot. We don't try to change anything with our protection. If we slide protect, we will slide away from the running back. In this case, the line is sliding to the left, since the back is aligned in the right slot.

The key to this scheme is we never read hot with our wideouts. Every route we run with our five wideouts has a built in hot route. If you get into that set, you don't want to put the burden on the receiver or a back that is not used to reading hot routes. Because of that, we build the hot route into our five-wideout scheme. What it does is give you some freedom to move your receivers in motion without asking them to read hot routes. That is an advantage because the quarterback is the only one who has to know anything.

The quarterback knows the protection is sliding to the left. His hot reads are any two blitzes from the left and any blitz from the right. That is his thought process.

If we call the five-down protection, it would be a slide protection toward number 51. The quarterback knows that if anyone blitzes besides the four down linemen and the linebacker, he has to throw hot. We put a lot of pressure on the quarterback to know all these reads.

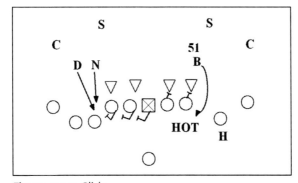

Figure 8-16. Slide

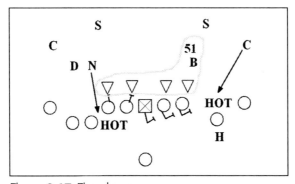

Figure 8-17. Five down

Some people think they gain protection by playing with a tight end. I don't disagree with that. The only thing I am saying is using four wideouts gives the quarterback a better chance to read the blitz. The safeties have a harder time disguising what they are doing. The quarterback can see it coming. Having receivers detached from the formation lets the quarterback see the blitz. The defense has to give it away to get to where they are supposed to be before the ball is snapped.

When you have a tight end aligned in a tight formation, they can cover him with the defensive end aligned on him and bring a linebacker. That is hard for the quarterback to see developing. That could be a well-disguised coverage. You can't do that when the defenders are aligned in space. The quarterback can see all their movements. They can't hide where they are going.

We have to handle the 32 defense from the empty set. We have a decision to make on the type of protection to use. We can use the slide or five-down protection. If we use the slide protection, we could get a quick blitz from one of the linebackers. If we get two blitzes from the left or one blitz from the right, the quarterback has to throw hot.

If we ran the five-down protection, the five inside people match up in an area zone-blocking scheme on the three-two look. If anyone outside of the three-two package comes on a blitz, the quarterback has to throw hot. In that case, all he has to do is watch the safety for movement to get the alert for the blitz. If the safety goes right, the blitz is coming from that side. If he goes left, that is the side he has to watch.

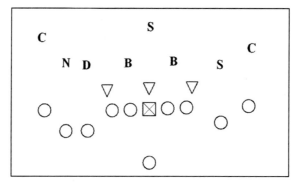

Figure 8-18

I'm going to go to some of our favorite routes in this offense. Our number one route is a double slant on the short side and the takeoff quick out on the wide side. The back has an option read, depending on his blocking responsibility to the widest receiver to the field lined up three yards outside of the numbers. The widest receiver to the short side aligns the same way. The slot receivers split the difference between the widest receiver and the offensive tackle.

Let's talk about where our thought processes were. I like slant patterns against everything except cover three. In cover three, the nickel and low safety, have an inside-out coverage on the slant routes. Both corners are going to the deep outside third. The free safety is going to the deep middle. You think the outside slant is open, and end up hitting the nickel back right in the chest with the ball. He is falling off on the outside slant, and the strong safety is coming under the inside slant. If we see cover three, we tell our quarterback to forget the slants and throw the ball to the other side. We look for the go route, to the out pattern, and to the dump off to the running back. We will throw the slant on every other coverage except cover three.

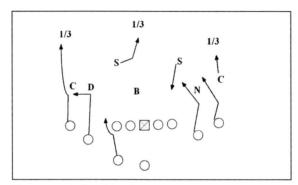

Figure 8-19. Double slant

We tell our inside receiver if he is getting a bump-and-run cover, he gets inside and slants right now. If the defender is off him, he comes off hard for three steps and breaks his pattern off into the crease between the defenders. All cuts have to be made at forty-five degree angles. The outside receiver has to win on his route. He gets off the line any way he can. If he has to come under the defender, it is all right. If he pushes up the field when he runs his slant, we want it flat. That keeps him away from the corner.

If the coverage is not cover three, we throw the inside receiver first and the outside receiver second. If we know it is cover two, the defender is doing every thing he can to keep the inside receiver out of the middle. When that happens, the outside receiver is open. The quick passing game comes from what we call a quick five-step drop. We don't throw any three-step passes. The corners are coached to watch the quarterback on his third step. If he stops on the third step, the corners are taught to break on the receiver. We want to take the drop past the third step to get the corner off balance as to what is coming. The timing is not that different for the pattern, but it looks different to the corner.

To the wide side of the field, we sit the inside receiver down if he see zone defense. If it is man coverage, he is running outside on the out. We always bring the back away from the slant routes in case it is man coverage. If it is man cover, that pulls the linebacker from underneath the slant routes.

The trips formation is the easiest way to teach a young quarterback. If he is a great athlete but can't read too well, this formation is the way to teach him. The first thing you teach him is the one-on-one to the backside. Most of the time, the best receiver is to the single receiver side. If that receiver has one-on-one coverage, throw the ball to him. If he is not single coverage, he goes to the trips side.

The receivers on the trips side are running a combination pattern. The inside slot is running a 12- yard to 14-yard in route and continues to run across the field. We don't want him to stop in the middle in a hole. The outside slot is running a shallow crossing pattern and comes across on the snap of the ball. The depth of the pattern is two to three yards over the line of scrimmage. The outside receiver is running a 6-yard to 8-yard in route. We want him to square off the cut and settle down in zone coverage if he finds a hole. The single receiver is running a 15-yard comeback pattern. The running back is running a swing route to the trips side.

We call this route all in, because all the patterns are going in except the swing pattern of the back. If it is man coverage, the shallow cross could rub off the defender covering the running back. Defenses don't switch coverage on those kinds of routes. If there is any contact between the receiver and either the defender covering the receiver or the linebacker, it could pop the running back free.

Our progression for this pattern is the split end if he is single covered. In the trip set, we throw the shallow cross first, the deep in route second, and the outside in route third.

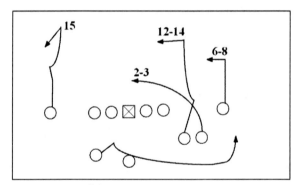

Figure 8-20. All in

This next play is the counter to the previous play. If the split end is single covered, we go to him as the first choice. If he has two defenders to that side, we flare the back to clear out under the curl. To the trips side, we run a go route by the outside receiver. Don't make the mistake of calling it a clear-out route. This is the pattern you have to throw. You don't have to complete it, but you have to throw it to keep the defense honest. This is the home-run throw, and you will hit it sometimes. Don't think it is a wasted pattern. The outside slot starts his pattern just like the shallow cross he ran on the all-in pattern. He takes three steps and breaks the pattern outside at a depth of two to three yards.

The inside slots pattern is the one we have to talk about. We spent more time running this route in the last eight years than any other route we have. I'm sure we'll do the same thing at Georgia Tech. We try to read coverages with this route. If the coverage is any kind of man coverage, the receiver breaks the pattern out at 10 to 12 yards. If it is any kind of zone coverage, he works his way up to 15 yards and bends it out and settles in the hole at 18, 3 yards outside the numbers.

The dime back keeping the inside slot out of the middle of the field is running to the deep middle. The receiver settles in the hole at 18 yards and stays out of the corner's zone. The nickel locks on the outside slot to keep him out of the middle and drifts with him outside. He is so preoccupied with the slot that he can't get back under the inside slot at 18-yards deep. This has been our number one route for the last eight years.

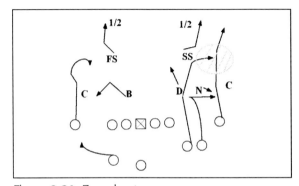

Figure 8-21. Zone beater

Well, we didn't get to the offensive game planning or the no-huddle offense, but if you would like to talk about those things come see us at Georgia Tech. Thank you very much.

9

Run and Pass in the Spread Offense

Skip Holtz
University of South Carolina
2004

I am going to talk about the spread offense. I will cover how we have progressed to this offense. Most of the time, we are in the multiple spread offense, and about thirty percent of the time, we are in a two backs set. When I coached at Connecticut I was in two back sets almost seventy percent of the time. I believe in running the football. I believe that is the way you win football games. There are a lot of ways to run the football. Some people throw the ball, some run the option, and some people run the power game. Regardless of whether are mentally tough, I believe they should be able to run the football.

In our first year at South Carolina, we were 0-11. We played the SEC teams, and we did not have the same talent they had. Hopefully we have closed the gap in talent somewhat. We were 0-11, and we were an awful two back offense. It used to be when teams got into a two back set teams went to an eight man front. Today, if you get into the two back set, you will see the nine man front. The two safeties are going to find a way to run downhill.

After the season, we saw the problems. We could run an isolation play and have everyone blocked, and the safetyman would come up and make the tackle for a gain of three yards. The next play, we would run the power play, and a defensive lineman would make the tackle for a loss of one yard. We would run another play, and again the safety would make the tackle for a gain of three yards. Now it was fourth-and-five, and we had to punt the football.

We sat down as a staff and tried to figure out a way to get the safeties out of the box. Teams are playing quarter coverages and match-ups that get everyone involved in the running game. That is why we went to the spread offense.

For us, the offense must complement the defense. Even though we are in the spread offense, we are not going to throw the ball 55 to 60 times per game. We are running the spread for a number of reasons, but we are in it first to complement our defense. We want to make first downs and control the football. Coach Holtz is an old-school thinker. He learned under Woody Hayes and Earle Bruce. They ran the ball for three yards and a cloud of dust, and then punted the football. They wanted to force the offense to drive the ball 80 yards to beat them. They were determined to win the game by a score of 10 to 7, or 14 to 10.

In the last four years, we have been in the top four teams in the SEC in rushing. We have converted over 40 percent on third-down plays. We are in the top three teams in the SEC in turnovers lost. This year, we led the SEC in the fewest turnovers, with only 15. When people think of the spread offense, they think of a high-risk offense where they throw the ball on every down. Last year we threw the ball 380 times and only got sacked 11 times. The spread offense helped us in this regard.

Productivity in the red zone has been our strength the last few years. The last two years we have gone 5-7 and 5-7. I am not standing up here beating my chest over those two years. But if you will look at our games, you will see the difference in winning and losing is only one or two plays. We were only three or four plays away from being a 9-3 team instead of 5-7. What we have done with the spread offense is to give us a chance to win in the fourth quarter.

First, I want to talk about our running game. We picked up a play last year that we call the mid zone. We had always been an inside and outside zone team. The reason we used the zone plays was because so many defensive teams were running stunts against us. Teams stunt to stop the run as well as the pass. We ran the mid zone last year 180 times. We averaged 6.0 yards per carry. But the way we evaluated the play was to see how many times we were able to gain 4.0 yards for us.

That is how we evaluate our run plays. We want to know the percentage of times we gained four yards on the play. Some plays may go for ten yards and then go for zero yards, and that comes out to an average of five yards. But that is a hit-or-miss play. In our mid zone play we had a 71 percent of plus four yards. On our inside zone play we averaged 6.2 yards, but we only converted the four yards on 80 tries.

The other running play for us is the counter, which is a misdirection play. Also, we run the outside zone play. It is not a big play for us because we are running the mid zone play. Then we have an option zone play. So you can see the zone plays are four of our five running plays. They are very similar, but the steps are just a little different.

When you get in the spread offense, you have two options. You can run play action and throw the ball down the field, or you can fake and throw the screen passes. You can fake the run and throw the ball, or you become a great screen pass team. It does not take talent to run the screen play. It does take execution.

We have a 15-minute session each day that we run our SDD period. We run nothing but screens, draws, and delays in this period. I will cover the bubble screen, the slow screen, the iso draw play, the reverse, and our middle screen.

I mentioned recruiting a few minutes ago. I want to tell you a story that I think will illustrate some of the issues we face in college recruiting today. The story is about a coach that dies and goes to the Pearly Gates and asks to see St. Peter. St. Peter comes to see the coach and says, "You have run a clean life, but when I look at the total picture, you are on the bubble. You could go to heaven or you could go to hell. You could do either one. I will give you a chance to decide if you want to go to heaven or hell. You can spend one day in each place and then decide where you want to go." The coach said that would be fine.

The first day he went down to hell. He got off the elevator and immediately saw a few of his old buddies. The people in hell were playing golf, playing cards, sitting around the pool, chasing women, and having a good time. His first thoughts were "It is not all bad down here in hell."

The next day he goes to heaven. The people were walking in the park, and going about their business. It was peaceful and quiet and everyone was content.

The next day he went back to see St. Peter. He said, "St. Peter, I never thought I would say this, but it was not all that bad in hell. I really think I would rather go to hell after visiting both places." St Peter told him that was fine and that he could have his wish.

St. Peter put the old coach on the elevator going back to hell. The elevator doors open and the fire and brimstone were shooting out at him as he got off the elevator. The people in the background were screaming and yelling something awful. He got off the elevator and saw Satan. He went over to Satan and said, "Satan, I was down here yesterday and everyone was having a good time. Everyone seemed so happy. What happened?" Satan replied, "That was your recruiting visit!" That always puts things in perspective when recruiting.

Why the zone play? We were a young team last year. We lost nine starters from our offense the year before. We lost four offensive linemen and our receivers. We wanted something on offense that was simple. You will see a lot of carryover with the rules on our plays. We want to make sure our players know what we are doing. This offense is good against all defenses. If the defense wants to move around or if they want to twist and run games, the offense is designed to handle those things.

We can run the offense of our multiple backfield sets. We can run the offense out of split backs, the I formation, one back set, motions, and multiple formations. We can get in the "I" formation. We can run 3 wide with 2 backs, we can run 2 tight ends and 1 back, we can run 1 tight end and 3 wide receivers, and we can go with 4 wideouts.

What we decided to do was to run the play about 200 times. That breaks down to almost 20 times per game. But we were going to run that same play from about ten different formations a couple of times. You cannot get in the same set and run the same plays over and over. We wanted to make it simple for the linemen, but at the same time, we wanted to dress the play up a lot of different ways.

As we go through these zone, plays, you must be able to answer a few questions to run the plays. You must be able to block frontside support. When you get into four wide receivers you must be able turn and block the frontside support to be able to account for all of the blitzes.

There are a number of ways to do that. You can keep the tight end in to block the support. If you do not have a tight end in the game, you can block with the motion receiver. You can use the back to block if you are in a two back set. Also you can use formations to block the support. You can put trips to the field and allow the inside receiver to block inside on the safety if he were an issue.

The other thing you must be able to do is to block on the backside. How do we block the backside? You can leave the 5 technique unblocked because you do not think he can run the play down from the backside. You can put a tight end to the backside. You can motion the wide receiver. You can put the quarterback in the shotgun set and have him read the backside end. These are the things you must consider when you are running the inside, middle, and outside zone plays.

Let me talk about the mid zone play. We call the play Ranger. We have set up our offense where we can call everything in a "no huddle" situation. We found that we were getting too wordy with everything, so we tried to make it simple. We are a rule offense. We give the players rules that will cover all defensive situations. Let me go over the rules for Ranger.

The frontside tight end has the D gap. It could be a 9 technique, or a strong safety outside. He has the D gap. He must listen for the tackle to make a call. If the tackle makes a help call, the tight end helps the tackle on a combo block. The end is going to block the D gap first with a midreach, or he is going to combo block if the tackle makes a call to the end.

The frontside tackle has on. He has the midreach. He has no help on the man over him. He can make an overcall to the guard if he does need help on the man over him.

The frontside guard has on. He works with the center. The center is on zero. He works with the frontside guard. Everyone on the backside, including the guard, tackle, and tight end, block the A, B, and C gaps.

The key to the mid zone play is the block. We have three zone blocks. We have a tight reach, a midreach, and a full reach block. That is where we spend most of our time with our offensive linemen.

You have seen the plastic donuts with the holes cut out in the center that Gilman Gear has for offensive linemen steps. We take those donuts and put the hole over the right foot. We want the lineman to take a lead step with the right foot, and take a step with the left foot gaining ground, and we try to put the left foot in the crotch of the defensive man we are blocking. If we are the tackle and we are trying to reach the 5 technique on the outside, we get the first lead step with the right foot, and then step with the left foot upfield. We want to step into the crotch of the defender. Then I want to get the shoulders square from there.

If it is a tight reach, we put the right foot just inside the defender's left foot, or inside of the defender's outside foot. Now the left step has to come almost straight upfield. We never want to cross our feet, and we want to keep the shoulders square.

On the full reach, we put the foot all the way on the outside of the defender's outside foot. We take a lead step, cross over, plant, and then shuffle up to the inside to turn everything back. When we talk about our zone blocks, I will call it a midreach, a tight reach, or a full reach block. We do a lot of drills on these three blocks. We work on the steps of each block over and over. That is the key with what we are trying to do with our offensive line.

For the receivers, if they motion to the play, they block the support. If they motion away from the play, they block the end.

The quarterback steps at 4 o'clock if he is under the center. The aiming point for the tailback is two yards outside the tight end. He is reading the hat of the tackle. His steps are a lead step, crossover step, and then he plants and takes it two yards outside the tight end landmark. You must hammer home for the tailback to read the hat of the tackle.

This is the way we would block the different defense on the tight end side.

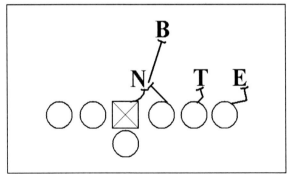

Figure 9-1

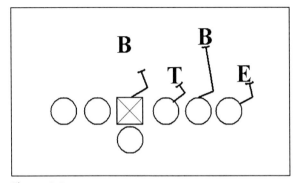

Figure 9-2

When we first put this play in, I was not totally sold on the play. I was taught never to chase a linebacker. I was taught to let the linebacker go, and to turn back and get the inside seal block. This is one play where we teach the linemen to chase the linebacker. We want to chase the linebacker and push him by the hole. We want to push him past the point of attack because about ninety percent of the time, the play looks like a cutback play. It is really a cut up the field and not a cutback.

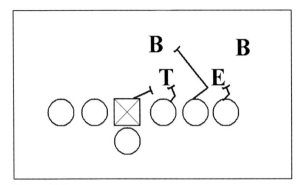

Figure 9-3

As the guard takes his three steps, he looks inside to help the center. He takes a lead step, a step with the back foot upfield, and then pushes off the inside step to get upfield to get to the linebacker. He does not run to scoop block the linebacker. He wants to kick him past the point of attack.

If our quarterback is under the center, we must find a way to block the backside end. We could turn him free or we can use the man in motion. The way we are going to block on the frontside is with the tight end. Our tailback is seven yards deep on the play. They take the lead step, cross over, and on the third step, they plant and cut upfield (see Figure 9-4). We are trying to give the defense the image that we are running the outside zone. On the third step, they are planting and going down hill.

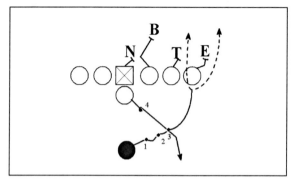

Figure 9-4

On the inside zone, the blocking is the same for the frontside. This play was a little more productive for us. For the front five men, the rules are exactly the same. The only difference is now it is a tight reach. We do not cross the feet on the tight reach. We are trying to get movement on the down lineman and move them out of the hole. We have tightened up the running back. He takes a lateral step, a crossover step, and plants on the third step. He is not going outside, so his aiming point is the outside leg of the guard. He is reading the first down lineman (see Figure 9-5).

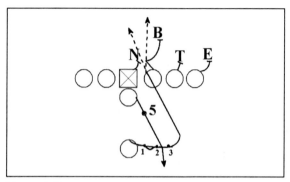

Figure 9-5

We can run the play toward the 3 technique or we can run the play toward the shade technique. It does not matter; he is still reading the first down lineman. The center and guard are working together on the shade or the 3 technique man. If we can not reach the 3 technique man because he is too wide, the back is going to cut back inside. If the 3 technique man goes inside, we take him down the line and the back cuts behind the block.

The quarterback is in the shotgun and he is reading the backside end. If he quarterback is under center, we ask him to step at 5 o'clock and then to go straight back to 6 o'clock. We do that because we do not want him to go back at six o'clock and then have to redirect, and come back to five o'clock. If he comes back at 5 o'clock, he does not push the running back too wide because we want the quarterback to give the ball to the tailback as deep as possible. This gives the tailback a better cutback lane. That is why we do not stay on the straight tract at 5 o'clock on the drop to hand the ball to the tailback. The tailback takes a lateral step, then a crossover step, then plants and cuts upfield reading the first-down lineman.

With this offense it is a great offense if you have a quarterback that can run. In high school, you want to put your best athlete at quarterback or running back because you want the ball in his hands. In this offense, the quarterback gets a chance to make a lot of plays.

Here is another concept that has been effective for us. We are running the zone play to the tight end side. We do not need a lead blocker because we have the tight end to block the alley. We run the zone to the tight end.

If we call "Orbit" we are going to run the option to the backside. The onside back fakes toward the tight end side. The quarterback goes toward the defensive end on the line. If the defense squeezes the play, the quarterback is going to option the support man on the outside. He does not option on the defensive end. He goes outside and options off the support man outside (see Figure 9-6).

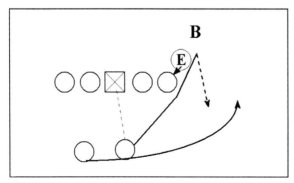

Figure 9-6

Let me get to the counter play. Although this play has not been our best play, since it ties in so much with what you do with the zone plays, it has been our most productive play for the last couple of years. We average over eight yards per carry. We run the play about 60 times per year. We probably should run it a whole lot more than that. It ties in so well with what we do on our zone play. If your run the one back this is one of the best plays you can run. It is nothing more than an isolation play out of the one back set with the backside tackle as the blocking back. That is what it boils down to.

The rules are simple. The tight end has the D gap. The frontside tackle and frontside guard have the number one and number two men on the line of scrimmage. The guard has one on the line, and the tackle has number two on the line of scrimmage. The center has the nose man or the zero man. The backside guard has the number one man on the line. The backside tackle pulls and kicks out on the linebacker.

The tackle pulls and turns up in the first hole past the center. He is looking to kick the linebacker. We are not going to log the linebacker. We want to kick him outside. (see Figure 9-7).

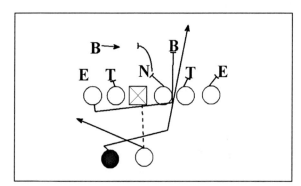

Figure 9-7

In a 4-3 defense, the middle linebacker has a hard time seeing the tackle pull. We have run the play with the guard pulling. Our tackles run decently. The problem you have with pulling the guard is two-fold. First, you have to block the center to the backside on the 3 technique man, and you do not get the point of attack blocked as well on the shade technique. The second point is the fact the linebackers do not read the tackles pulling like they do the guards (see Figure 9-8).

In the backfield, we are trying to do is to take the movement on our zone and ranger plays and step away from the call to give our tackle time to get into the hole.

If we see a double eagle defense, we call "Bear." That is an exception the blocking rules. We are going to double the center back or the 3 technique on the playside, and that tells the tackle to kick the defender outside instead of leading through the hole on the linebacker.

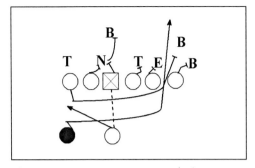

Figure 9-8. Counter vs. a 3 technique

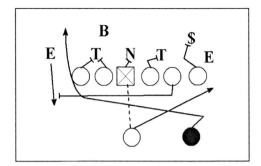

Figure 9-9. Counter vs. bear defense

We found this was a better play to the shade than it was to the 3 technique man because of the double team block. We have run the play both ways, so we do not give the play away when we are running it to the shade technique.

We tell the ballcarrier he has to take a hop step away from the play. If that tackle does not move very well, he may have to slow the run down to give the tackle time to get to the block.

We can run the plays with the running back or with the quarterback in the shotgun. We can let the quarterback keep the ball on the bootleg if the backside end does not stay at home and honor the bootleg.

When we line up in the shotgun, we can have the running back on either side of the quarterback. We can run the quarterback on the zone one way, and the running back on the counter play the other way. We can run the zone either way, and you can run the counter play either way.

Running the football is tough and it is a mindset. The thing I worried about getting into the spread offense and becoming a zone team was that everything would come down to a finesse game. A lot of teams run the zone offense and that have the linemen drop stepping and all of the other finesse moves. We do not drop step. We want to move forward and come off the ball. For us, it is toughness and a mindset of coming off the football to run the ball. We get in a mindset that we are going to run the football when we get in the spread offense.

Once we were able to establish the run, the thing we wanted to do was to eliminate our turnovers. After, we were able to do that we wanted to make sure we had a high completion percentage. That is where the next package comes into play. I am talking about our screens, draws, and delays.

We break the offense down into these areas. We have our run game, which I covered. Then we have our screen game, our quick passing game, and our dropback passing game. I will not have time to cover all of this here, but I will talk about our screen game.

Everyone that has ever been in the spread offense runs the bubble screen. We run the bubble a number of different ways. We will run the bubble out of a 2 X 2 set and a 3 X 1 set (see Figure 9-10, Figure 9-11, Figure 9-12, and Figure 9-13).

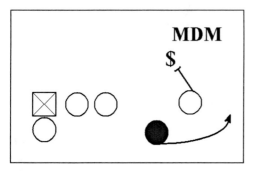

Figure 9-10

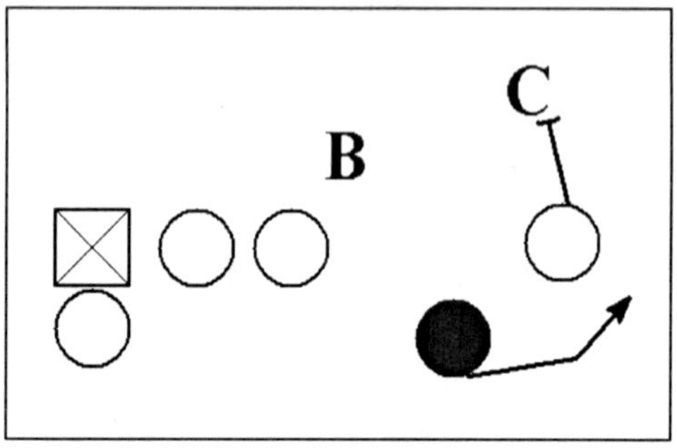

Figure 9-11

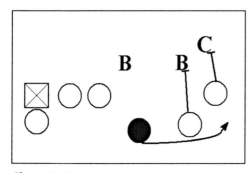

Figure 9-12

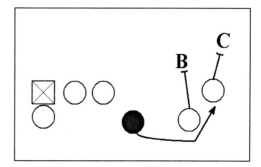

Figure 9-13

Predominately we will bubble to our inside receiver. We will also bubble to our middle receiver and our outside man. We are going to make you cover our receivers down low.

Some teams associate this play with the running game. Teams will move a linebacker outside and split the difference between the receivers. They set the man outside and have him key the quarterback. If he sees the quarterback come up to throw the ball, the linebacker comes outside to play the pass.

In the 2 X 2 set, we bubble the inside guy. The rule for the man on the outside is the most dangerous man. In the three deep, that is the strong safety. In a two deep, that is going to be the cornerback. The quarterback's read is on the down defenders outside. We never throw the bubble if both receivers are covered down low. If they put the linebacker on the inside man and the strong safety on the outside man, then we can't run the bubble screen. I will talk later about our options when that happens.

In our trips set, the only rule we have is if everyone is covered down low. The rules are the same for the receivers on the blocks. We block the most dangerous man. We block the strong safety and the corner. We let the alley defender go.

What teams started to do to take away our bubble was to play us in three deep. They took the strong safety and put him on the inside shoulder of our middle receiver. As the play develops, the blocker stalks the strong safety. As the ball is released, he comes up the field and does not allow us to get any width on the play. That forces the receiver to turn back inside, and that is where the pursuit comes from.

So what we started doing was to run the crack block on the inside man (see Figure 9-14). The outside receiver came down inside and stopped the penetration of the strong safety. The middle receiver prevents penetration until the block is made, and then he releases and goes upfield to block the corner.

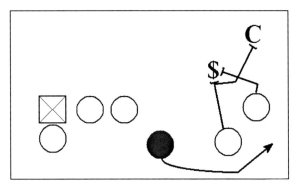

Figure 9-14

That is what we did when we started getting heavy outside leverage on our number two receiver to run the bubble. We run the play from trips and get the ball to the third receiver. We can run the play to the split end side. The play has been good to us in all three sets.

The play that is dynamite is our bubble deep. It is a great play to get the ball down the field. I talked about our talent level. We do not have the talent to say we are going to play four wide outs and throw the ball down the field until we score. I wish we had that kind of talent, but we don't. Our talent is not quite as good as our opponents in most cases. So we must find ways to get the ball down the field. This is a good way to do that

We have the inside receiver stalk block on the under defender. He will stop to set his block, and then he will take off down the hash mark. The outside man will stock block and stop and go down the sideline. The receivers stalk the man head-on and then they go vertical down the field. The quarterback pumps the bubble and then lays the ball up for the receiver to run under.

One of the problems we have is our receivers all run the bubble differently. One receiver will run it hard down the field, and the next man will run a soft pattern down the field. So we have tried to give the receivers some guidelines to make everything uniform. We tell the bubble man to put his inside foot up. As the ball is snapped, we are going to turn our back to the quarterback and sprint three steps sideways. This gives the quarterback a target, which is the middle of the receiver's back. He takes the three steps straight across the field toward the sideline. The quarterback is throwing the ball right at the receiver's back. When the receiver gets to the third step, he shuffles gets turned around, and faces the football, where he can catch the ball and run with it. We should be able to complete that pass. I do not have very much patience with an incompletion on this play.

I tell you what makes the play special. The offensive line and the running backs run the inside zone play. If the defense moves outside and covers down on all of our receivers, we are going to run the inside zone play. We make a zone-bubble combo call. The quarterback can make that read from the shotgun. We do not run the play from under the center. We only run the play in the shotgun. We have a combination check to give the quarterback some guidance on checking to the run. We can run the zone play toward the bubble, or we can run the zone away from the bubble. It is a great play, with the tight end to the backside, and trips to the wide side of the field.

We ran the bubble play close to 80 times this year. We are going to make the defense go outside and cover everyone down. When we went to this offense, we wanted to be able to run the ball. We wanted the defense to cover our outside receivers down so we could run the football. With our quarterback in the shotgun, we can run the ball against the six man front even though we only have five blockers.

The bubble pass is really a sweep play for us. It is getting the ball out on the perimeter where we can make yardage. It is not a big play for long yardage for us. We want to get eight or nine yards on the play. If you have a sweep play that gives you eight or nine yards per carry, how many times do you call it?

We can run the play from the empty set. We run the double bubble and let the quarterback run the zone play. If the defense covers the bubble, we are going to have the quarterback run the ball on the zone. If they do not cover down on our wide receivers, we run the bubble screen. It is a good play to run on first down and it is a great third-and-short call, and it is a good second-and-medium call. You cannot go wrong calling the play. If you are going to run the spread offense, you must be able to get the ball outside in a hurry.

If you asked us to tell you the thing we have done the best job with in the last three years, it would be our slow screen pass. Our linemen are not great athletes, and they are not speed guys. But this has been a good play for us. There are a couple of coaching points on it that I want to cover. Here are the rules for the slow screen play.

The receiver that is closest to the play crack blocks. If we are in a tight end and flanker set, then the tight end would be the closest receiver, and he would crack block on the first linebacker in the box. If we run the play to the split end side, then the inside receiver is the man that crack blocks back inside on the linebacker. If we run the play to a single receiver side, then that single receiver crack blocks inside. The closest receiver to the ball, inside out, is the man that is going to crack the inside linebacker. If we run trips to the right and call the screen to the right, the inside receiver is going to crack block inside on the linebacker. All of the other receivers are DMMS, Deep Man My Side. They get downfield.

The tackle sets the depth. He sets up and cuts the defender at six yards (see Figure 9-15). The guard jams, locks, and releases. That is our timing on the play. JLR is what we call it. If the defensive line comes, we want to jam them, lock the arms out, and then release them. We do not give a count of 1001, 1002, and 1003. We have found that does not work well for us. We call it JLR. The guard is going to go flat and kick outside.

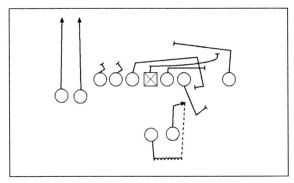

Figure 9-15. Slow screen

The center is going to go JLR and then go flat and turn up. The backside guard does the JLR and then he peels and seals. He comes down the line and peels back, looking for any defensive lineman that is chasing the play from inside out.

Here is a big coaching point. We want our guard, center, guard alignment to be no more than two yards apart. We want those three men running straight down the line. The running back sets up like he is blocking on a pass play. He sets up behind the guard. He does not leave until the guard goes. When the guard goes, then the tailback leaves. The running back wants to be behind the wall of the blockers, so he never takes a shot. He turns his back to the line of scrimmage, and we are going to protect him as he catches the ball.

When the quarterback puts the ball in the air, the tailback makes a "Go" call. He steps up and fakes the block. As he sees the ball in the air, he calls out, "Go-Go-Go." Now we want everyone to turn and go upfield. If he has not called "Go," then the linemen are not allowed to turn upfield.

The quarterback is in the shotgun. He takes a three-step drop. He takes three steps and holds he ball as long as possible. We want the defenders coming to the quarterback. We want the quarterback shifting to the side of the call. He wants the defenders coming toward him before the throws the ball to the back setting up behind the guard.

We run the iso draw. We run the play out of the two backs set, or we can run it out of our one back set with the quarterback. We use the same rules as we use on our counter play. The quarterback flashes the quick pass to the side away from the play side. The running back isolates on the frontside linebacker. The quarterback takes the snap, drop steps, and shows pass to the side of the back that is getting the ball. We do not run an isolation play, but we do run the isolation draw. If you run the isolation, the linebackers come up and try to fill the hole, and there is no separation. By showing pass, we are trying to get a little hesitation to hold the linebackers.

The reverse play may be one of the best things we do because we run it out of so many different formations and different backfield actions. We have a lot of fun with the plays because we only run the reverse one way in each game. The players want to know who is going to get to carry the ball on the reverse each week. We can run the reverse off the speed option and the zone plays.

When you do not have the talent of your opponents, you have to find ways to move the football. We have tried to be simple with our zone concepts so we all know what we are doing. We let the defense dictate where we are going to run the ball instead of trying to push teams around that have us outmanned. We have done that with our screen and delay game. I do not know if I have helped you with this session, but if you could just take one thing back, it would be this.

This is what we do. Get something you can live with. Get married to it, teach your players what you are doing, and stay with it. Don't change so much. We all are guilty of adding things we see during the year that we think worked well for someone else. Do what you do best and take that philosophy and be simple. Thank you for your time. I really appreciate your attention.

10

Establishing the Spread Offense

Craig Howard
Nease High School (Florida)
2006

First, I want to give you some information about my background. I have coached at the small single-A school, and I have coached in the PAC 10, and the Southwest Conference. To me, every stop along the way was the same. You are coaching kids, and loving them. It is having a passion and a love for coaching the game.

I could spend hours telling you about coaching jobs. The one thing I want to get across to you is perseverance. We were fortunate to win a state championship. All of our staff was involved; I just happened to be the head coach. I am 52 years old and have been in the game for a while. We had come close to winning it all in some other situations, but we did not win the state. In all of the jobs I took on, I never took over a school that was the perfect situation. As in most cases, in all of the jobs that are open, the person that gets the head coaching position must build a team up. Otherwise, those jobs would not be open.

Four years ago, I went back into coaching at the college level at Edgewater College in Jacksonville. They wanted to run our offense. After coaching there for one year, I applied for a junior college in California. I flew out to California in July and interviewed. I did not get the job. I told my wife that I was just going to take a year off from coaching. I had been coaching for 30 years and I decided to take a year off and go around to colleges and study high school programs, and watch football practice. That all sounded good after 30 years of coaching.

When August came around, I wanted to coach again. I looked on the FHSAA website and found there was only one head-coaching job open in the USA. That job was at Apalachicola, Florida. I went there at the age of 49 and took the job two days after the practice season had started. Now, I had made a long journey, to say the least. I went from applying for a junior college job in California, to the head-coaching job at Apalachicola High School in Florida.

After I got the job, I drove up to the field and there were 12 players out on the field practicing with four dads. The grass on the field was as high as this table. I told the dads the first thing we had to do was to cut the grass. I told the fathers if they would cut the grass, I would take the 12 players and work with them. I told the fathers we had to get the grass cut to run the spread offense because the grass would slow us down. We did not have very many athletes in that group. However, it proved to be an interesting situation. When I took the job, I had made up my mind I would retire there. I was going to buy a house there, buy a boat, and I was going to eat oysters and shrimp, and drink Bud Light for the rest of my life.

Now, some of you that are in the big programs that have a big budget cannot imagine that situation with the grass that tall. The grass had not been cut all summer. The lawn mowers would not cut that grass. We had to go down to the prison and get some inmates to cut the grass with big mowers. The prison had the guards out on the field with their shotguns watching the prisoners. It was just like the scenes from *Cool Hand Luke*.

I told the team we were going to run the no-huddle spread offense. We only had 13 kids out for the team. I did not have an assistant coach. I was 50 years old and I was coaching the team by myself. I looked at the schedule and we were playing Ft. Walton Beach in our 10th game of the year. They were a 4A power in the state. We had to play some of the best teams in the area with those 13 players.

My wife and children were still living back in Jacksonville, Florida. After the games were over on Friday, I would drive back to Jacksonville to see my family over the weekend. Then I would go back to Apalachicola on Monday morning.

After that season, the Nease High School head-coaching job came open. I applied for that job. I drove up to Nease High School in my 1968 Volkswagen Beetle. All of the cars in the parking lot were Hummers and Mercedes. Those cars did not belong to the assistant coaches; they belonged to the players. I did not think I would get the job, but I did.

At the time of my arrival at Nease High School, we got a noseguard who transferred in from Trinity Christian School. He was a home-schooled kid by the name of Timmy Tebow. We made a quarterback out of him. He turned out to be the best quarterback I have worked with.

One day after practice, the coaches were in our staff meeting. I looked out on the field and saw a player throwing the football. He was working on his passing skills by himself. I took a closer look and saw it was Timmy Tebow. He had the greatest work ethic I had ever been around as a coach. Not only did he work his guts out, but also he had the ability to influence others with his work ethic. Tim has already gone to the University of Florida this semester and he has made an impression on the coaches in the weight room.

The one thing I was able to do at Nease, besides getting the opportunity to coach a player like Tim Tebow, was that I was able to surround myself with a great staff. I have a staff that loves the game of football. They have a passion for the game, and they have a passion for the kids. It is difficult to find great assistant coaches. We work as a staff in everything we do. We went to two-platoon football. At the time we went to Nease, we had 60 players out for the team. Now we have 160 kids out for the team.

In the time that I have for this lecture, I want to talk to you about our no-huddle spread offense. I want to talk about our strength program and how our kids started getting scholarships by becoming stronger. This past year we had 12 players that signed scholarships. When I first arrived at Nease, the college recruiters would not even come by the school. Now our kids are much stronger and they are being looked at by most of the recruiters.

As a head coach it is difficult to find assistant coaches that are dedicated enough to develop the players in all phases of the game. The head coach wants to know if you are the type of assistant coach that is going to be there when needed. He must be loyal to the program, and he must love kids, love the game of football, and be willing to learn the game. It is difficult to find a staff with all of those qualities. On most staffs, you are lucky if you have two or three coaches like that.

We did a study of the teams that were similar to our situation to see what they were doing to make their programs better. Here are the things we looked at as we researched the available information.

The first question we want to know was how many players those teams have out for football. We wanted to know how many levels of teams they had in their program. How many teams did they have? What type of off-season program did they have? How much money do they have for their football budget? How do they have the booster clubs organized? How much money does the booster club give the football program? How many assistant coaches do they have?

By compiling all of this information, we came up with a formula. Here are the things those schools have that are similar to our program. When I went to Nease, the budge was $11,000 and we were $15,000 in the hole. When we looked at those benchmark schools, we found out the booster clubs were raising $100,000 for their programs. We played Hoover High School in Alabama on ESPN and their budget is over $500,000. It is like a college situation.

We looked at the number of coaches these schools had. Nease had five head coaches in seven years, but they had new assistant coaches every year. When that happens, the kids are learning new techniques every year.

So we decided we wanted to have a touchdown club that was separate from the booster club. We want to start raising money to elevate our program from an $11,000 budget to a $100,000 budget. We want 15 assistant coaches instead of three assistant coaches. Instead of 60 players on the JV and varsity, we wanted 160 players out for our frosh, JV, and varsity teams. We have been able to do most of the things we set up as our goals.

The big thing to me that I think has really made a difference in our program is getting those assistant coaches. One good assistant coach is worth five good players. We have 12 assistant coaches now and hope to add to that total. I am bringing in coaches with whom I want to be associated. I want coaches who want to talk football. We are going to run the spread offense. We are going to run a 4-4 package defense, and we are going to coach three levels of football. That is what we do. We do not have a freshman team that practices all by itself. All of our coaches work with freshman team, JV, and varsity levels. When we play a JV game, all of our coaches are on that sideline. I am the head varsity coach, but I am also the head JV coach. We have a year-round program. We have a great off-season program.

Our kids must dress in the parking lot. Even though we won the state, our kids still have to dress in the parking lot. Our fields are mowed, and it is not as it was at Apalachicola. The first thing we did with the money we raised was to put it into safety equipment for the kids. We got safety equipment such as helmets and shoulder pads. Then we started putting money into our weight room. We took over an old dance room that was not being used and made it our weight room. Our kids bought into our program. We work hard and we are going to compete. When we walk into our weight room, we coach in there just as we would in a game. We have the entire staff in the room and they all work. Our staff is dressed in coaching uniforms and works with the players they coach in the games. We compete in the weight room to make it more interesting.

Our kids come from nice homes and have many luxuries. The first thing have to do when we get them is to get after them to do what we want them to do on the field. That carries over into the weight room as well. We put them on the mats and have them compete against their teammates. Our kids learn to fight and they learn what it means to compete. The basis for our spread offense was to get our receivers to learn to fight and to compete on the field. Now, we were not throwing the football. We were working on the mats. Tim Tebow, who is 6'3" and weighs 245 pounds, would get in the group with the linebackers and he learned to compete on the mats. Now we will hear from Danny Cowgill on our strength and conditioning program and David San Juan will talk about our recruiting program.

Danny Cowgill – Strength and Conditioning Coach

(Highlights of the presentation on the goals of the Nease High School strength and conditioning program.)

- Build team unity through our strength and conditioning sessions.
- Develop functional strength.
- Teach the players the difference in strength and power. Football is a game of strength and speed.
- Build core strength.
- Develop flexibility, especially in the hips.

David San Juan – Recruiting Coordinator

Our recruiting program at Nease High School is related to the way we go about getting our players recruited to colleges. It is not about bringing in high school players from other schools to the Nease program. Our motto is, "If a kid wants to play college football, there is a place for him to play."

I want to go through a couple of basic points I think could help you in your program. I will give you a list of my contacts and a website that you can go to that will show you what we do in our recruiting program.

We educate our players and parents early in their high school program about the recruiting process. We give the parents a book that I will be glad to send you. We use the same basic approach with players such as Timmy Tebow. We put the players in our system and try to attract the colleges to our players. We do not wait for the colleges to find us.

Our website is: www.neaseprospects.com. That is the website I developed for our athletes. The cost to us was nothing. It only cost five dollars a month to host this site. We are up to 27,000 hits on the site. The site has my e-mail address on it.

I work with Derek Williams of Sunshine Preps. If you are interested in getting your kids recruited, it is a free service to your kids. He does a great job. You can reach him at: www.sunshinepreps.net.

Here is one quote I want to leave with you: "We coach for a loving and not for a living."

We had 30 seniors on our team this past fall. Five of them did not have a desire to go on to college to continue with football. Some 17 out of 25 of the other seniors are going to be playing football in college this coming fall at some level. We have 12 players that will be playing at Division IA programs. We figure we are gaining $300,000 per year in scholarship money using this system. Now I will turn it back over to Coach Howard.

Coach Craig Howard

After spending 15 years as a college coach, and then coming back to coach in high school, I thought having a recruiting coordinator would be worthwhile for our program. Our kids were smart, but they were not being recruited. We started the strength and conditioning program and that helped us a great deal. Our kids are being recruited because of the improvement we have made in our program in the last few years.

I think it is important for your best players to be your hardest workers in the program. You take the player you think is the best player in your program, sit him down, and tell him you think he is the best player in the program and that you want him to be the hardest worker on the team. That will change everything in the program. The college coaches tell me we have the best website they have seen to promote the high school players.

We all know about some of the recruiting services that come into the school and want to charge the players parents $1,000 to get a player on their list. The question I ask those services is this: how many athletes have received scholarships using this service? I think the NFL should pay for this service. With our website, we can tell our kids they will have a chance to go on to play at the next level if they are good enough. We will see to it that they are exposed to the colleges through our website.

We all have the choice of the offense or defense to run in high school. We call our offense the spread offense now. I am going to give you a brief overview of why and how we have used the offense.

In 1978 and 1979 when I was running this offense, it was called the run-and-shoot offense. Today the basis of our offense is the run-and-shoot. We have averaged 45 points per game (three-year total). However, I want everyone to know the reason we won the state championship was our defense and not just our offense.

Items	Year	Year
Wins	11	13
Rush Offense	183	211
Pass Offense	347	250
Total Offense	**530**	**461**

We think we are balanced between the run and the pass. We are not just throwing the ball on every down.

We have combined our spread offense with the no-huddle offense. We use a lot of words to teach our system. We want the words to describe our plays as much as possible. Here are the features of our offense. Again, we are a no-huddle spread offense. We two-platoon on all three levels. We want to run as many plays as possible, as fast as we possibly can. We have not huddled in three years at Nease High School.

We run multiple formations. We use personnel groups to create adjustments, chaos, and confusion. We use code words or hand signals. We are not going to use cards. We like the short pass and the long run. We want to throw the ball short and make a long run on the play.

We want to find the flaw in the defense. We do not look at a script to call the play. We look at the defense to call the plays. The flaw may be a player. The flaw may be the way a team lines up. We do not want to find the flaw on defense on Saturday in the film. We want to find the flaw before the game so we can take advantage of the flaw.

Another thing we do very well is to "coach the game." If you play two-platoon football, what do you do with the players when they are not on the field? We meet with our offense when the defense is on the field. We meet by positions. Each player meets with his position coach. We can make any adjustments during the game. We set up the chairs on the sideline to allow us to meet in small groups.

Attack. What? We do not just call plays. We attack. We force the defense to show their hand. We do not use blind calls. We do not run all of our plays against every defense we face. We are only going to run certain plays against different defenses. Again, we do not call plays off a list. We call the plays off the look the defense gives us.

By running the no-huddle spread offense, conditioning becomes a factor earlier in the game by running a lot of plays. It allows the offense to control the tempo of the game. We can run our offense very slow or we can go very fast. We control the tempo. We want to score 50 points per game and we want to make the defense throw up. This offense is not complicated. We are using the same offense all the way down to the fourth grade.

By running this system, we see fewer defensive looks. Players enjoy it and it builds confidence with the team. We want to get max reps in practice. We see mostly a nickel and a cover-3 look. We may see a nickel and cover 4.

We can run plays in sequence. We call this stampede. That means we are going to call three plays and run them without saying a word. We come up with some kind of acronyms the week of practice to help our players remember the order of those three plays. We can run five plays in stampede if we choose to do so.

We have another deal where we call "El Paso." This means we are going to run our concepts passing game in sequence until we call the code word to get out of that phase of the offense. We may run 10 plays in a row without calling anything. All the linemen need to hear is a direction occasionally.

Another thing we use is called "rock and roll." This means we are going to run the zone read and then we will go back to El Paso. This is how we practice so we can do these things in the games. We never huddle in practice.

Here is what we are looking for in play calling. We are going to run with the numbers. These are our rules.

- Five or six players should be in the box.
- Check for the four-man side and run away.
- Run to the three-man side.
- Run to the bubble: Shade or 1 and 5 techniques.
- Angles—Down block and kick-out. Reach them and stretch them.
- Grass—Get the ball to athlete in most open space.

We throw with the numbers. If the defense has six in the box, we can run or pass against a single safety. If they have seven in the box, we throw the ball if they do not have safeties. If they have five in the box, we run the ball. We run the ball against a two-safeties, four-shell look.

I want to talk about our running game. Here is what we did in the running game in two years.

Play	Tries	Average Yards
Quarterback Wrap (Dart)	79	10.0
Isolation	66	6.8
Zone Read	51	6.6
Quarterback Isolation	39	9.7
Speed Option	39	6.4

We can run the dart several ways (Figure 10-1). The way we run it against one team will be different from how we run it against another team.

Our next running play is our isolation play (Figure 10-2). Our quarterback reads the defensive end.

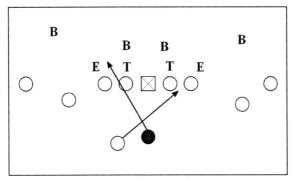

Figure 10-1. Quarterback wrap (dart)

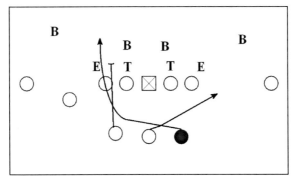

Figure 10-2. Isolation play

The third running play is our zone-read play (Figure 10-3). Again, the quarterback must read the defensive end.

We also run the quarterback isolation play (Figure 10-4). We have not used the play as much as some other plays, but we still average good yardage on the play.

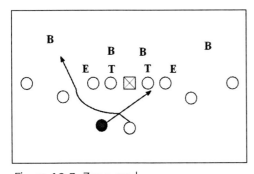

Figure 10-3. Zone read

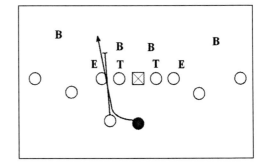

Figure 10-4. Quarterback isolation

Next is our speed option play (Figure 10-5). The quarterback can keep the ball or pitch it to the halfback like most option teams do.

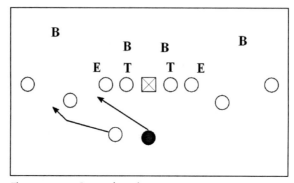

Figure 10-5. Spread option

In our pass production, this is what we have accomplished in three years:

Years	2003	2004	2005
Yards	2566	4604	3528
Touchdowns	20	51	38
Interceptions	5	3	2

Our system comes fully equipped with the following types of plays. Different elements of this offense will show up with each quarterback. We adapt to our quarterback.

- Quick game
- Half roll
- Five step
- PAP
- Gun dash
- Screen game
- Running back
- Wide receivers

We want to throw one screen pass out of every four dropback passes we throw. If we throw the ball 40 times in a game, that means we are going to throw the screen pass eight times. We run the screen to the running backs and to the wide receivers. We will even screen the ball to the quarterback.

We feel that adapting the offense to the quarterback is important. Not every quarterback has the same abilities. You must run the offense that fits the quarterback who is in the game. We are still going to run the no-huddle spread offense, but we may not run those same plays.

The big question is why we move the pocket in high school. We do not want our quarterback sitting back in the pocket all of the time. We practice the scramble drill each week. If the defense has players that are better than the players we have, blocking them it is better to move the quarterback. We want the quarterback to have the ability to run out of the pocket to avoid that 6'8", 290-pound defensive lineman coming full speed at him in the pocket. By running away from that big dude, we accomplish several things. One, we are still running our no-huddle spread offense, and all of that running chasing the quarterback is hard on that defense man. We are not limited in our offense. We have versatility built into the system.

Another way to move the pocket is with the play-action passing game. If I had to eliminate some of our offense, I would go back to our run-and-shoot offense and roll the quarterback out on several plays. He can roll to his best receiver and he can roll to the side he throws the best from.

We have 10 basic concepts in our passing game. We are going to take shots at the deep ball in every game. Again, that is part of the game plan. The question we must decide is how many shots to take in each game. We do that in our staff discussions. When we take those shots is determined by several factors that relate to the game plan. We have a plan on the rationale of taking those shots. Our shots will be different each week.

I talked to you about our screen passes. We also use the flood routes and play-action concepts. We teach these concepts all year in our program.

Passing-Game Concepts

Concept	Number
Slot Option	0
Single Isolation	1
Screen	2
Play-Action	3
All Go	4
Smash	5
All Stop	6
Smash Bender	7
Bounce Scat	8
Deep Single Isolation	9

- First digit is the concept.
- Second digit is the protection.

- The "4" indicates the vertical concept.
- The "50s" are our dropback protection.
- The last digit tells our running back which side he lines up on.

For example, the call is 450. We are running four vertical routes, with dropback protection and the running back is on the right side. On even numbers he is on the right side, and on odd numbers he is on the left side. We spend a lot of time going over this with the players in the classroom. It is not that complicated once they understand the concepts.

If we can help you, we would be glad to share what we do in our program at Nease High School. Thank you.

11

The Spread Formation Option Game

Paul Johnson
Georgia Tech
2009

Along time ago when I used to go to clinics, I felt if I could get one or two things from the clinic that was great.

The topic, in general, is the Georgia Tech option offense. We could take four or five days and not cover the topic thoroughly. I will go over our base play from the option package. Our base play is the inside veer or triple option. I will try to break it down into some fundamental techniques and rules.

We call our offense the *spread-option offense* (Figure 11-1). Our base formation is the double-slot set. The splits in the offensive line are three feet all the way across the offensive line. We call the slot backs A-backs. The split receiver to the right is the Z-receiver, and the one to the left is the X-receiver. The tailback aligns behind the quarterback and is the B-back. Most every formation we use has a quick motion by one of the slot backs.

The receivers are interchangeable. The reason we give them names is for the passing game that comes from the formation. We call both the slot backs A-backs. The splits between the guards and the center never change. However, on occasion we may split the tackles wider in their alignment. We have played the tackles as wide as six or seven feet. If the defense will go with us, we take them as wide as they will go.

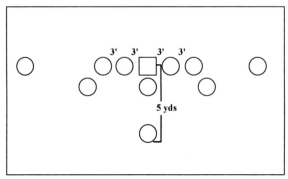

Figure 11-1. Base formation

We are a true option team. We read our way out on this play. We read #1, pitch off #2, and block #3. The backside wide receiver's rule on the triple option is to cut off the backside corner. The backside A-back is the tail motion for the pitch. He is the pitchback. The B-back is the dive aspect of the play. The A-back goes in motion off the cadence. Our cadence is, "Ready, set, hike." The A-back goes in motion on *ready*. We have done it that way for 20 years.

If we call the cadence on two, the quarterback repeats the cadence twice. The A-back comes in motion on the second *ready*. He tries to get a step and a half into the play before the ball is snapped. He comes in motion at full speed and aims at the depth of the B-back. He runs through the butt of the B-back. The B-back aligns with his heels five yards from the front of the football.

The pitch relationship between the quarterback and the A-back is tough to coach. If the slotback is fast, he gets wider than a back that is slower. Once they reach the butt of the B-back, we coach them to take three more steps and turn up with the quarterback. When he catches the pitch, he becomes a football player and runs with the ball. We are not trying to outleverage anyone. If the seam is inside, he takes the ball inside. If it is outside, he takes the ball outside. He reads the blocking on the play and runs accordingly.

The beauty about the offense is from week to week, we do not have to worry what defense we face (Figure 11-2). The backside tackle and guard have the same rules. They scoop their inside gap. We call the gap from the tackle's crotch to the guard's crotch. We are not trying to cut off defenders—we try to knock them back. We want to step down at a 45-degree angle. The next step is at 60 degrees, and the third step is up the field. We try to move the line of scrimmage even when we cut off.

The center has the playside A gap. He scoops into that gap and blocks anything that appears. If he is uncovered, he steps into the A gap and looks for linebackers on a run-through technique. If he is covered by a nose defender, he tries to get through the playside armpit and up to the second level of the defense.

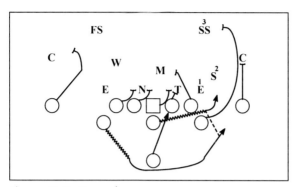
Figure 11-2. Base play

We use the same system of numbering the defensive techniques that Coach Bear Bryant did. If there is a defender head-up the center, he is a 0 technique. If he aligns on the center's shoulder, he is a shade technique or a 1 technique. Moving outside from the center, all the head positions are even numbers. Head-up the guard is 2, the tackle is 4, and the tight end is a 6 technique.

The shoulders of the offensive linemen are the odd-numbered techniques. The outside shoulder of the guard is 3, the outside shoulder of the tackle is 5, and the outside shoulder of the tight end is a 9 technique. The inside shoulder of the tight end is a 7 technique. No one knows why that is the case, but Coach Bryant numbered it that way, and no one has had the guts to change it. There are two special techniques that align a defender on the inside eye of the guard and tackle. They are 2i and 4i.

The playside guard has a base rule. If he is covered, he base blocks the defender trying to get six to eight inches back off the ball. If there is a shade technique on the center, in our base rules, the guard goes straight to the linebacker and the center reaches the shade technique. If the center cannot block the shade, the guard comes down on the shade and the center and guard block an ace combination for the shade nose and the linebacker. However, as a rule, we want to reach all shade techniques.

I do not think the center can reach the nose and block him by himself. Generally, the nose is a better player than the center. If he was not better than the center, he would be playing center. We know the center will probably not reach the shade, but the way we run the B-back, it does not matter. All the center has to do is get in the way.

The tackle's rule is to block the first inside linebacker to the playside. He uses the best release he can to get off the ball. If he has a 4 technique or a heavy 5-technique defender, his easiest release is an outside release. If the tackle takes an outside release, the guard has to be climbing on the linebacker. If he does not and the linebacker runs through the gap, he drills the B-back.

If the tackle cannot release inside, he goes outside. The guard gives a call that tells the tackle he can keep the linebacker from running through the B gap. He cannot get him if he scrapes, but he can keep him out of the B gap.

It is important to understand how we count for the handoff key and the pitch key. The first defender touching the playside tackle in his alignment is #1 or the read key. The next defender outside is #2. He is the pitch key. The run support defender is #3. The playside A-back blocks the run support. He counts from the tackle going outside. He counts *one, two, three,* and blocks #3. However, we do not ask him to block a rolled-up corner.

The A-back takes an arc release. He takes a drop-step and a crossover step. The A-back aligns with his inside foot back and splitting the outside leg of the offensive tackle. We align them with their inside foot back to keep them from false stepping when they come in tail motion. When he comes in tail motion, he digs his outside foot into the ground and pushes off it.

With his outside foot up, he drops the outside foot, crosses over with the inside foot, and looks for the run support defender. Teams try to change up their run support to confuse the blocking of the A-back. If the A-back reads the corner firing off the edge, that is the man he blocks. The wide receiver sees the corner fire to the inside and knows there is someone coming over the top of the corner. That is his block.

The A-back tries to cut the outside leg of the run support defender. We tell them the aiming point is six inches outside the outside knee. He does not throw on the defender until he can step on his foot. I do not want the A-back taking a dive on the ground. I want him to get in close and throw. I know in high school, you cannot cut. We do not cut all the time. If a defender knows we are going to cut him, he plays it. As a change-up, we block him high on occasion. The playside wide receiver blocks the near defender. He blocks the deep defender. That is how we block the option.

The quarterback's responsibility is to read #1. He opens at 4 o'clock and pushes the ball back as far as he can. He wants to get his second step in the ground, looking at his read key. We get the ball back as far as we can so we can ride the B-back. We put the ball in his pocket and ride him to the line of scrimmage. He rides the B-back until he reaches his front leg. The quarterback has to make the decision to leave the ball with the B-back or pull it by the time the ball reaches his front foot.

My quarterback is 6'3" and his steps are not going to be the same as the quarterback who is 5'11". You have to rep the play so the steps work out. The most important thing the quarterback can do in the ride is get his second step on the ground.

When we coach our quarterbacks, we coach them to give the ball if the defender does not take the B-back. I cannot read the face mask, his head, his numbers, or any other clinic-talk key. If the defender cannot get his head in front of the ballcarrier, we give the ball. A lot of those decisions depend on who you have at quarterback. When I have had good running quarterbacks, we use the phrase, "If in doubt, pull it out." If you have a quarterback that is not a good runner and there is doubt, hand the ball off.

The quarterback reads #1 and options #2. If #1 and #2 are coming hard from the outside, I love that situation (Figure 11-3). It turns the option into a toss sweep. That is why the second step is so important. If the quarterback does not have his second step in the ground, he gets killed or has the pitch knocked down. With the second step in the ground, the quarterback can create space away from the defender. He steps straight back and creates more distance between himself and the defender.

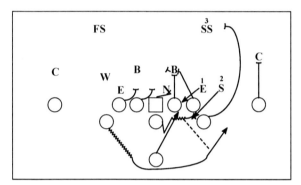

Figure 11-3. #2 crash

If the quarterback sees the #2 defender on a crash, he does not care what the #1 defender is doing. He pitches the ball off of #2 and he is crashing. He disengages from the B-back, steps straight back, and pitches the ball.

The second reason the second foot has to be in the ground is due to the mechanics of pulling the ball. If the read key closes hard to the inside, the quarterback must have his weight on the front foot to pull the ball, seat it, and step around the closing read key. He has his weight on the front foot so he can give some ground and step around the collision.

Once he pulls the ball, he options the ball off of the #2 defender. We tell the quarterback he has the ball, so run with it. We do not care who he options. We do not care if he pitches it or keeps it. We want the option key to come to the quarterback. We are not going to chase him. He does not try to get to his outside shoulder so he can pitch the ball.

The goal line is north and south, and as soon as he gets the chance, that is the way he is going. We do not want him run laterally. As soon as the pitch key turns his shoulder to the quarterback, he pitches the ball. We do not have to be close to the defender. All we want is leverage on the pitchman. When the pitchman has leverage on the support player, we pitch the ball.

If we attack the pitch key, we attack the inside shoulder. That is the shortest distance to the goal line. We teach the quarterback to pitch the ball any way he can. When we teach the pitch, we seat the ball in the chest and pitch it with the thumb down. We pitch the ball from the seat position on the inside with the thumb down. The ball gets there quicker and is less likely to be knocked down.

The quarterback has to deal with stunts trying to confuse his read key. Defenses stack the read and pitch key and exchange their responsibilities (Figure 11-4). If you run the option, you will see that stunt. It is not that hard to read. We call that an easy stunt. We rep it enough so that we pull the ball off #2 and pitch it off #1.

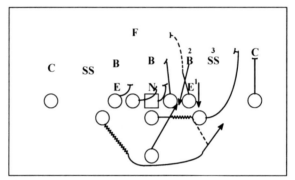

Figure 11-4. Easy stunt

The B-back's aiming point is the inside leg of the playside guard. His technique allows us to block with the scheme we use (Figure 11-5). He aims at the inside leg, but he reads the first down lineman inside the read key. If we have a shade nose on the center, that is the center's block. His block is to reach the shade nose. We know he will probably not reach him. If the quarterback has a give key to the B-back, he leaves the ball with him. The B-back reads the nose working toward him. The center continues to drive on the nose and the B-back breaks the ball behind the center's block into the backside.

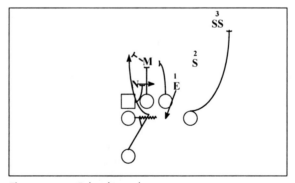

Figure 11-5. B-back read

The B-back's heels are five yards from the tip of the ball. We have not aligned deeper than five yards. However, we have moved slower backs closer to the line. If you have a good back, that is the right depth for running the ball and pass protecting the quarterback. That depth gives the B-back a chance to read the block of the first down lineman inside the quarterback's read.

The B-back learns the blocking schemes of the offensive line. If the defense is a 50-shade defense, the B-back knows we will load the scheme and double the nose with the center and playside guard (Figure 11-6). The read key is the 4-technique tackle, and the pitch key is the rush end. If the quarterback gets a give key, he hands the ball to the B-back. Since we double-team the nose, the B-back does not cut the ball back. He hugs the double-team and keeps the ball to the frontside of the play.

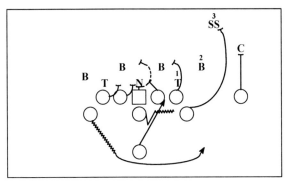

Figure 11-6. Load

The B-back will learn the blocking schemes and know what we are going to do in the offensive line. But even if he does not know who is blocking who, he can find the seam. Our B-back this year was the ACC player of the year. He is a good player, but he could not tell you who is blocking anybody. He might not be able to spell the word cat if you gave him the C and the A. That was a joke. He is a good player and will probably be playing on Sundays eventually.

Our B-back aligns in an even stance. He has to go both ways from that stance. He has some weight forward in the stance. If he goes to the right, he curls his left toe into the ground or turf. I want him to curl the toes of the off foot into the ground so he has something to push off and does not false step. We tell him we want him approaching the line of scrimmage like a plane taking off.

We drill him in the chute so he learns to run from low to high. He curls the toes and explodes with his initial step at the inside leg of the guard. We do not want him to overstep, and his first step may be six inches. We want him full speed until he passes the quarterback's front leg. From there, he reacts to the blocks of the linemen.

When you run this play, the defender you must account for is the playside linebacker. He makes most of the tackles on this play. The second defender you have to block is the backside linebacker. However, if he makes too many plays, we will run some counter at him.

When the playside tackle takes his release, he tries to release through the outside armpit of the 4 technique. That is the angle he takes, but he wants to avoid contact with the 4 technique if he can. The tight 5 technique or 4 technique will not allow the tackle to veer release across his face to block the linebacker. That is why we work behind his alignment. If the defensive tackle tries to step with the offensive tackle and slow him down, the read will be a give to the B-back.

Teams have tried to stop the tackle from getting to the inside linebacker by stepping the outside linebacker down on the outside move of the tackle. If they do that, we use the quick toss to the outside and get around the corner.

If we find the #3 defender in the middle of the football field, the tackle and A-back can run a combo block for the playside linebacker (Figure 11-7). The playside linebacker can get over the top quickly and is a hard block for the tackle. In this diagram, the tackle has to combo with the guard on the 3-technique defender before he can block the linebacker. The support player is the single high safety. The A-back takes an inside release and seals the inside linebacker and the tackle chases the safety.

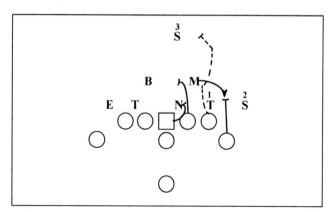

Figure 11-7. Tackle/A-back combo

We give teams that play that kind of front something a little funky. When they play the eight-man front on defense, they tie the safety and outside linebacker to the release on the playside slot. They tell the linebacker if the slot runs straight up the field, the strong safety takes the quarterback and the free safety runs for the pitch. If the slot arcs, the linebacker stays outside on the slot and the safety runs the alley for the quarterback. That is not a bad way to play and is probably smart. If we find them doing that, we automatic with a safety call. We run the slot on the inside release, but he passes the linebacker and blocks the free safety. The defense has two defenders on the quarterback and no one on the pitch. We did that a bunch against Georgia in our last regular-season game.

If we figure out how the defense is playing us, we have counter and blocking schemes to handle all types of defensive adjustments. But that is a double-edged sword—if they figure out what you are doing, they will get you.

If #3 is in the middle of the field and we are having trouble getting the linebacker blocked with the tackle, we have an adjustment. We release the A-back on the linebacker. However, if the tackle cannot catch up to the safety, we can call a crack scheme. We load the play and call crack. The wide receiver cracks the safety.

If the defense aligns with a four-across look in the secondary, we tell the playside guard and tackle they have the playside linebacker to the backside safety (Figure 11-8). People that play four across try to roll the secondary to get the backside safety into the box as the extra alley runner. If the guard has the block on the linebacker and the linebacker scrapes, the tackle blocks him. The guard climbs to the backside safety and cuts him off. If the linebacker blows the B gap, the guard blocks him and the tackle climbs for the safety.

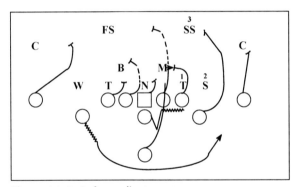

Figure 11-8. Safety adjustment

There are many complementary plays that go with the base option. If the defense loads up to stop the option, we have ways to run the complementary plays to take advantage of what the defense gives up. That is the old argument of who has the chalk last.

If we want to go unbalanced, there are a number of ways we can do it. If we take both wide receivers to the same side, we call over (Figure 11-9). Both wide receivers will be on the line of scrimmage and the rules for the play stay the same.

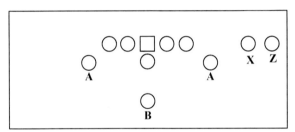

Figure 11-9. Over

If we want to change the eligible receivers, we drop the X-receiver off the line and move the A-back on the line of scrimmage. We call that formation *green*. We can get into a trips formation by moving the backside A-back up on the line and dropping the playside A-back off the line. We call that formation *brown*. If we find the defense not covering the ineligible receiver, we huddle call *green to brown* (Figure 11-10). We come to the line in a green formation. At the last moment, the backside A-back moves up on the line of scrimmage and the playside A-back moves off and all four of the receivers are eligible.

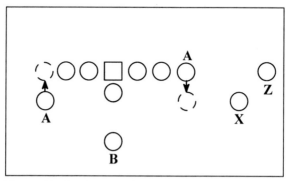

Figure 11-10. Green to brown

If we call a trips set as the huddle call, the A-back is on the same side with the backside wide receiver as the single receiver.

Question: How do you practice and teach the read?

A typical practice is made up of five-minute periods. When we start in the fall, we go 23 periods, which is about an hour and 45 minutes. Later in the year, we practice 14 periods, which is an hour and 10 minutes. Periods 1 through 4 are our fundamental periods—our individual periods where we work on our individual skills. The quarterback and B-back, during the fundamental period, are working on footwork and ball security. They work their steps and mesh with one coach. The coach is the read key in that drill.

Period 5 is a 1-on-1 period with receiver and defensive back, with the quarterback throwing. Periods 6 through 9 are live-option periods. We do this every day. This is a live 11-on-11 period. When we are playing, we go against the scout team. In 20 minutes, we get 45 plays. We script the plays for this session and run two huddles. The coaching is done on the fly. We do not stop the period for individual instruction. During this period is where the quarterbacks get all the live reads. We hit the quarterbacks all year. We do not take them to the ground, but they are hit. If #1 and #2 are coming hard from the outside, we light up the quarterback. Everything has to be above the waist.

You have to practice at the speed you are going to play. If we play Miami, we know they are a 4-3 defense—everything we run is 4-3 blocking. However, we throw some double-Eagle and eight-man fronts into the mix of the periods. We must know how to block all those defenses. That is how you find out if they know the scheme or whether the second-team player is just watching the block of the first-team player. If he blocks the same defender and the defense changed, he is wrong.

After the option period, we take a break because it is 20 minutes going as hard as we can go. After the break, we go to pass skeleton for two periods. The rest of the practice is team time. During that time, we run our entire option package. We run the triple, midline, counter, speed, and belly options. The count system stays the same for all the options and that makes it easier.

Question: How would you attack the 3-3 stack defense?

The first thing I am going to do is move either the slot or the split end to the other side. That makes the defense move a defender to cover the unbalance. That would be the first thing we would do. By using the unbalanced set and motion, we force the defense into a numbers game with the option read. We outnumber the defense to the backside of the formation.

Question: What adjustments did you make to move the ball on Notre Dame when you were at Navy?

When we played Notre Dame the last year I was at Navy, they played a 3-4 defense. The outside linebackers were taking the quarterback. The defensive ends came hard inside and took the B-back. The outside linebackers played the quarterback but were jamming our offensive tackle trying to loop behind the defensive end for the linebacker. The tackle could not get on the linebacker and he was running free in the alley (Figure 11-11). Without changing anything we did with the blocking scheme, I brought the wide receivers down into a flex position, which is a five-yard split.

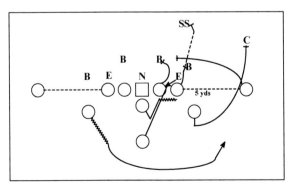

Figure 11-11. Double flex

That put the outside linebacker in a bind. If he stood inside to jam the tackle, we cracked him with the wide receiver and ran the toss sweep. When we went to the double-flex formation, they went from a four-across look to a two-deep look. When we ran the option, we swapped the block of the A-back and Z-receiver. The A-back arced and blocked the corner, the Z-receiver cracked the linebacker, and the tackle went up on the safety.

The double flex has been a good formation for us. We get them tighter and run the toss play. That is a good play because you do not have to block anyone. You pitch the ball and run to the corner.

Question: What is the best defense against this offense?

The best defense against this offense is good players. All the offenses and defenses are similar in concept. The key to any scheme is knowing how to fix what goes wrong. I love playing football teams whose offense is football's best 20 plays. They have a bunch of plays that look good, but none of them mesh together. If you have a system and understand it, you have a chance to fix it. It is like the Notre Dame game. They had a good plan to run against our base offense. However, when we fixed our problems, they could not refix their scheme.

The simpler you can keep it on offense and defense, the better it is. Just rep what you do and get a total understanding of the scheme so when one thing goes wrong, you know how to fix the scheme. When we go into a game, we run six or seven plays. We have many wrinkles off them so people think it is more than that. If you execute what you do, it does not matter what the defense does. If they can get better in three days of stopping it than you can get in 19 weeks of running it, they are going to beat you anyway.

You do not win too many games by surprising people. You win by outexecuting them and playing harder than they do. Too many times we, as coaches, think there is a magic elixir. I see it at our level all the time. Each week, we play against the defense of the week. When you do not play the option week after week, you have to make adjustments in your scheme. We played North Carolina in Chapel Hill and they beat us. We had 440 yards of total offense but only scored seven points. For the next three weeks, we saw what North Carolina played against us on defense. In the Miami game, they lined up exactly like North Carolina. We played better and they did not play as good and we beat them.

The play-action pass in this offense is designed to get the #3 defender (Figure 11-12). The backside A-back runs tail motion and blocks or is involved in the pattern depending on the blocking scheme. The backside tackle has a base block as his assignment. He blocks the technique down and the guard will pull outside for the edge rush. We can use a white scheme. That is gap protection. If the tackle has a 4i technique aligned on him, he makes a white call to the guard. The guard fans back for the 4i and the tackle fans for the defensive end. We do not do that too much because it does not look like run. The center's rule is onside gap. The playside guard's rule is base to down. The tackle has a base block.

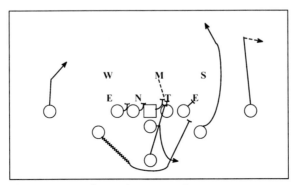

Figure 11-12. Play-action protection

The quarterback opens, meshes with the B-back, and comes straight back. We used to go two steps down the line of scrimmage before we dropped. The quarterback cannot see as well so we changed it. The B-back runs his track and has the playside linebacker in the B gap. The A-back in tail motion has the C gap.

The patterns are combination routes. If we call vertical or seam, the playside A-back runs his arc track and tries to run by the safety. The Z-receiver runs a take-off and tries to run by the corner. If he cannot get deep, he breaks his pattern off to the sideline at 14 to 15 yards. We can tag routes for the backside receiver. We can call 312 X post. We get the same patterns on the playside and an X-post on the backside. If we tag the pattern, the quarterback comes back to him. We can throw the ball on a hitch to the X-receiver because most defenses roll their secondary with the tail motion of the A-back. That leaves the wide receiver 1-on-1 on the corner.

We try to give the defense the same look on the pass as we do on the run. If we had been cracking with the wide receiver, we run the switch call (Figure 11-13). We try to give the defense the same look. The wide receiver runs the post, and the A-back runs a wheel route on the corner.

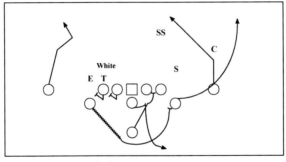

Figure 11-13. Switch

We are not a big midline team but we do run it. We call it 10-lead (Figure 11-14). If we run it to the 3 technique, we read him. The B-back runs up the center's butt. The backside tackle cuts off inside as he does on the option. The center and backside guard block an ace combination on the shade nose. The playside tackle turns out on the defensive end. The playside A-back blocks the Sam linebacker the best way he can get him. The tail motion comes up into the B gap and leads the quarterback. The playside guard seals inside on the Mike linebacker.

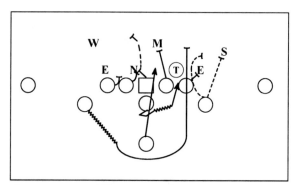

Figure 11-14. Midline to 3 technique

The quarterback digs his toe into the ground and swings his playside foot back without moving his backside foot. The backside foot is on the ground and is the same technique as the second step on the option. The quarterback reads the 3 technique and gives or keeps the ball. If he keeps the ball, he follows the A-back on the lead block.

We can run the midline to the shade-nose side (Figure 11-15). We double the shade nose back to the Mike linebacker. We read the first defender outside the 2i technique. Everything else on the play is the same.

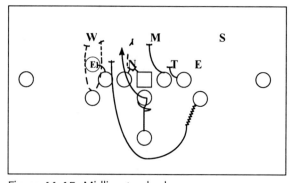

Figure 11-15. Midline to shade

If we call 10, it is the triple option from the midline read. The blocking is the same except the tail motion is the pitchback and not the lead back. We run trap, toss, and all the option plays, but we do not run much midline.

If a team runs a double-Eagle defense, they have effectively canceled the dive back (Figure 11-16). We still run the triple option, but we do not read the dive back. We run a two-way option. We base block with the playside guard and tackle and run the B-back in on the linebacker. The A-back arc blocks on the corner and the wide receiver cracks inside. The quarterback pulls the ball and runs an option on the safety.

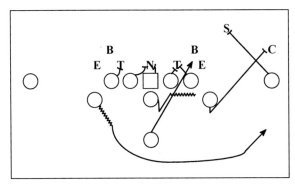

Figure 11-16. Triple vs. double-eagle

We run *28-option* and area read the play. If there is a stud at the 3 technique, we double-team him with the guard and tackle. That leaves the linebacker and defensive end to take the B-back. If the defensive end comes down to take the dive, the quarterback pulls the ball and pitches off the linebacker. If the defensive end squats and the linebacker is running, we hand the ball off. Somebody has to take the dive. When they do, they run out of people on the outside.

I enjoyed sharing some of what we do with you. Thank you.

12

The No-Huddle Spread Offense

Mick McCall
Bowling Green State University
2005

Thank you for the introduction. I want to talk about our offense and some of the things we did that helped us to become a better team last year. We led the country in third-down conversions. There were many reasons for that. That is a huge deal for us. Our defense has a goal to be successful on 40 percent of the third-down plays. We averaged four yards per run on offense, which gave us a 55 percentage.

I am going to talk about our spread offense and our running game. When most people think about the spread offense, they think about throwing the ball all over the yard. The last two years we have had a runner gain over 1,000 yards each year. We were the only team in the country that had 4,000 yards passing and a 1,000-yard rusher. We are going to run the football. Two years ago, we were second in the MAC in total rushing offense. We are going to run the football and we are going to run it efficiently. It is not about how many yards we get; it is about how efficient we are.

We scored a touchdown 66 percent of the time when we reached the red zone. When you get in the red zone, you must score and we teach that to our players. On Wednesday, we work on the red-zone offense. On Thursday, we work almost exclusively on red-zone offense. We spend a lot of time on our red-zone offense.

We averaged 26 first downs per game. We had five plays of over 20 yards or more per game. We do not stress the big plays. We are not worried about the long plays. Those things will happen if we are doing the other things right. We have to find a way to make big plays.

I will give you some of the running plays we use, but I want to go in the direction of the "no-huddle offense." I want to give you an idea of where we come from in our thinking. We like to use the no-huddle offense. That is what we do. That is who we are. It is not something that we just dabble in occasionally. Here is why we use the offense.

First, it is about controlling tempo. Being an offensive coach, I have a problem allowing the defense to dictate what plays we have to call. I do not like to call plays just to get us out of a bad play. I want to dictate to the defense what they can do to our offense and what they cannot do to us on offense. That is our mind-set. We want to control the tempo and I will cover that later.

Using the no-huddle offense gives us more time in practice. We signal the plays to the offense in practice. We can run a ton of plays. We get several reps in practice. Our practice tempo includes several reps and we get it going very fast. Practice is a lot faster than games as far as the tempo is concerned. When we get in a game, it is slow to our players because the officials have to set the ball ready for play.

We tell our offensive line and receivers to lineup and conserve energy until we signal the next play. They like it when they do not have to go back to the huddle on each play. They like setting up at the line of scrimmage and ready to go. We conserve a lot of energy doing this simple thing in a game. The defense still has to go through all of the things they usually have to do.

The two-minute offense is no big deal to us. That is what we do. The difference is that we are stopping the clock. Therefore, we are used to running the two-minute offense. That is who we are.

Running the no-huddle offense, it minimizes defensive packages. We do not want the defense to be able to call everything they have in their defensive package. If we force the tempo, it limits the defense on what they can use against us. We want to simplify what the defense can do against our offense.

We are able to look at the defense and call the play. At the start of the 25-second clock, we can look at the defense to make a decision on what play we want to run. We can call the play from the box down to the sideline or we can actually call the play from the sideline.

Our offense is different for the defense. They must hurry to line up and be ready to set their defense. They must hurry to get set against our offense. We want them to play defense for 25 seconds of the shot clock. As soon as the whistle blows for the

25-second clock, we want them to be ready to play defense. We may snap the ball in the first few seconds when we line up on the ball. We can let it run down to 15 seconds and then snap the ball. Or we may let the clock run down to the last couple of seconds and snap the ball just before we get a delay of game call. We want to force the defense to concentrate for most to those 25 seconds. We do not have that many players that can concentrate that long. Our offensive players know when we are going to snap the ball. That is how we are going to control tempo.

Our offense fosters communication skills. It does not matter what you think; the players still have to get the job done on the field. It is the ultimate team game. Coaches may actually have less to do with what happens on the field in football than they do in baseball or basketball. In football, players must communicate. We practice the same way as we play the game and the players must concentrate in practice to know what is going on with our offense. Our defense has to be on the field with their players in practice to get them lined up in the proper positions. The offensive coaches are off on the sideline signaling the plays in to them. They must communicate in practice as well as in the games.

I know kids want to spread the field and throw the football. In our offense, it is not just one man getting the football. It is not just one receiver on the boundary sideline that is going to get the football all of the time. Our four wide receivers had 50 or more catches each this past year. I told you we had a running back that gained over 1,500 yards rushing. He also caught 40 passes. We spread the ball around and we throw the football to more that one receiver.

There are negatives to running this type of offense. You need to know these points and you have to work on them. The first negative is that we are limited in what we can run on offense. We cannot do everything running this offense. I have studied several programs and I have visited several different schools looking at the things they do on offense. It amazes me to see some big-name schools that run a play in a game and have great success the first time they run the play and they never come back to the play again in that game. I have seen teams that have run 70 different plays in a game without duplicating a single play. To me, that does not give continuity to your offense. However, you have to minimize the plays you can run from the offense we use. Players can only get so many concepts down for the games.

We know we are going to have communication breakdowns. You are going to have them. You must negate the possibilities that you are going to have those breakdowns. We still have a player that misses a signal. We may have a player miss the direction he should have gone. The quarterback can miss a call on the check off. We understand this and we must live with it and go on.

The other drawback is that we have to be secret about our method of signaling the plays to the quarterback. We may have two coaches giving signals and we can have another player giving the signals. Only one person is going to be giving the live signal. The other two people giving the signals are dummy calls. That is how we beat the secret aspects of the system.

Our system must have unifying principles that are simple and identifiable. The system must use common words and they must be easy to say. We use words such as city, state, color, numbers, or mascot. It can be what you want them to be. It is your terminology. We want to use short, one- or two-syllable words. These words may represent blocking schemes, formations, plays, and other information.

The signals should be distinct and they should follow a pattern. They must mean something to the players. A lot of the time we have the players make up their signals. Our wide receivers get different signals than what the quarterback, running back, and tight end get. It means the same play but the signal is different

The system is the same today as it was three years ago. It is the same system. We build on it and we subtract from it. If you can keep the same system for four years, the players should be good at the system by the time they get to be seniors.

We want the signals to be simple and through so the players can play without thinking so much. We want to keep it simple, yet give them some flexibility in the system. We want them to be able to focus and play, and not think so much.

If you get anything from the lecture today, this would be the point I would consider worthwhile. If you were thinking about running the no-huddle offense, these would be the reasons why you should run it.

Our no-huddle offense consists of five phases. It is important to know why each phase of the offense is used. We can use these phases anytime during the game. First, I want to talk about our procedure on the line of scrimmage. I am not going to give you the exact detail of how we call our plays, but this is how you implement the phase.

The quarterback will be responsible for alerting everyone for the change in tempo. We are going to change the tempo as we go up and down the field. The quarterback will always give the play to the offensive line. We are not going to ask those five big bulls to look to the sideline to get the signal on the play. The quarterback will tell the line the play.

The receivers and tight ends get the information from the sideline. As soon as the previous play is over, they start looking to the sideline to get the signal where they are to line up and what the play is. The quarterback gives the snap count to the offensive line. All of the receivers, including the tight end, must watch the football.

The first tempo is what we call our "sugar" huddle. We are three to four yards behind the ball. The line faces the football. The quarterback can line up in front of the line or he can actually line up behind the line. It is a normal "sugar huddle." We do not use this very often. We use it when we are milking the clock, or trying to slow down the game.

The second tempo is our "fastball." We line up and run a play in any formation in our offense as fast as possible. The quarterback calls out "fastball, tastball," and everyone lines up as quickly as possible. He does not have to give them the formation because they know the formation from the signal from the sideline. The quarterback only has to tell the linemen a few words. He may call out to the linemen, "read right, read right," and that is all they need to know. We can snap the ball on a regular count or we can go on a fast snap count.

We want to go as fast as we can when we call fastball. We can change the formation on fastball. We can call "right to left" and change the formation but we are going to do it as fast as we can. We want to catch the defense looking to their sideline to get their defensive signal and we run the bubble off the back door. We want to create those for the defense where can take advantage of those type of situations. We want it very simple so we can run the plays.

Our third phase is our "super fastball," or a "two-minute offense" tempo. We line up and keep the receivers on the same side of the formations. We are going faster and we are going to snap the ball as fast as we can get set. We can call "smash - smash" and the line knows what we are doing. We snap the ball and away we go. Again, the receivers stay on the same side of the formation.

The next phase of our tempo is what we call "glance." Now, I am not going to give all of our codes or signals here today. They will get back to our opponents fast enough. This is how we do this tempo. The quarterback calls any play and we line up on the ball. He continues to go through his signals for a set amount of time on the 25-second play clock. When the play clock gets down to about 18 seconds, the quarterback and the receivers all glance over to the sideline to get the signal for the play we are going to run. We snap the ball with three or four seconds left on the play clock and away we go. That is our simulated glance tempo. We want the defense to get use to the fast and then we slow it down. We call a lot of our offense from that tempo.

The next thing we do is to simulate check. It is the same thing. We go "fastball, fastball" and then the quarterback calls a color. That alerts the offense that we are not going to go on a quick count. The quarterback may call out "red - 15, red - 15." Then the quarterback looks to the sideline and if the play is what we want he will call the snap count, "Go." We are snapping the ball at 14 to 15 seconds on this tempo. We do not want to give the defense a chance to reset their defense.

In our tempo, we can snap the ball from the beginning of the play clock all the way down to the end of the 25-second clock. We want the defense to show what they are going to do and we want them to play defense all the way through the 25-second clock. Now, it is like shooting fish in a barrel.

The offensive coordinator is in the press box and he can see what the defense is doing while we are waiting for the defense to line up. As soon as he sees how the defense is going to play us, he can look at his chart and make the best call for that situation. It gives the quarterback a chance to look at the defensive rotation and figure out what is going to happen on the play. Our quarterback could make the all without looking at the sideline based on what we have worked on in practice for that week.

We have four base running plays. I may not get all the way through the four plays. We have a "read" play, which is our zone play. It is a zone read play. We have the "speed option." We have a "trap" play and we have a "rep" play. I will only have time to cover the first three plays. We run these plays in a one-back set. We run the zone plan in our one-back and we run our zone plan from our empty set with our quarterback. We run some of the other plays out of the empty set. We can run the trap with our one-back set or we can run the trap with our quarterback running the "two-trap."

First, I want to talk about our zone plays. I am coaching with the best offensive line coach I have ever coached with in my coaching career. He is phenomenal. He does a great job with our zone plays. On our zone plays, we must be able to run the plays out of the spread look with a tight end or without him. We must have the flexibility to run the play with or without the tight end.

We can do the same thing without a tight end. We have a covered principle and an uncovered principle. It starts outside. If the guard is uncovered, he helps the tackle. The tackle is going to make the call. The guard can make a call to override the tackle.

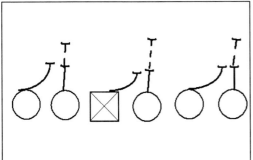
Figure 12-1

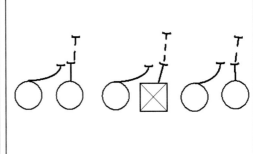
Figure 12-2

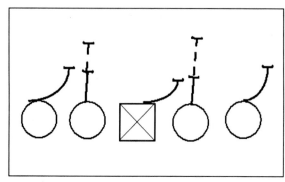

Figure 12-3

If the guard can come outside and help the tackle, he is going to make the call. That tells the tackle he has a block with the guard. It is the same when the tight end is in the game. If the tackle cannot go help the tight end, then the tight end has the man one-on-one. The rules are very simple to follow. Our linemen can play any of those positions because they know the type of blocks to use on the line. We could play them at any of the line positions if we had to do that. We are going to play our five best players at those line positions. If a player gets hurt, the next best player is going in the game.

Our first play is "14 read." We are running this to the playside. The deep-back is set at five and one half yards deep (Figure 12-4). He lines up over the offensive tackle. Last year we went to big splits in the line. If the tackle splits wide, the mesh point is a little different. We give the back the freedom to adjust on the play. He must be three steps to the mesh point. He has to have a feel for that mesh point. We work on mesh point everyday with our backs. We do ball handling everyday. We run "14 and 15 Read" everyday in our individual period.

Our quarterback lines up with his toes five yards deep. He is slightly ahead of the running back. He catches the snap, takes a rocker step, and rides the tailback as he comes through the mesh area.

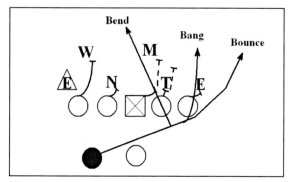

Figure 12-4

Everyone up front is zone blocking. It does not matter if we have a tight end or not, we are still blocking zone. The key to the play is the tailback. He must get two steps past the mesh. He takes three steps to the mesh then he must go two steps toward the line to set the blocks up for the linemen up front on the linebackers. He must make the linebackers move.

The back has to make the play go. After he sets up the play with the two steps past the mesh, he must make a decision on where he is going to run. He can bounce it, bang it, or he will bend it back. He reads the first covered lineman past the center and then his eyes must expand after that. He gets as close to the tackle as possible before he makes the cut. We use the term "bend back," but it is more of a bend up on the cutback. That is what we do for the tailback.

The tailback must be patient on the play. The closer he can ride the tail of the tackle, the better the play will be. He must allow the play to develop and that takes time. At the very last minute, he breaks the play to the open area.

If the tailback breaks too quick, it makes it tough for the linemen to block their man. It is the responsibility of the tailback to set the blocks up for the linemen.

As long as we have five defenders in the box, we are going to block five defenders. We see six defenders in the box most of the time. We see some type of shade with six defenders in the box. There are two things we are concerned about when this happens. First, if you are in a 4-2 front we are going to block the six defenders near the line and read the outside man with the quarterback (Figure 12-5). Everyone else blocks zone. The quarterback must determine if the defensive end can make the play at the point of attack just behind the tackle or on the line of scrimmage. If the end can squeeze the play down enough, the quarterback must determine if he should pull the ball or not, or if he is going to give the ball to the back on the zone play. It is the same as if you were running the triple option. It is no different.

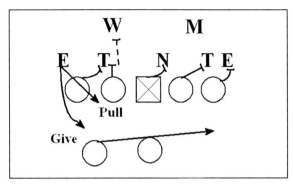

Figure 12-5

This is what I tell the quarterback. One, width is more important to judge than depth or turning the shoulders. If the end can squeeze the play down and stay inside with his shoulders square to the line of scrimmage, he can stop the handoff. If the end comes up the field and does not squeeze the play down, he may not be able to get back inside to stop the play. We tell the quarterback width is more important than depth. It is more important than how much he turns his shoulders on the play.

The other thing we tell the quarterback is to read the eyes of the defender. The quarterback is not responsible for the mesh. The back is responsible for the mesh. If the quarterback can see the end's eyes looking at him, he gives the ball to the running back.

The other thing that we see is the odd alignment. As long as there are five defenders, we are going to block five defenders (Figure 12-6). That is easy.

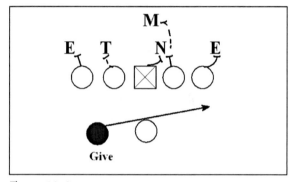

Figure 12-6

Normally on the perimeter, if we are running "14 read" and we keep the ball against the six-man front, the slot man blocks the second defender off the line of scrimmage. He does not know if the quarterback is going to keep the ball or not. It is straight zone block for the H-back (Figure 12-7).

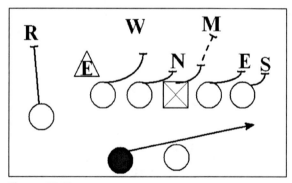

Figure 12-7

The other thing we do is to run the read play and tag it with the option. Now we do not block the end. If the quarterback sees the end is outside, he is going to give the back the ball on the zone play. If the call is a read and the end stays outside, the quarterback hands the football off on the play.

If the end comes down inside now, the quarterback pulls the ball and comes outside toward the end. We said we do not block the end on this play. Now the quarterback is going to option on the end (Figure 12-8). That is another way to incorporate the read or the option.

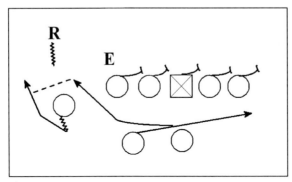

Figure 12-8

I will cover a couple more things on the option play. The offensive line inside is still running our zone schemes that we talked about before. This is our equalizer. We check to it when we expect the blitz, or when we are in the red zone. We can run it with or without a tight end.

The big key is this. The tackle and the end receiver must both be on the same page. The first thing we want to do is to option the end man on the line of scrimmage (Figure 12-9). If the defensive end is not coming, the tackle drives to the Will. The outside receiver is going to cruise upfield and check to make sure the tackle has taken care of the Will linebacker. If the Will is blocked, the receiver takes the next man that shows.

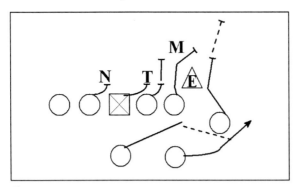

Figure 12-9

If the linebacker is wide, and there is someone else backing the blitz such as the strong safety, then the tackle is not going to drive for the Will linebacker. He can see the strong safety has a chance to blitz. The defensive end lines up tight. He is coming inside. We still want to option the end man on the line of scrimmage. Now we option the Sam linebacker. Now we are going to "gang" it.

The receiver sees the same thing. Now, we "gang" the play down the line. We pitch off the end man and away we go on the speed option. If the tackle is in doubt about what to do, we tell him to gang the play.

We can run the play with a tight end in the game. He has the same rules as the linemen. We still want to pitch off the end man on the line of scrimmage. Now it is just one hole removed for the play.

The end works upfield to the linebacker. He may not get the linebacker. He may end up blocking on the safety. We want to get a hat on a hat.

This is how we approach the pass protection. We have principles to cover the blocking. We work on this from day one in the spring and fall. We have a period where we are going to work on the quarterback checking to as many bubbles as we can. That is the first thing we are looking for.

We go through the following things in checking to the play we want to run. Our thought process at the line of scrimmage is this. First is the bubble route. If our inside receiver out-leverages the defender over him enough to catch the bubble pass and run away from him, we are going to check to the pass and run it.

The second principle we apply is to check the second level defender (Figure 12-10). If the defender is 10 yards deep, we will audible to a buddle call. We can check off to the play from the shotgun or from under the center.

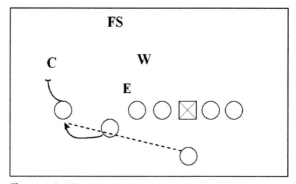

Figure 12-10

We would like to run everything from the shotgun, but that does not always happen. The bubble is a lot quicker if we run it with the quarterback under the center.

If the quarterback is under the center of the bubble, he is going to crow hop back and throws the ball. He gets rid of the ball very quick.

The receiver has a normal alignment with the inside foot up. He opens and crosses over, and then starts downhill. He must know he is going to get the ball a lot quicker if the quarterback is under the center than he would if the quarterback is in the shotgun. The quarterback wants to throw the ball to the front shoulder of the receiver.

If the quarterback is in the shotgun, the pass is going to be slower now. That means the receiver is going to change his route on the play. Again, the quarterback takes the long snap and crow hops. He wants to get his momentum going toward the receiver. He wants to get the ball out to the receiver as quick as he can.

The receiver knows the quarterback is in the shotgun so he knows the pass is not going to come as fast. The receiver must adjustment his alignment. It is not a big adjustment, but he does back off and gets a little deeper. His first step is an open step. The second step is a crossover step. On the third step, he continues laterally on the route. He wants to stay on the same path as before. We do not want every receiver running the route differently.

If the receiver is "uncovered," it is different for the receiver. At the snap of the ball, if there is no first level defender on the receiver, we run the play the same as we do on the bubble. If the second defender is over 10 yards deep, we run the bubble. The quarterback and receive must be on the same page. The receiver opens up his shoulders and turns his head toward the quarterback as he comes off the line. The quarterback must deliver the ball immediately on the snap. We call this awareness. If the quarterback does not throw the ball to the receiver, he must continue on his step on the route called.

We go over the different defenses we see and give the quarterback the responsibility of making the decisions on throwing the bubble or not. He has a couple of things to consider in making his decision to throw the bubble or not. He must consider down and distance. On first and second downs, we will show the "awareness" no matter what the defense does. On third down, he must decide if the receiver will be able to get the first down or not. We do not give the receiver the choice to run the route or not. We let the quarterback determine if he is going to throw the bubble pass or not.

The third consideration is the "hitch" route. It is the easiest throw in football. We will throw the hitch route to any receiver as many times as we can all the way down the field. We are going to throw the hitch route as many times as we can. It does not matter if we throw it to the field, to the boundary, or in the middle of the field. If it is an inside hitch we want the receiver to run five steps, turn around, and catch the football. We will continue to throw the hitch until the defense comes up and takes it away from us. When they do that, we go to some of our other plays in our package.

Our players know we are going to have a period each day where we work on the three principles. We work on the bubble, the uncovered, and the hitch routes.

I touched on running certain concepts a bunch of times. We want to run a few things and run them well as opposed to running a large number of different plays all over the place. We ran some form of four verticals over 100 times. Our players got good at running four vertical routes. They knew the adjustments on the routes. We are going to run four verticals as many times as we can.

The basic premise of the four verticals is to stretch the field. The two outside receivers are going to be at the bottom of the numbers. For the two inside men their alignment is two yards outside the hash marks. That would be on the high school hash marks. The back runs a "dump" route over the middle of the football (Figure 12-11). We are going to have someone in the middle so the quarterback can dump the ball off if he is in trouble.

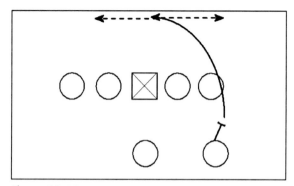

Figure 12-11

We do a couple of things a little differently. The outside receivers are going to run a vertical route. If the outside receivers cannot beat the defender by 12 yards, they are going to run a drop out at 15 yards. This keeps the defender from turning and running up the field as hard as he can go.

The two inside receivers are going to get on their seams and run the route deep. That is an easy throw if there is only one safety playing deep. If there are two high safeties playing, we want to have one of the receivers run a "bender post route." It is a post route back into the middle of the field. Normally that bend receiver is our straight side receiver. He is going to run the post back inside.

If we are running 60 protection, which is six-man protection, the back can stay in and block on the play. If we have 50 protection, it is a little different. The read for the quarterback is important. He knows how far his drop is going to be. He knows his movement key and what he is looking at, and he knows he has a progression on the read. For all of our routes the quarterback has those three points to consider.

We work against the safeties. We go one high safety, or two high safeties. The quarterback looks at the two inside seams if we get only one safetyman. He looks the safety one way or the other. He is going to throw the ball to the open seam receiver. If the seam is not open, he reads the outside receivers. If they are not open, he looks for the back on the route. Those are the reads for the quarterback.

If he reads a "two high safeties", he looks for the "bender" receiver. He looks for the inside post and then to the outside fade route, and then to the back. Those are his reads with two deep defenders. He is going to read the safety to the boundary side. It could be "bender," "drop out," and then the back. Those are his progressions.

The last look is our three-by-one deep look in the secondary. We have our "all go" routes called across the formation. This tells certain receivers they are on certain landmarks. You will have to determine that with your terminology. Normally we are working shortside to the wideside of the field. Against the three-by-one, if it is a one high look, the read is the same. We read the free safety one way or the other and read the inside seams, to the drop out on the side the quarterback looks toward, and then to the back on the "dump."

Let me go to our empty set. It really gets interesting in this look. Between these two concepts, we threw the four vertical routes over 100 times. We are still going to set the receivers on their landmarks. We call a receiver's identity tag and throw him a special route. We still have the two deep routes on the outside, and we have the two inside receivers on the seams. The called receiver runs a simple "jig" route (Figure 12-12). The receiver running the jig route comes across inside. He slams on his brakes, comes back outside as if he is going to run a pivot route, and then he works across the field. He has some parameters in this area. If no one comes outside with him, he can settle and look for the pass. If the defender goes with him on the pivot, he comes back underneath to the inside and look for the football. That is the jig route.

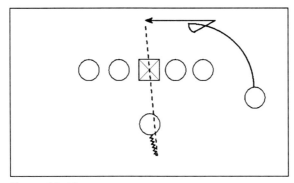

Figure 12-12

The quarterback is still reading four verticals. Now his reads are a little different because he has to read the jig route. If it is a one high look, he is still reading the seam or the free safety. He looks one way and throws the ball back to the other side. If he does not throw the ball to the inside, he still has the man on the outside on the drop out route, and we have the man on the inside on the jig route. If we face two high safeties, we still have the bender route deep. He is reading bender to jig and then to the drop out route.

The movement keys are the same for the quarterback. It is no different for the quarterback. He has thrown the pass over 100 times, so it is no different for him.

Let me show the tape on our passing game. If you have questions, I will be out in the exhibit hall. My time is up. Thank you.

13

Establishing the Spread Offense

Urban Meyer
University of Utah
2004

I am going to talk about the spread offense. We are in a shotgun set where we look to run the ball first and pass second. It is a spread-the-field type of offense we used at Bowling Green University and we carried with us to Utah.

I am going to talk briefly about philosophy. The spread offense began about seven years ago to become a primary set for a number of universities. I think it is getting harder to move the ball because the defenses are catching up with what is happening. The spread is like the wishbone and West Coast offense. The more the defense sees an offense, the better they are able to defend it.

When we recruit a quarterback, we want a throwing quarterback who can run with the ball. I think people make mistakes when they try to fit personnel into an offense that does not fit his talent. If your quarterback does not fit your offense scheme, you are in the wrong scheme. It is amazing that it may take you two years to finally recruit the A-one quarterback to fit your offense, and that is just before you get fired. In college football, if you do not turn the program in two years, you are gone.

We adapted our offense to fit our quarterback's talents. When we were at Bowling Green, we had a non-athletic quarterback. That year we sneaked up on people in the Mid-American Conference and the Big Twelve Conference. People in the MAC had not seen the spread offense. We beat the hell out of Missouri, and I am still trying to figure out how we did it. We finally recruited a great running back, moved him to quarterback, and the offense blossomed.

When we recruit a quarterback, we look at the tape. I want to see the ten or twenty plays on the tape, where there is no chance for the play to be successful. When I find the quarterback who found a way to make those plays gain yardage, that is the quarterback I want.

When I went to Notre Dame, we were an I formation team. We could beat teams we are better than. We could beat Rutgers and Navy because we could run the ball right at them. If you cannot run the ball, you are in trouble in the I formation. That is why we went to a shotgun formation.

When I came to Utah, we had three dropback quarterbacks who were very non-athletic players. Do not run a West Coast offense if you do not have West Coast quarterbacks. Do not run a spread offense unless you have a runner that can throw. Our coaching staff did a tremendous job of adapting the offense to fit what the quarterbacks could do.

They did some neat things to take the ball out of the quarterback's hand. That is hard to do in the spread offense. Not one play exists in the spread offense where the quarterback just hands the ball off and gets out of the way. Every snap in the spread offense, the quarterback has to be a decision maker, an athlete, and a smart signal caller.

When you run the spread offense, you have to equate numbers to run the ball. We want to avoid the bad play by using an audible. We spent four to five months this year studying the offense, and we are going out next year and studying with other teams. Our quarterback is a good thrower. It is the first time in nineteen years of coaching I have had a legit thrower who can run the football.

In the spread offense, we force the defense to defend the field. The purpose of the game is not to get 22 people inside the hash marks of the field. We want to spread the field, create mismatches, and force the defense to defend the field.

We are going to run the football. To do that, we equate numbers so we do not end up running into unblocked defenders.

We put the ball in the hands of our playmakers. Identify your playmakers and find ways to get the ball into their hands. If you have to direct snap the ball to them, get the ball in their hands.

We played California this year and the score was see-sawing back and forth. In the third quarter, we hit a lull and could not move the ball. We went two straight series with three-and-out results. We put one of our best wide receivers in the backfield and direct snapped the ball to him three plays in a row. We went right down the field. It changed the tempo of the game. It was not plays we made up because we had them in the offense. However, it was a way to get the ball in the hands of our playmakers.

This offense is hard to prepare for in two days. If you do not see this offense often, it is hard to prepare the defense in the limited time before the game to handle everything the offense does. You have basically two days to get the game plan in and tweak it to what you do well.

The worst thing that happened to us this year occurred after we received our bowl bid. We won the conference and everyone was excited about playing in the bowl. I watched the TCU-Southern Mississippi game on TV because we played the winner in the bowl game. I was pulling for TCU because of the defense Southern Mississippi ran.

Southern Miss had one of the best defenses in the country, but they ran that wild three-three defense. At one time during the bowl game, they had ten people standing up at the line of scrimmage. When we played BYU, they ran the same type of defense, and it was really confusing to our kids. We want to do the same thing with our offense.

Every year I ask defensive coordinators what they hate to see the offense run. I want to know what gives them knots in their stomach. The first thing they always mention is option football. All the stunts a defensive team likes to run are not good against an option. Man coverage is not good against option football teams. Option football teams force defense to be very vanilla in what they run. We are going to be an option football team.

The second thing that defenses do not like to see is the empty set in the backfield. We have an empty set package. Defenses do not like to play teams that unbalance their sets. We are very seldom in a double slot formation. We line up in the trips set because it allows us to better identify what the defense is doing. We want to be an offense that makes it hard for the defense to prepare.

In the spread offense, we create mismatches with the defense. Our best receivers are our inside receivers in our sets. We run the ball at the defense, which requires the defense to play linebackers. When they play linebackers, we force them into coverages which are mismatches for them. Our inside slot in our trips set has caught close to 100 catches the last three years. That is the position that defenses have to stop. The second receiver on the team is the split end or the one receiver in the three-by-one set.

If you come to Utah and watch our staff work, you will be impressed. I think Pete Carroll is a fantastic coach. He knows football, but if he did not, he still would be a good coach because he is so enthusiastic. If you ever hear him at a clinic, he is so upbeat and enthusiastic that you are ready to play when he finishes talking. I think every coach in America is a great X's and O's coach. Knowing those types of things does not win games.

Being energetic in practice is the way I want my coaches. We only have the players for two hours a day, and I want my coaches to be able to give them two hours of work and enthusiasm. At our practices, you will see coaches that are fresh and energized, coaching their tails off. They are chasing players down the field and coaching like their hair is on fire. If that is not the way they want to coach, I am going to fire them because they are cheating their players. Next year we will win because of the attitude we have right now.

I am going to give you a very simplistic explanation of how we equate numbers in our running. One-high to us means there is a single safety between the hash marks more than 10 yards deep. Two-high means two safeties in the middle of the field on the hash marks more than 10 yards deep. No-deep means the defense is playing zero or man coverage with no one in the middle of the field.

If the defense has one safety in the middle of the field against a double slot set, we say that equates to an equal set and we run the ball (see Figure 13-1). The thinking is that the defense is covering your set with a three-deep and four-under zone scheme or a man-to-man with a free safety. That means inside the tackle box, the defense has six players. Since we have five offensive blockers and the quarterback's read counts as a blocker, we are equal in number and run the ball.

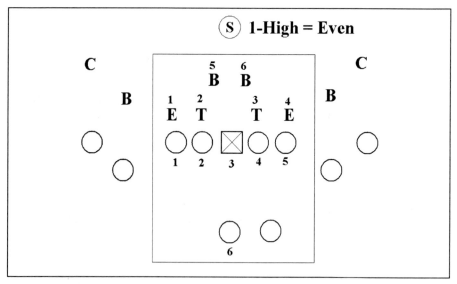

Figure 13-1. One-high

If the defense has two high safeties in the middle of the field, that equates to a plus one in our counting (see Figure 13-2). The defense is playing with five men in the tackle box, which gives us a one-man advantage in the number of blockers compared to the number of defenders. We run the football.

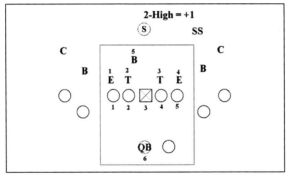
Figure 13-2. Two-high

The last look, which we will see more and more until we get more speed at wide receivers, is no safety in the middle of the field (see Figure 13-3). That means the defense has dropped the safety into the box and is playing man-to-man with no free safety. The defense has seven men in the box, and we have only six blockers. That is a minus one and we have to run a speed option or throw the ball.

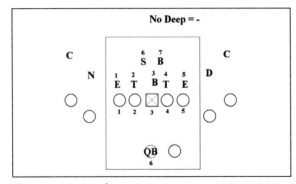
Figure 13-3. No-deep

The play I am going to show you is called 14-15 read (see Figure 13-4). We run this play 17 to 25 times a game. The 14 play is run right, and the 15 play is run left. It is like the wishbone, which can be run from a multitude of sets. This play is a zone play. The blocking assignments for the onside guard and tackle is what we call Tag. When we give a tag call, the tackle and guard are working together on the block.

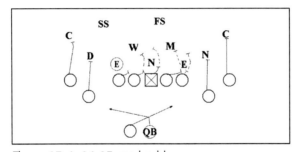
Figure 13-4. 14-15 read odd

In the odd front defense, the guard is uncovered. The tackle and guard are zone stepping and reading the hip of the 5 technique. The guard's aiming point is the inside hip of the 5 technique. He steps to the hip and gets his outside hand on the defensive end. If the hip comes to the guard, he takes the block over using two hands, and the tackle goes up to the linebacker. If the hip stays outside, he works up on the linebacker.

If the center has a shade to the playside, he calls "Scoop." (see Figure 13-5). That tells the guard he needs help. The guard now calls "Badger," which tells the tackle he is by himself. The backside guard and tackle are working a tag scheme on the backside.

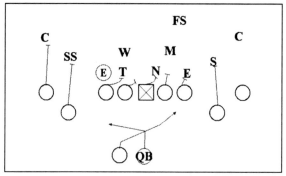

Figure 13-5. 14-15 read even

The running back is aligned at five yards from the line of scrimmage behind the offensive guard. The quarterback's hands are at 5 yards, and his heels are at 5.5 yards. The running back is responsible for the mesh. The quarterback is keying the backside hand-off key, which is the first man outside the backside tackle. The running back cannot get in a hurry getting to the hand-off position. He takes a crossover step, which is described as a slow, slow step. The next two steps are called quick, quick steps. He cannot get in a hurry pressing the ball to the line of scrimmage. When he turns up, he does not cut until he reaches the heels of the offensive linemen. At that point, he runs to daylight.

In a double slot, the slot back to the backside has a keep block. He is playing for the quarterback to bring the ball back to him. He is blocking on the inside number of the walk-away player aligned on him. If that defender runs away from him, he does not chase him. He waits for him to come back, and then he seals him inside. To the front side the slot back is blocking the support, which is the defender's head up to the inside.

If we go to the trips set, nothing changes in the box. The inside slot blocks the MDM, or most dangerous man. This play can be a great misdirection play. The quarterback reads the backside end. If the end is chasing the ball down the line of scrimmage, the quarterback pulls the ball and runs off the slot back's block. The threat of the quarterback running the ball to the backside slows down the inside linebackers.

I want to show you something that we did to take the ball out of the quarterback's hand. This play did not depend on the quarterback making a great run. It is a play called 14-15 triple (see Figure 13-6). We are running a triple option depending on the read of the quarterback. The offensive line is zone blocking on a track. They are blocking the inside zone and nothing else. We are counting the men outside the tackle. The number one man is the hand-off key. The number two man is the pitch key, and the number three man is the wide receiver's block.

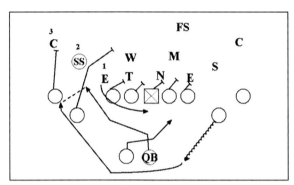

Figure 13-6. 14-15 triple

The pitch man is the slot back coming back in motion behind the quarterback in the shotgun set. He is in the position of an I-back when the ball is snapped. The quarterback runs a 14 read play. If there is any doubt of what to do, the quarterback leaves the ball with the running back. If he keeps the ball, he is pitching off the run support to the weakside. This is an excellent play and an easy read on the pitch man. He attacks the inside number of the pitch man as fast as he can. The slot back is five yards outside the quarterback and one yard behind him.

The next play I am going to give you is called 14-15 read option (see Figure 13-7). On this play, we are not motioning anyone. We are running the 14 zone play again with the read on the backside defensive end. If the quarterback pulls the ball, he runs the triple option off the run support and pitches to the backside slot back. The slot back is two yards off the ball in his alignment. As the quarterback is making his ride on the running back, the slot is taking three steps backward. He shuffles to get timed up on the quarterback. He is in the pitch relationship of five and one yard from the quarterback.

This play is called 6-7 shovel option (see Figure 13-8). This play actually started at Notre Dame. We ran the play at Syracuse when I was there. At Syracuse, we ran it from a two back set. We block this play as an off-tackle power play. We are blocking gaps in the offensive line and pulling the backside guard through the hole. It used to be that if you ran the shovel pass and the defender dropped to the inside, the quarterback was screwed. This play gives the quarterback something to do with the ball.

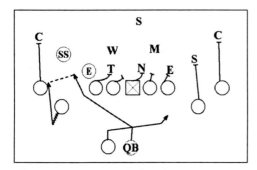
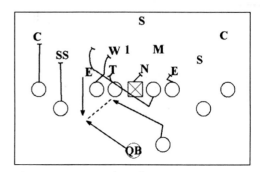

Figure 13-7. 14-15 read option   Figure 13-8. 6-7 shovel option

The 7 shovel option is run to the left. The running back aligns to the right behind the outside hip of the guard. He is five yards off the line of scrimmage. The quarterback is in the shotgun set with his hands at five yards. His heels are at 5.5 yards. The quarterback runs the speed option down the line of scrimmage toward the read key. He is attacking the outside number of the read key.

If the defender attacks the quarterback, he gives ground and shovels the ball back inside to the running back. The quarterback has to go hard toward the defensive end to make the defense commit one way or the other. If he is lazy, the defensive end can hang in the middle, and he can play both the quarterback and the shovel back. The pulling guard leads up inside on the linebacker.

If the defender does not attack the quarterback and falls back inside on the running back, the quarterback continues to run the option and brings the ball to the pitch key (see Figure 13-9). He is running the read option with the slot back as the pitch man. The slot back is reading the key defender so he knows whether to block or become the pitch back.

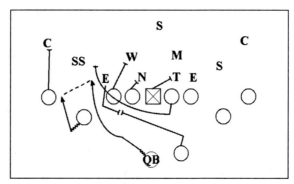

Figure 13-9. 7 shovel option

The thing that people have to consider if you are thinking about installing some of these ideas in your offense is the center snap. We had a center at Bowling Green University that was so good he led the quarterback in the direction he was going. The snap is a blind snap and is a dead type of snap. We do not spin the ball. That is one aspect of the play that can destroy the timing of the play quickly.

If we get into the trips set and bring motion by the inside slot toward the quarterback, it looks like the triple option toward the motion (see Figure 13-10). We snap the ball and run the shovel option back to where the motion came from with the outside slot back as the pitch man.

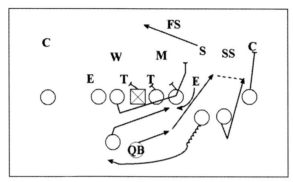

Figure 13-10. 6 shovel - motion

If we get in the empty set, we can still run these plays using motion. When we go empty, we like a two-by-three formation. The formation is a double set one way, and a trip set the other. We can run any of these plays using motion and achieve the same results. Nothing gets changed for anyone in the offense. The backs in our sets are interchangeable in the running game. They know how to run the read option as the pitch man. By using multiple formations and motion, you can run the same plays with different looks for the defense.

This year we were not as physical on the offensive line as we will be next year. This year we really played with offensive linemen that were not very skilled. They worked hard and improved as the year went along. We will be better next year. I appreciate your attention, and thanks for coming.

14

The No-Huddle Spread Offense

Chris Moore
Appalachian State University
2008

I want to give you a short background of our program since we have been at Appalachian State. Most of the staff have been there for the past 10 to 12 years. We have a good staff and we work well together. We managed to win a few games over those years.

In 2003, we had several talented athletes on the team. On offense, we lined up in the I formation with a tight end and two backs. We were trying to run the power game against the defense. The defense was lining up with 12 men in the box against that offensive set. Teams just stoned us with everyone up tight on our offense.

We knew we had some good athletes coming back, and we decided to explore the things we needed to do to feature those athletes. We visited West Virginia University when Rich Rodriquez was there. We went to Bowling Green University, and we got the tapes from the University of Utah when they were running the zone read. We went to visit the University of Florida after Urban Meyer took over down there.

We adapted to the no-huddle and the spread formations to run the football in 2004. Now, we are trying to throw the ball 50 percent of the time. We would like a 50/50 balance on offense. However, we are going to take whatever the defense dictates to us.

We always had to defend Georgia Southern when Paul Johnson was there. They liked to run the triple option. We just could not cover everything they did on offense. We tried to adapt our spread offense to the type of offense that had always given us problems.

There is no secret to our offense. We are going to spread you out and run the ball. We are going to run the option. We have an offensive line coach who likes to play with two tight ends. We have a quarterbacks and receivers coach who likes to run the empty set. I like the two-back attack and the option game.

We do not have an offensive coordinator. We are always bickering with each other in the staff meetings. However, when we leave the coaching meetings, we all understand we are going to run what will be effective for us that day and in that game. We practice all of those things, and it works for us. In our offense, we do not try to hide anything. We know our opponents are going to get a copy of our tapes.

We had a great spring and pre-season practice. We were feeling good about our offense. That first game in 2004, we played at Wyoming. In the first seven minutes, we were behind 28-0. We did not change the plays at the line of scrimmage, and we did not read the defense. It was as if we were still in the I formation. We threw the bubble screen pass and it was intercepted. It was really getting bad for our offense. Then, we had a lighting delay for one hour. We went to the locker room and the players were looking at each other as if they did not know what was happening. We knew we did not have a chance.

We came back the next week in practice and decided we had to go all-out to run the offense. We had to change the plays at the line, and we had to read the defense. We had to get the offense into an upbeat tempo to get the offense going. We scored 50 points in the game. Now, they felt better about themselves.

We really did not know how to practice when we started the no-huddle offense. They tried to go as fast as they could at all times. We did not have time to talk with the players to correct mistakes because we were concentrating on going fast in the no-huddle. Our defense did not know what to do and how to play practice because our offense did not present the picture we needed to improve on defense. It took us about a year to learn how to practice against each other where it would benefit each of us.

We threw the ball 80 percent of the time in the no-huddle. We had a receiver catch 120 passes to lead the nation in pass catches. However, we were not effective as a team.

After the 2004 season, they fired the athletic director. We got an interim athletic director. We were 6-5 that past season, and we knew things were not what they should have been for us. The people got on us about not winning more games. So we had a closed-door meeting with the entire coaching staff. The head coach said this, "Men, we are going to win. We are going to throw the ball, and we are going to run the ball. All of you must line up and circle the wagons. We do not have to tell anyone what we are doing or what is going on with the football program. If the school wants a new coach, that is fine with me." So we decided we had to find a way to win some games.

In 2005, we stressed the true zone option and the passing game that goes with the offense. We have won three straight national championships since that time. Here are some stats on our offense to give you an idea about how effective we have been. This is for the 2007 season:

- 288 yards rushing
- 200 yards passing
- 488 total offense
- 43 points per game

We try to spread the field. We are always in the shotgun formation. We actually took a knee from the shotgun last year. We do not get under center. We have not huddled in four years. We make our calls so simple so the defensive players understand that the field is 120 yards long and 53 yards wide. We are going to play the *whole* field.

During the game, we mix our personnel grouping up to create confusion on the part of the defense. We are going to throw the ball deep two times per quarter. If we are having success on one phase of our offense, we are going to stick to that part of the game.

We feel the game has become the NBA style of playing. It has become man-to-man defense. If you want to outnumber a team in the box, we feel you must play a blitz/man type of coverage. You must understand we run our quarterback. If we are in a one-back set, that really is two backs to us. We say that because 30 percent of our running plays are to the quarterback. If we go four wide, we never see seven in the box.

We spread to run the ball first. We either see five or six men in the box. We must be good enough to run the ball with six men in the box.

Here is our running game—these are the only running plays we have. We have an *inside zone* that we wear teams out with. We run the inside zone 80 percent of the time. We didn't run the *outside zone* for two years. Then, defensive teams started cheating their ends down inside to stop the inside zone. Last year, we put the outside zone in and gained a ton of yards on the play. Now, teams have to play us more balanced because they know we can run both the inside and outside zone plays.

We run the *truck play,* and it is always with a tight end. The truck play is based on technique. We pull two linemen on the truck. We like to pull our center if possible. We pull the guard or tackle on the play. We kick out, wrap around, and hand the ball to the back.

We want to run the *speed option*. We want it to be a quarterback play. In our speed option, our tackles cannot go out and get a linebacker. It is almost an outside zone play to the tackles. We run the back outside to get the linebacker to move outside. If the linebacker stays inside, we pitch the ball. We are not expecting the quarterback to pitch the ball. It is a quarterback run to us.

We run the draw because we run the four vertical routes. We run the *dart play* some, but we did not run it much last year. Our dart play is when we pull the tackle. Also, we have a *speed sweep*. I will cover those plays later in the film.

Our basic philosophy is to take what is given to us. Our signals for our plays make us effective—we are not very complicated. Our staff up in the box can signal information down to us on the sideline. Our signals to the players are very simple.

The quarterback looks to the sideline to get the signal. The receivers are watching the sideline as well. The linemen do not care what we call on the sideline. They hear *40* or *41*, or red or blue, which are our zone plays. They hear one number and they know *28* is our truck play. If they hear *28, 50, 28, 50,* they know we are running the truck play. Nothing else matters to them. They need to know about five things in our offense.

We want to have the ability to throw the ball 50 times per game or run it 50 times per game. We are not caught up in game planning. We take what the defense gives us. We are going to run our base plays every week. The plays that are working that game are the plays we are going to run.

Let me cover the process of calling plays. We have two coaches in the press box and two coaches on the sideline who signal in the plays. The play comes to the quarterback. The quarterback looks to the sideline, and we give him a signal. He tells the line what we want to run. Then, we run the play. It is as simple as that.

The way we call the plays gives us an opportunity to check out of bad plays. The quarterback does not check any play. The coaches are the ones watching the films and studying what the defense does. The players only get about one hour a day to look at the opponent's defense. We put the pressure on the coaches to get us out of a bad play. We feel we can signal the quarterback, and he can call the play we want to check out and give it to the linemen. We think this is a better option for us. We can still change the play with six or seven seconds on the play clock. This takes the pressure off the quarterback.

We work on the tempo each week for the no-huddle offense. We have four speeds. We practice these early in the practice session.

- Jet: Fast tempo
- Normal (to Fast): Check sideline

- Indy: Freeze play
- Scan: Call formation (no play)

In our jet, we call the play and the team lines up on the ball. Most of the time they are waiting on the officials to mark the ball ready for play. They are not looking back because they are running the play called. We go as fast as we can go.

The normal is a regular call. We call the formation and the play, and we are lined up ready go. Now, they look to the sideline, and we may change the play or we may not change the play. We are in this tempo about 80 percent of the time. If we get a team that is out of condition, we will run the jet instead of the normal.

The Indy is a dummy call. We call the formation, but we do not call a play. It is a freeze play. Our snap count never changes. It is, "Ready, set, hut," every time. When we are in Indy, we call the cadence, "Ready, set, hut." If the defense jumps offside, we throw the ball deep. We have gone on the first count on the Indy, but that causes us problems.

On scan, we call the formation without a play. It is a faster tempo than Indy. We want the offense lined up before the officials are off the ball. They look to the sideline, and we call the play, and away we go. We do not run scan that much.

Using multiple formations, we want to change the defense by stretching them throughout the game. We have 22 different formations that we use. We like to run different formations early in the game to see how the defense is going to play us. We want the staff of our next opponent to spend a lot of time breaking down our film and pulling out all of the different formations we run. The jobs for the front five linemen do not change that much. We want them to be comfortable in their assignments.

We want to get the defense out of their comfort zone. We want to create confusion for the defense. We do have to spend a lot of time on the different formations we run.

I love the aspects of option football. The defense must be sound to play assignment football against the option. We like to have the ability to bring a slot back around for the pitch on the option. We want to have some type of motion so we can force the safety to be responsible for the pitch.

We like to see the safety running downhill so we can take our shot 1-on-1 with our speed players. We want to make the secondary *run conscious*, and they must know where to fit against our option game. We do not think they can keep both safeties high against us. We expect to see one of them down low. We run the ball enough to expect at least six men in the box. We do not think you can outnumber us in the box. This is especially true with our motion offense. We have the ability to get to our two-back set with our slot formations. We anticipate where the defense will align against us.

We had several skilled players, and we decided we needed to get the ball to them. We decided to spread the offense and create speed in space. That is the trademark of our offense. We want to get the ball to the playmakers and create 1-on-1 situations for them. We feel the inside zone play does this for us. We reduce the number of blocks that must be made on the play. Because of the quick passing game, the outside linebackers must respect that area of the field, and it helps us on the zone play.

By running the spread offense, we can exploit match-ups. We show the formation early in the game and then find mismatches.

We preach toughness. We have always believed that we were tougher than the teams we play. Our players have a mindset that we are tough. We are a finesse offense by appearance. Running the ball makes it that way.

There is no indecision in our offensive line as far as their blocking is concerned. That has been a big advantage for us. Those big linemen do not have to do a lot of thinking. They know what they are doing every play. They have five things to remember, and they have three types of pass protection. They are doing the same things repeatedly every day. They do not have to think much to do what they do.

We work on short-yardage plays all of the time in practice. We are third and two yards to go more than we are third and seven yards to go for the first down. We put the ball on the nine-yard line and give the offense three downs to score. We do this more than we scrimmage against each other. We stress the short-yardage situations. We feel that builds toughness into the players. We do not want the defense to think they have preemption on toughness.

People ask us why we run the spread offense. We give them several reasons why we like the spread: it will maximize the speed of our team, it is the best way to create speed and get the ball on the perimeter, and it creates 1-on-1 match-ups.

It allows us set the tempo of the game. We feel our tempo is unique because we are going at a fast pace for most of the time in a game. We run the heck out of our players. Many no-huddle teams do not condition their players.

We get better conditioning with our players by not using the huddle. We run for 30 yards on each play in practice. The players run the play and get back to the line ready to go again. They see the signal for the formation on the way back from running the last play. They do not get much rest between plays. The conditioning part takes care of itself. However, we are old-school and we still run them after practice.

It puts the defense in a bind in terms of personnel, match-ups, stunts, coverage, and overall communication.

I will cover the way we call our plays later, but we only give one receiver a pass route. The other receivers must remember what they do on the play called for each receiver. If the end is running an option route, they must know what they do on that call. That takes some time in practice, but it allows us to change the plays very quickly in games.

We feel we can check to any play in our playbook without any problems. We feel we can get the play off if we change it with six or seven seconds left on the 25-second play clock.

By not allowing the quarterback to check off on a play, we should never be in a bad play. *Should* is the key word because we do make some mistakes in this area.

By running several different formations, the defensive coordinators must spend time in setting up their alignments against the formations.

The spread offense that we run appears to be complex, but it is easy to install. This goes back to the way we get the plays to the kids. We have key tag words that tell them what to do. The players learn the offense very early. They understand what we are doing after a few days of practice.

We went to visit West Virginia to see what they were doing on the spread. We wanted to go to the spread as a tempo change-up. At first, we were only going to run the no-huddle seven or eight times a game. When we visited with West Virginia, they told us we needed to be committed to the spread and run it all of the time. Our head coach, Jerry Moore, did not want to change from the I formation and two-back set. We finally convinced him to make the change. We got into that mind-set, and now he likes the concept. Now, he likes the hard-nosed aspects that we stress with the spread offense.

Our offense is a hybrid of the option and the West Coast offense. We got most of our triple-option offense from Georgia Southern's double slot offense. We can run almost the same plays as the double-slot/triple-option game from our two-back-option offense. It does not hit as quick, but we are forcing 1-on-1 situations across the field. We make the defense defend our triple option. They must have their defensive responsibilities down correctly or we can hurt the defense.

With this offense, it is easy to find offensive players. They do not have to be the best athletes to play for us. A good example of this is with our center. He was a linebacker five years ago. He is a short, squatty individual. He is 5'11" and weighs 260 pounds. He is not big, but he can run. We are not asking him to knock defenders off the ball. We are asking him to run. Our line is not that big, but they can run.

When we went to the no-huddle spread offense the attitude of the skilled players changed. They wanted to play. They enjoyed what we were doing on offense.

We wear headsets in practice every day. We are always signaling the plays to the players. It makes the kids pay attention. Even if the players are not in on the play and they are on the sideline, they have to pay attention to keep up with what we are running in practice. The kids know exactly what is coming. They are having more fun and they are into the game more.

That Michigan game was just crazy. We were just a small school from a windy two-lane road up in Boone, North Carolina. When you get to Boone, it is Podunk up there. An ESPN truck was at Boone for two weeks after the Michigan game. We did not know how to act while they were there. Really, we did not have a place for them to park at our place. They would not leave Boone. It was a lot of fun, but it was crazy.

Let me talk about the practice schedule. We have a horn in the locker room. That lets everyone know practice is going to start in five minutes.

Practice Schedule

- Walk–through: 8 minutes
- Stretch: 5 minutes
- PAT/FG: 4 minutes
- Zone period: 10 minutes
- Indy run: 10 minutes
- Team run: 15 minutes
- Team run vs. defense: 7 minutes
- Special teams: 8 minutes
- Indy pass vs. air: 7 minutes
- 1-on-1: 7 minutes
- Skelly: 15 minutes
- Red zone pass: 5 minutes
- Special teams: 5 minutes
- Team pass: 24 minutes
- Win: 4 minutes
- Special teams: 5 minutes

Total Time: 2 hours and 19 minutes

When we get to the practice field, we start with the walk-through. We go over what we covered in the meeting rooms. It is a relaxed session. The stretch period is the same in that we are not intense in this session.

We go to the PAT session and that is where the tempo starts up. We have done the PAT live for the last several years, including on Monday. We go live until Thursday when we back off the live drill on the PAT.

In our zone period, we go for 10 minutes, and we run nothing but the inside zone play. We run the plays out of all of our formations.

We go to the Indy run and spend 10 minutes. We go to the team run for 15 minutes. Now, we run our other three running plays. We do run the inside zone play during this period as well. The zone play is what we are hanging our hat on.

Next, we go to the team run against the defense. It is the same thing with the plays. We run the same plays.

Next, we go to special teams. We used to run the special-teams sessions at the beginning of practice and at the end of practice. Most of our defensive players are on the special teams, and they did not have a good feeling for special teams. Three years ago, we inserted the special-teams session in the middle of our practice time. This has been effective for us. The kids know when the period is coming, and they are ready for it. Everyone is not tired and they can do a better job on special teams.

Then, we go to the Indy pass session. It is routes on air. The running backs may work on blocking in this session.

From there, we go to 1-on-1 with running backs and linebackers. At the other end of the field, we go with the receivers against the defensive backs.

During the season, we do our skelly drill against the scout team. From there, we go to the red zone passing game. It is always against our defense. We put the ball on the 20-yard line and move it closer to the goal line each play. We keep moving it until we get it down to the three-yard line. We always go good-on-good in this drill. We never go ones versus twos.

We come back and run another special-teams drill. We work on things we did not have time to work on before. Then, we go to team pass. Our defense has a hard time covering our receivers. They send bullets at us most of the time in this drill.

We have a period we call our *win period*. We put this in our practice sessions two years ago. It is used for whatever we want to stress that day. Many times, it is goal-line situations, or our two-point play. The next day, we may work on coming out of the end-zone offense. We may have a special play we use in this period.

We always end the practices with the kickoff and kickoff-return game. The total time is about 2 hours and 20 minutes. We are trying to cut it back, but the head coach does not think we are out on the practice field enough. So it is a happy medium for everyone.

I want to go over our basic formations. When we call *Y trips*, the Y end always goes to the wideside of the field. That is trips with a tight end.

Our spread formation is the tight-end formation. The X goes away from the call. The Y goes to the call on the ball. The tight end and flanker are on one side, and the slot and split end are on the other side.

We do not signal personnel to switch tight-end sets or four-wide sets. We just signal our formations in to the team. If we call trips, the Y receiver must understand he is coming off the field and the tight end is coming in the game for him. They must memorize the personnel. On *trey*, we are in trips with a backside tight end. If we call gator formation, we put our tight end in a wing set where we can move him around.

If we want to run the empty set, we have the two backs to the same side (Figure 14-1).

If we run *lock*, we have a tight end on the side with the two backs (Figure 14-2).

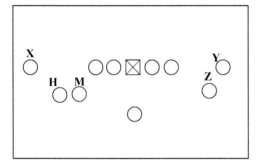

Figure 14-1. Empty set

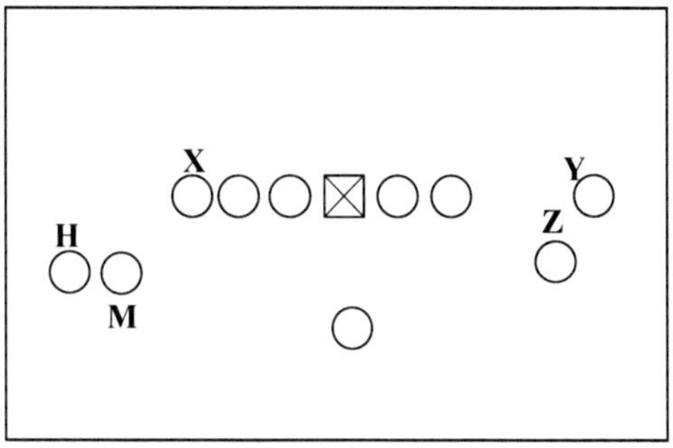

Figure 14-2. Lock

If we call *Lisa*, we have two tight ends with two backs split to one side, and one back to the opposite side (Figure 14-3).

This is our right stretch. We have both ends split. The Z back is wide and the M back is in the slot on the left side (Figure 14-4).

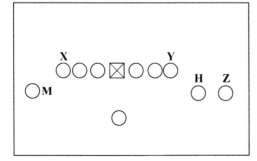
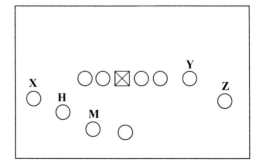

Figure 14-3. Lisa

Figure 14-4. Right stretch

If we call *right ace*, we have both ends split. We have both slots on the inside (Figure 14-5).

If we call *kings*, we have the slots lined up on the outside (Figure 14-6). The ends are still split, but not as wide because the slots are on the outside.

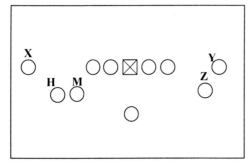

Figure 14-5. Right ace

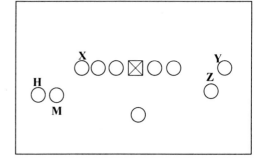

Figure 14-6. Right kings

This gives us the ability to take a good receiver and put him in any of those positions to get the match-up we want. The Y end is always to the callside. This is the way we can get the ball to the receiver we want the ball to go to.

Trio is our 3 x 1 formation. We can run this to both sides. The two-tight end sets are very simple. We can run those with two backs to one side or the other. The *doubles formation* is our 2 x 2 formation. Our offense does not use a two-back set with a tight end. That is one personnel group that we have never been. Most of our M receivers are high school running backs who have some strength. We do not have a problem sending them in motion from the backfield. We never put two true running backs in the game with the tight end.

This is our *left and right open sets*. We have two backs in the formation, but we have both ends split. We can call, "Open far," or "Open near." If we call, "Left, open, far," the back lines up in the slot away from the call.

This is how we call our motions. We have a right wristband and a left wristband. One is red and one is yellow. If the red hand goes up in the air and I am on the right slot, he is going to go toward the play looking for the pitch. If he is on the slot on the left side and the red hand goes in the air, he is going toward the quarterback.

Motions for the Receivers

Z = Zoom, zip, zap

M = Move, motor, mix, mex, rip

H = Hop, hiccup

S = Radar, laser

The hop is for the tight ends. We do not want them to get confused with the slot backs.

We call our running back the *S back*. We use radar and laser to get to our empty set with him. This moves the running back to the right or left outside. We may only throw the ball to the back twice a year on this set. It is a way to get to empty.

Here are the running plays we use. This is it. We do not run the dart and the speed sweep very often.

Running Plays

40/41 = Zone

48/49 = Mid zone

28/29 = Truck

18/19 = Spread/zone option

16/17 = Load option

Dallas = Draw

22/23 = Dart

98/99 = Speed sweep

36/37 = Counter

We never called the 48 or 49 zone plays until late this past year. We have been running about five plays for three years. We are rushing for 260 to 290 yards per game. Teams that watch us play feel we are running a lot more plays than we really do run.

We can add the letter *Q* on our plays. If we call 28 truck and point to the quarterback, the back that was supposed to get the ball is going to block because the *Q* tells us the quarterback is going to run the ball. This does not matter what the call is to the linemen. They know it is a 28 play.

Let me give you our protections. If we call *river* or *lake*, it is the five fat linemen with one back in the protection. The *R* and *L* tell the line which side the back is on that will be helping them. We go big-on-big.

Our 100 protection is our play-action plays. It is similar to the river and lake, but we tell the line the back is going to the opposite side. Our 400 protection is our naked calls. The 500 calls are our bootleg protections.

The *load* is our seven-man protection. It is load Roger or load Louie. This tells the tight end to stay in to block. Roger and Louie tell them which side the back is going, and the load tells the tight end to stay in and protect. On *canyon*, the back is releasing. When we are in empty, it is five men to protect and that is it. On 94 and 95 roll, we are running the sprint-out series. We are not very good at this, so we do not call it very often.

On *dynamite*, it is a catch-and-throw situation. It is a quick pass, and we cut the defensive line. Everything is on the outside knee. We are trying to get the defense to get their hands down.

That is all of our protections. We do not slide protect. Against the 50 front, we may call *solid fan*. It makes it hard for the back to read the play, but we are trying to get the ball out quick.

Next, is our quick passing game.

- Quick stop: If the corners are going to play off the receivers, we are going to throw the ball to them. We are going to make the defense walk up on the wide receivers.
- Spacing: This is a Quick Stop pass. We have landmarks and numbers we use, including inside and outside the hash marks.
- Quick flare: Is our Bubble Screen play.
- Dragon: We take our three-receiver side and send the inside slot deep. If the defense plays the defender on the slot inside more toward the box, we can call Z Now, or M Now. The quarterback catches the snap and throws the ball to the slot receiver as quick as possible. If the defense does not cover the slot, we are going to get him the ball.

We run the *slant* and *swing passes* with the different receivers. It is basic pass plays. We run our flat routes. Everyone must know what to do on the flat routes.

We run several shallow routes. We can designate any receiver to run the shallow. The other receiver on the same side of that receiver will run a *get-open-behind-him* route.

The under and shallow routes are the same play. We are telling the back which way to go on the call. Shallow and back away both have *W*'s in the spelling. If it is a shallow call, you flare away, and if it is under, you flare toward the play.

We throw tons of option routes. We give the Z-back or our M-back the option routes. If it is the Z receiver and we have the option route, he has from the opposite hash all the way across the field to get open. The other slot man has from the near hash mark to the near boundary to get open. If we call the Z option route and the receiver is not open, the quarterback is running the ball. We do not give him a third option. He looks for the Z back first, the M back second, and if they are not open, he runs the ball. We call this backyard football. It is very simple to run.

We throw two vertical passes, at least two per quarter. We send out four receivers deep because we do not see two deep safeties very often. As soon as we snap the ball, one of those two are coming down in the box.

On the inside zone running play, the right tackle must never get beat inside. The center must step toward the guard on the frontside. The guard is blocking man on by himself. The tackles have the linebackers reading inside. The running back reads the first man leading up over the center. We want the backs hitting inside the tackles. We do not want them bouncing outside on the play.

I really enjoy running this offense. We have a lot of fun with the players. It could help anyone who is interested in running this type of offense.

You will be able to see what we are doing in the film session. I will stop the film and answer any questions you may have.

I appreciate your attention. I will be around for questions later.

15

The No-Huddle Spread Offense

Gary Pinkel
University of Missouri
2006

Today I want to talk with you about our philosophy. It is not so much our philosophy, but it is what we believe in and how we practice. I will go over the different things we do and I will get into what we do with the spread offense.

We are a no-huddle offense. We changed a couple of years ago. We did not huddle one time last year.

I want to talk to you about why we went to this offense and some of the concepts of why we went to this offense. I could spend 30 minutes just talking about our zone play. I am not going to do that. I am going to give you some concepts on why and how we run the zone play.

I have been the head coach at the University of Missouri for five years. The first couple of years we struggled. We have been to two bowl games in the last three years. We have gone 20-16 in the last three years. Has it been easy? No! It has been very difficult.

I played at Kent State University. I was a captain with Jack Lambert. Jack and I played for Coach Don James at Kent State.

I was an assistant coach at Bowling Green State University before I rejoined Don James at the University of Washington as an assistant. We went to 11 bowl games in 12 years.

To say the least, I am a Don James disciple. Without question, our program is based on that same philosophy. The program was taken from Kent State and then to Washington and then back to Toledo. We took the same program to Missouri.

The first thing I want to cover with you is the University of Missouri practice and teaching philosophy. Our goal is to outpractice our opponents. We do this in the following ways:

• Practice harder
• Practice smarter
• Practice with game-day intensity

We have a walk-through before practice that lasts 15 minutes. Then we go practice. Every drill we do is with game-day intensity. We get after it. That is what we believe in. We want our practices tough so once we get into the games it is easier.

In addition to practicing hard, we want to practice smart. When we go into a drill, our players know what the drill is about and the speed with which we are going to approach the drill. The players know if we are going into the drill in "thud," or if we are going to back off on the drill. They are going to know the speed with which we are going into the drill, so we do not get anyone hurt in the drill.

I want my coaches to teach their players that they are the best position coaches in the league. If they do not believe it, we are not going to win. We must sell the players on this concept. We have to be organized and look like experts in front of the players. If we can do that, the players are going to play at a higher level.

We must be great teachers. I tell the coaches this: "What you see on the video is what you coach." You are a teacher and your evaluation is measured by your players' performance. Professors can have students that make A, B, C, D, and F grades. We must have all A's and B's. We must keep things simple. We do not want to overcoach. We want to find the best way to teach. We must teach fundamentals. Our goal is for each player to master the fundamentals at his position.

We know what must be taught. Staff growth is important. We must improve our schemes. We strive for our players to improve daily. We have a philosophy that players must master the fundamentals at their positions.

We must utilize teaching aids. We change up procedures for our meetings. We must use different techniques in our teaching methods. We know what must be taught.

We must use the different methods to teach what we want the players to learn. We have video breakdowns. We must find a way to use them. We make boards and use diagrams to illustrate the points we want to cover. The accuracy of diagrams is critical. We know that 75 percent of learning is visual. How you draw up a play is important, because the way you draw up a play is the way they are going to run the play.

We must find ways to be positive. We do not want our enthusiasm just to be cheerleading. We want everything explained to our athletes. We criticize performance. We do not want the players to take the criticism personally. We want to find things to be positive about. We know that 99 percent of our communication and motivation should be positive. If this is not true, then we need to change the way we communicate with them. We want our coaches to be positive most of the time when dealing with the players.

We must be consistent. All players must be team players and abide by the team covenant. We must be consistent in our player interaction. We must praise and criticize—all players. Players will notice any inconsistency in your player interaction. We must coach toughness, coach toughness, coach toughness. We must coach 100 percent effort on every play—every play, every day. We must play hard. Players must be on time for every scheduled meeting or practice. They must pay attention to detail. We demand players to compete in everything they do.

We want hard workers on the field and in coaching. Coach every play! Coach every play! Coach every play! Coach every play! Don't stand in one spot. Hands in pockets, arms folded is not permitted in our program. Get to where the action is. If the coach stands around, so will the players. We do not want a coach to give a clinic on the field. That is why we meet and have walk-throughs. Coaches will run drills to drill just like the players do. Players must run on the field, never walk. Players don't lie on the ground. Demand enthusiasm, intensity, and make sure the players know their assignments.

Control the hitting! Tag offense. Play ball. Live off. Thud. The best coaches in the country take their players' performance personally. Missouri coaches take their players' performance personally!

Why did we go to the spread offense? First of all, it went against the ideas I was brought up with in football. After the last game in 2004, I went down to Texas Tech to visit. They have a great offense. Because of their offense, they have gone to six or seven bowl games in a roll. I watched the offense change over the years. Urban Meyer at the University of Florida was running the spread offense and they were scoring a lot of points each game.

We decided to use the spread offense for the 2005 season. Our goal for this past season was to score 35 points per game. We knew that we had to have a system that would allow us to accomplish this goal. Before last year, we ran some one-back and two-tight-end offenses. We ran the zone, the counter play, and the naked bootleg play. I felt that we needed to attack and score more points. This is how we evolved to the changes we made on offense. I spent a lot of time talking to other coaches about the system.

The reason we ran this offense was because of the following:

- More attacking
- Point potential
- Offense average of 35 points per game
- No huddle
- Equalizer: spreads people
- Presents problems for defense
- Splits
- No backs
- Option
- Vertical and horizontal stretch

I talked to a lot of other coaching staffs before we added the no-huddle. The advice most people gave me about the no-huddle was this. "If you are going to run the no-huddle, then run the no-huddle. Do it with every play you run." So in the spring we put in the no-huddle with every play we put into our offense. We all knew the signals for the offense and we used the no-huddle on every single play.

We like the no-huddle because we can get great tempo with this offense. We ran more plays than anyone in the country last year. We want to get first downs with our offense. The big thing about the no-huddle is that it allows you to control the tempo of the game. Also, it allows you to slow your tempo down to enable you to see what the defense is doing, so you can take advantage of your offense based on what the defense is doing.

We like to split our linemen to give us running lanes. Defenses do not like teams that split the linemen. They do not like teams that run from the one-back. They do not like teams that run the option.

One of the things we want to do is get the defense playing on their heels. When teams play on their heels we feel we are more effective in using the running game.

We believe you can run the ball 50 percent of the time and pass the ball 50 percent of the time from this formation. We have noticed an expansion of the running game from the no-huddle offense. Now the no-huddle offense has become more complex.

We can go from no backs to one back. We line up with no backs and then motion someone in the backfield into the one-back look. You can motion in and out of this offense, which makes it more complex.

The one thing about this offense is this. If you spread people out, you must force the defense to cover them. If they do not cover the wideouts, throw them the football. Also, you must throw a lot of hitch routes in this offense. If the defense does not cover the wideouts, we want to get the ball to the open man. What does this do? It spreads the defense out all over the field.

We have two rules on the no-huddle. If a receiver is open, make the throw to the open man. If the hitch route is open, make sure you throw the open receiver the ball.

When we game plan, we want to give three basic concepts. First is our 2 X 2 concept (Figure 15-1). We could motion one of the other backs and change the formation. We are going to set our game plan where we have the opportunity to run the 2 X 2 formation.

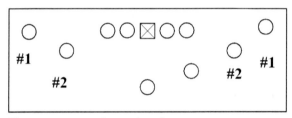

Figure 15-1. 2x2 formation-deuce

We can call this formation six different ways to get our tailback outside. You could just do it one way, but we have several ways to get into this formation. We can get our personnel in the positions we want them in by using different calls.

The next thing we are going to do is look at our 3 X 1 formation. We have the plan where we can go to our 3 X 1 look (Figure 15-2). We may motion out of this formation and go to a 2 X 2 look. We are going to use this to give a different look to the defense. It is our trips look. The defense would prefer for us to stay balanced, with two men on each side in a 2 X 2 formation.

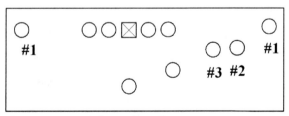

Figure 15-2. 3x1 formation-trips

The next look we have is our 3 X 2 formation (Figure 15-3). We can line up in four or five different ways to get into this formation. We can get into the bunch formations and move our receivers out in different ways. That is our diamond formation.

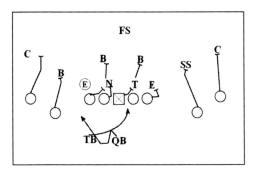

Figure 15-3. 3x2 formation-diamond

The base running plays we can use from these formations include the following: inside zone, speed option, shovel, toe, dive, and the trap plays. We can run the outside veer, which I do not have listed here. We can run the inside veer as well. I really believe in this offense. Obviously, if you have a quarterback that can run and pass as well, the offense is awesome. I think the best way to run the offense is to get the defense playing off their heels. This makes it possible to have large running lanes.

We take the large splits to spread the defense out. On the inside zone play, we do not block the end man on the nose tackle's side unless the defense has five defenders on the line (Figure 15-4). Our quarterback opens to the tailback, extends the football, and reads the end man on the line of scrimmage. Against the five-man line, he hands the ball off to the running back. The tailback reads the first down lineman beyond the center. Then he wants to bend, bang, and bounce.

If the defensive end cannot make the tackle on the play, we want to hand the ball off (Figure 15-5). We want the wide splits, because it helps us on this play.

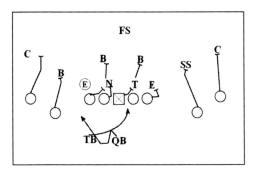

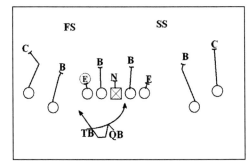

Figure 15-4. Inside zone

Figure 15-5. Vs 30

We tell the tailback to go two yards, and then bang, bounce, and bend. The tailback takes two steps beyond the quarterback and then he is going to bang it upfield, or he is going to bounce it back inside. We would prefer to press it and bounce it outside.

Against the 30 defense, the read is different. Now we are blocking the end man outside of our center. You will be able to see our splits in the film.

Next is our speed option. This is our 3 X 1 formation (Figure 15-6). Basically, we use the drive technique with the tackle. We use that as a game call. If the defensive tackle comes down inside, it becomes a straight man block for us. It becomes a quarterback keep play. The quarterback catches the snap, recognizes the pitch key, and attacks his outside shoulder. He makes the pitch off the center gap defender. He must be ready for a quick pitch. We do not know who is going to be the C-gap defender. Also, we must be ready for the quick pitch.

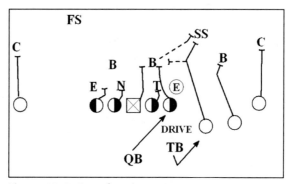

Figure 15-6. Speed option

One thing that helps us in this offense is the fact that the quarterback can see what is coming on defense. It really is not a complex play.

The next play is the shovel play (Figure 15-7). We pull the backside guard around on the play. Everyone else blocks back on the play. We want the tailback to get a relationship of six yards deep on the pitch phase. The tailback comes over in a six-yard phase underneath the quarterback. You must work on this pitch relationship. We want him six yards deep and one yard in front of the quarterback.

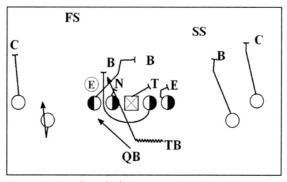

Figure 15-7. Shovel play

We want the quarterback to force the defensive end to move when he comes down the line. If the end just sits there, we are in trouble. If the end sits there, he can take both the quarterback and pitch man on the play. We want to force the end to get a little wider and move one way or the other. If the defensive end comes upfield and outside, we want the quarterback to pitch the ball underneath.

If the defensive end comes upfield toward the quarterback, we want him to shovel the ball underneath to the tailback underneath. The quarterback is five yards deep. He takes the snap and gets width. He pitches off the end man on the line of scrimmage. If he takes the pitch to the tailback away, he keeps the ball. If he squeezes the play inside, the quarterback keeps the ball and runs the option in the alley. You can make the play as complex as you want, and you can also make it simple.

Our trap play is from our 2 X 2 formation. The quarterback steps at the playside leg of the center and reads the pulling guard (Figure 15-8). We trap the 3 technique. We do this in our tempo drill.

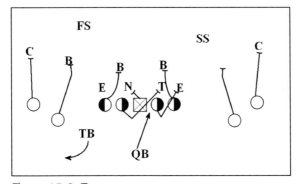

Figure 15-8. Trap

I want to talk about our base passes. We want to run our spread-offense passing concepts. Our specific plan is this. We want to spread the field and attack the open zones. The general idea is this: We want to spread the full-field concepts—a group of routes intended to spread the entire field and create open zones. It does not matter if it is our dropback passing game or a running play.

Next is our half-field concepts. They are a group of routes intended to fill open holes on one side of the field. There are always paired with another half-field concept to allow flexibility against different defensive looks. You can run one game plan on one side of the line of scrimmage and another concept on the other side of the line. You can move the play from one concept to the other concept.

Basically, we have two three-step-drop protections. One is the no-back, and it is from man protection, and the other is the concept of turn protection. These are the only two protections we use in our dropback passing game. We cut a lot in the passing game. These are the two concepts we use.

I will show you a couple of plays from our two formations (Figure 15-9). Next is our quick game protections—350-351.

- Playside tackle: Covered, block man on. Uncovered, block man outside.
- Playside guard: Covered, block man on. Uncovered, make fan call.
- Center: Covered, block man on, and listen for fan call, then turn back and protect the gap backside.
- Backside guard: Covered, block man on, and listen for fox call. Uncovered, turn back and protect the gap backside.
- Backside tackle: Turn in protection, block outside. Set to the widest defender.

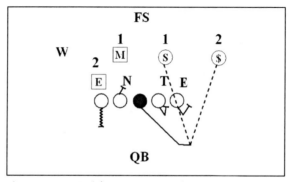

Figure 15-9. Quick game protections—350-351

Next is our quick game protection. It involves our 360-361 protections (Figure 15-10).

- Playside tackle: Set aggressively, get hands down. Covered, block man on. Uncovered, block man outside.
- Playside guard: Set aggressively, get hands down. Covered, block man on. Uncovered, make fan call.
- Center: Set aggressively, get hands down. Covered, block man on. Listen for fan call. Turn back and protect gap backside
- Backside guard: Set aggressively, get hands down.
- Backside Tackle: Set aggressively, get hands down. Turn in protection and block outside. Set to the widest defender.
- Tailback: Read playside A gap out.

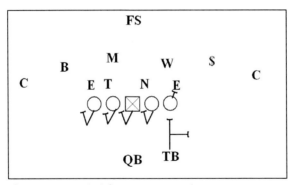

Figure 15-10. Quick game protections—360-361

I want to move along on these next plays. First is the 2 X 2 quick pass. It is our deuce right 360 gold-tan (Figure 15-11).

- Quarterback: Catch and throw. Safety zone, go to tan side (slant/bubble). Two safeties, go to gold side (vertical/speed out). Versus man, take best-located defender: 1-vert, 2-slant, 3-speedout.
- Tailback: Protection, double read the first two linebackers to the playside.
- 1B: Vertical release to six yards. Slant route.
- 2B: Drop-step release, stay flat and parallel to the line of scrimmage until the ball leads you to the LOS.
- 2F: Slight outside release, breaking at six yards from the line of scrimmage.
- 1F: Protection release through the far shoulder of the defender. The landmark is the outside edge of the numbers.

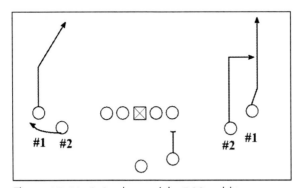

Figure 15-11. 2x2—deuce right 360 gold-tan

Our next look is the 3 X 1 quick routes. It is trips right 360 spacing-black (Figure 15-12).

- Quarterback: Catch and throw progression, and slant to the spot to extended hitch. Always look for the slant to give spacing time to develop.
- Tailback: Protection, double read on the first two linebackers to the playside.
- 1B: Vertical release to six yards. Slant route.
- 3F: Come inside flat to four yards over the ball.
- 2B: Run a six-yard hitch route with two yards of width (6x2) from the original alignment.
- 1F: Run a six-yard hitch route with two yards of width (6x2) from the original alignment. We must convert vs. press or hard corner.

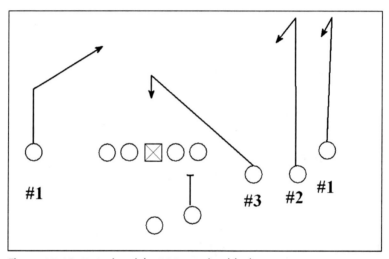

Figure 15-12. 3x1 trips right 360 spacing-black

On the 3 X 2 quick, we call diamond right 351 sit-gold (Figure 15-13).

- Quarterback: Catch and throw. Hitch rule. One safety zone, take sit side (outside in). Two safeties, take gold side (vertical to speed out). If the defense is in man coverage, take the best-positioned defender: 1-vert, 2-speed out, and 3-hitch vs. soft coverage.
- 1B: Protection release through the far shoulder of the defender. The landmark is the outside edge of the numbers.
- 2B: Slight outside release breaking at six yards from the line of scrimmage.
- 3F: Run a six-yard hitch route with vertical push.
- 2F: Run a six-yard hitch route with two yards of width (6x2) from the original alignment.
- 1F: Run a six-yard hitch route with two yards of width (6x2) from the original alignment. We must convert vs. press or hard corner.

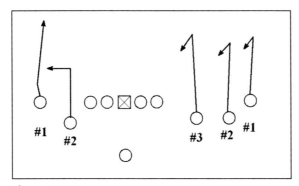

Figure 15-13

Here are our dropback protections—50-51 (Figure 15-14).

• Playside tackle: Covered, block man on, be aware of outside linebacker coming underneath for SIFT.

• Playside guard: Covered, block man on. Uncovered, Molly unless fan call is made.

• Center: Needs to identify the five most dangerous defenders. He makes a Mike call against four-down fronts.

• Backside guard: Covered, block man on. Listen for our fan call from center.

• Backside tackle: Covered, block man on.

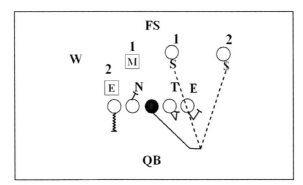

Figure 15-14

Our next protection is our dropback protection—60-61 (Figure 15-15).

• Playside tackle: Covered, block man on. Uncovered, block man outside.

• Playside guard: Covered, block man on. Uncovered, make fan call.

• Center: If covered, block man on. Listen for fan call, turn back, and protect gap backside.

• Backside guard: Covered, block man on. Listen for fan call. Uncovered, turn back and protect gap backside.

- Backside tackle: Turn in, protection block outside. Set to the widest defender.
- Tailback: Read playside A gap out.

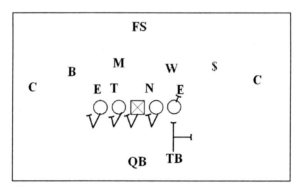

Figure 15-15

Next is our 2 X 2 dropback. It is our deuce right 60 choice (Figure 15-16).

- Quarterback: Step drop (one big, two little). Hitch rule—Progression: Hitch-choice-dump. Versus two safeties, chance of post. Versus one safety, only a corner. Versus no safety, think post.
- Tailback: Protection: first or second linebacker playside. Route: No blitz, dump five yards over the ball.
- 1B: Run a six-yard hitch route with two yards of width (6x2) from the original alignment. Run a delay vs. press man coverage.
- 2B: Protection release, vertical push to 10 to12 yards and run a corner route with an aiming point of 25 yards on sideline. Must get open vs. man.
- 2F: Vertical push to 10 yards, make a decision to break to corner or post by doing the opposite of the near safety. Break route at 12 yards.
- 1F: Run a six-yard hitch route with 2 yards of width (6x2) from the original alignment. Run a delay vs. press man coverage.

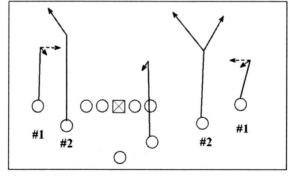

Figure 15-16

Our next look is the 3 X 1 dropback. Here is our trips right 60 cross (Figure 15-17).

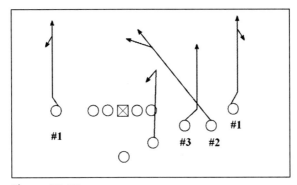

Figure 15-17

We were more successful running the crossing routes than we were on the other plays. We are in a 4 vertical and we are going to push it deep. If it is against a two-deep secondary, we are going to throw the ball off the backside safety. If the safety crosses outside, we want to hit the number 2 receiver in the hole in the middle. If the linebacker gets deep, we throw the dump to the tailback.

- Quarterback: Three-step drop (one big, two little). Against two safeties, read boundary. If the safety gets width, think crosser to the tailback (feel linebackers depth). If the safety sits, go outside to vertical (BND #1) Go to the dropout to the tailback on the dump. Against one-safety zone, read the single safety. If he picks a side, he looks off and drives into the other inside vertical. (Be aware of the corner and linebacker depth.) Against one safety man, he works against the best-positioned defender for us. Against one boundary he goes to the press route. Against man coverage he goes to the two crosser on the man route. His third option is to go to the tailback shooting away from the linebacker.

- Tailback: Protection: first two linebackers playside. Route: five-yard dump route.

- 1B: Vertical release (best release) to 12 yards. If you are hip-to-hip with the corner or past him, continue with the route. Go to the outside edge of the numbers. If the corner is deeper than you are, then convert to dropout at 15 yards.

- 3F: Width release behind F2 and get to a landmark of plus-two outside the hash. Stay fixed and use best release.

- 2F: Release inside to eight yards on alignment of F3 stick to 20 yards. Run the seam route on the backside hash at plus-two.

- 1F: Vertical release (best release) to 12 yards. If you are hip-to-hip with the corner or past him, continue with the go route on the outside edge of the defender's numbers. If the corner is deeper than you are, then convert to dropout at 15 yards.

Our last play is our 3 X 2 dropback. This is our diamond right 51 smash (Figure 15-18).

- Quarterback: Three-step drop (one big, two little). Hitch rule: Read from the boundary—hitch-corner-safety seam. Against a bail corner, throw the hitch on the third step. Against a hard corner, take your eyes to the corner and see where the coverage is coming from: under (corner bounceback)—come back to hitch; on top (safety)—get back to safety seam. Against man: corner route needs to beat the defender.
- 1B: Run a six-yard hitch route with two yards of width (6x2) from the original alignment. Run a delay vs. press man coverage.
- 2B: Protection release: vertical push to 10 to 12 yards and run a corner route with an aiming point of 25 yards on the sideline. Must get open vs. man coverage.
- 3F: Push vertical for eight to 10 yards. Run a seam post to the backside hash vs. two safeties.
- 2F: Protection release: vertical push to 10 to 12 yards. Run a corner route with an aiming point of 25 yards on the sideline. Must get open vs. man coverage.
- 1F: Run a six-yard hitch route with two yards of width (6x2) from the original alignment. Run a delayed route against press man coverage.

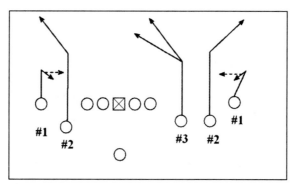

Figure 15-18

I want to show the film clips of these plays so you can see them in a game.

We do run play-action passes from these formations. We run the wheel route on top to keep the defense honest. Also, we run the sprint-out route with these sets. We move the quarterback around. It helps the quarterback and the offensive line.

I really appreciate your attention. I played for Don James in college. My position coaches in college and my high school coach from Akron, Ohio, were the most influential coaches in my career. We live in a world today where the kids do not have a whole lot of direction. In November of this past year, the one-parent homes surpassed the two-parent homes.

When I was growing up with my 15 buddies, there was not one of them that did not have both parents at home. Life is different now. What do the athletes do today? They turn to their coaches as role models. Our kids turn to me. You have great impact on these kids. I want the kids to say, "My coach is a man of integrity, and he is a coach that cares about us. He is a good person. If I can follow the life he does. I will be a good person as well."

Later in life, they are going to evaluate you as a role model. Coaches have great influence over people. This is true because you are a coach. You must take the responsibility. Help the young kids. Thanks for your attention and may God bless you.

16

The Versatility of the Spread Offense

Gary Pinkel
University of Missouri
2008

I appreciate all the things you do for the players you coach. With the backgrounds they have and the lack of role models, they need our help now more than ever. One of the people these kids look to is the position coach or the head coach. You can have a tremendous influence on kids. Today's players need positive role models around them. Never sell yourself short as to the importance you have in these players' lives.

In every area of our program, I try to be the best in the country with every thing we do. On Tuesday and Thursday, we run a conditioning program called "The Winning Edge." It is 63 minutes in length. It is the toughest thing our players will ever go through.

For every system we have, we try to be the best at running it. Eventually, that will help us win football games. We have a plan to win at Missouri. The first part of that plan is to *protect the football*. There is no statistic that determines whether you win or lose football games like the turnover margin.

I believe turnover margin is all coaching and attitude. We were eleventh in the nation in turnover margin. That does not mean you will win football games. However, if we can get the turnover margin in our favor, that increases out chances of winning.

You need to know how to protect the ball and learn how to get it out. We do that with every play of every drill we run. You must have a plan to get that done.

The second item in our plan to win is *win the kicking game*. You cannot allow yourself to be beaten by the kicking game. However, having a good kicking game can help you win football games. The only way to develop a great kicking game is to work you butt off.

The third thing we talk about in the plan to win is *eliminate mental errors and have the fewest penalties*. Missouri was the third-least-penalized team in the nation last year. We had a good bunch of players who paid attention. We worked at it, and they knew it was an emphasis. We did not want Missouri beating Missouri. That is what happens when you pile up penalties. Before spring practice this year, I showed our players the stats from the Big 12. There was 400 yards of field position between the least penalized team and most penalized team. You could win a game or two with the field position difference between teams.

A coach asked me how many mental errors are acceptable in a football game. I told him zero. Mental errors are inexcusable and a lack of preparation. The last thing you must do to win is *finish in the fourth quarter*. You have to become a fourth-quarter football team. If you cannot finish a football game, you will not win the game. The only quarter in which you can win a football game is the fourth quarter. You cannot win the game in the first, second, or third quarters. These are the most important things that put you in a position to win. If you have a good offense or defense, then you improve your chances. These are the things that work for us. All those things I mentioned are all coaching.

When I put this offense in at Toledo, we were more of a running team with a good quick-passing game. When I came to Missouri, I knew we were going to struggle because we were not very good. As we began to build the program at Missouri, I watched Mike Leach at Texas Tech. Mike is a great football coach, but he does not care if he runs the ball at all. The point is they win at Texas Tech because of their offense. I was looking for the edge at Missouri. We went to a bowl game in our third year, but we struggled the fourth year. After that year, I talked to a bunch of defensive coordinators. I asked them which offense they did not like to face. Almost every one of those coaches said the spread offense.

They felt the spread offense was an equalizer. If a team could not match up physically or talent-wise with the defense, the spread offense helped them compete. I took that information and soul-searched before I got my offensive staff together to talk about it. I watched Urban Meyer run the offense at Bowling Green and Utah, before installing it at Florida. West Virginia was having great success using that scheme.

The running game has changed in the spread offense. If you have a running quarterback, you can be a great running team. There are many versions of the spread offense. If you go to the spread offense, you must commit to it. You cannot run it as a part of another scheme. It is such a versatile offense that you can determine whether you want to be a great running team or passing team. We went to the spread, and I do not regret it at all. I did a tremendous amount of research on the spread. When I made the decision to go to the offense, I did it for the right reasons.

In our offense, we want to be able to run and throw the football. We wanted to lean on the people who are athletic and could make plays. The best thing we did with the installation of the spread was to go to the no-huddle scheme. Our players are into the no-huddle, and our quarterback did not check a play this year. Our staff controls the entire play calling. In three years at Missouri, we have not huddled.

Everyone who runs the spread has a different twist, and we are no different. We want to spread the field with our passing game to create running lanes. That is what happened in our bowl game against Arkansas. They dropped eight men into coverage and did everything they could to stop the passing game.

Our running back ran for 287 yards and set the Cotton Bowl record. It was the second-best rushing performance in the history of bowl games. Our coaches had enough patience to get away from our great receivers and our quarterback and stick with running the football. We ran it because that is what they gave us.

We tell our players they must be able to play catch. If you cannot play catch, you cannot run this offense. If the quarterback cannot throw the ball to the wide receiver and he cannot catch it, that is Missouri beating Missouri. I know that sounds fundamental, but it is very important.

A big part of the spread offense is play selection. Last year, we ran the ball 43 percent of the time, and we had 21 percent dropback passes, 16 percent quick-game passes, 10 percent screens, and 10 percent play-action passes. That is what Missouri does in our offensive scheme. We ran the ball for an average of 177 yards a game and threw it for 314 yards a game. We threw the ball 57 percent of the time. If you look at teams like West Virginia, who run the option phases of the game, you will see about the opposite of what we did.

We want to spread defenses. Our base set is a two-by-two set (Figure 16-1). The personnel in those positions will change with situations and game plan. The #1 receiver to the wideside will align at the edge of the numbers. The #2 receiver will be on the hash mark. Into the boundary, the #1 receiver aligns on the outside of the numbers. The #2 receiver to that side splits the difference between the tackle and the outside receiver.

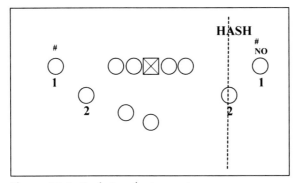

Figure 16-1. Basic two-by-two set

We try to run seven to eight plays a game in unique formations. Teams have to spend time in practice preparing to play us. We use different sets for five straight weeks and the players love the diversion. It adds to our offense, and it is difficult to defense.

The next formation we use is the three-by-one set (Figure 16-2). We number our receivers from the outside to the inside. The boundary receiver is the single-receiver side of the set. He aligns at the edge of the numbers. We have three receivers to the wideside. The #1 receiver aligns at the numbers. The #3 receiver is two yards inside the hash mark, and the #2 receiver splits the difference between the #1 and #3 receivers.

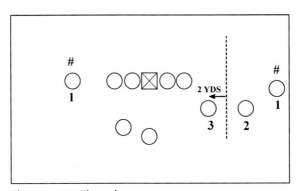

Figure 16-2. Three-by-one set

The other formation we use is the three-by-two set (Figure 16-3). The three-by-two alignment gives us an empty set in the backfield. In the empty set, we use the same boundary rules as the two-by-two set. The wideside receivers align in the three-by-one set, and the boundary receivers are in the two-by-two alignment. The #2 receiver into the boundary splits the difference between the tackle and #1 receiver. It is not complex, and the rules are very consistent. In this set, we can bunch the receivers to either side, but 90 percent of the time, we align in a normal formation.

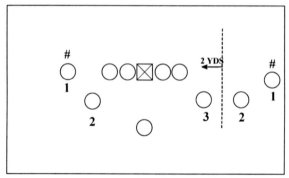

Figure 16-3. Three-by-two set

The first time the offensive line coaches see these sets, it makes them a little nervous. There is a lot of space between our offensive linemen. We split the guard two to three feet from the center with the tackles splitting three to four feet from the guards.

In the shotgun, if you align your quarterback and running back at four-and-a-half yards, you cannot run the ball with those splits in the line. The quarterback has to be six-and-a-half yards deep. Our tailback aligns six-and-a-half yards deep on the offensive tackle. We cheat his alignment on some plays, but 90 percent of the time, that is his standard alignment. With those splits in the offensive line, there will be penetration. Our offensive line comes off the line with a zone step, but it is more of a back step. That means we cannot prevent some degree of penetration by the defensive line. We must have the extra depth by the quarterback and the tailback to run the ball.

We experimented with the splits when we first started running this offense. If your splits are too tight or the tailback is too close, you cannot run the football. The penetration in the line will not allow the back to see the creases. The depth allows the line to get their hands and shoulders on the backs of the defenders and push them out of the way. When we run the zone play, the tailback takes two steps to receive the ball. From there, he has a number of places he can take the ball, depending on how the defenders charge. He can take it frontside or backside to the inside or outside. All of the zone plays break a little differently.

The idea about the offensive line splits came from Texas Tech. However, the additional depth gives us a chance to run the football. In this set, when we align our backs at five yards, that leads to a lot of negative yardage.

When we add motion to the sets, it gives us a new dimension. We start out in the empty set about 75 percent of the time. We motion players back into the backfield and run the football. Defenses like to play a set alignment when we are in the empty set and another alignment when we have one back in the backfield. We use the quick motion to our advantage. We show the empty set and run the play from a one-back set by using motion. Using motion will keep some teams from moving around in their defensive alignments.

We use the motion to go from a one-back set to a two-back set. We use it to go from an empty set to a one-back set and from a one-back set to an empty set. Many people say that causes the defense to move and that causes problems. That is one of the best things we do.

Defenses play us differently when we are in the one-back set as opposed to the empty set. We call the motion "far motion." If the tailback aligns in a receiver position and motions back toward the quarterback, that is far motion (Figure 16-4). The quarterback uses his hand to set the back in motion. We want the ball snapped five seconds after the back moves. That motion puts him on the opposite side from where he aligned. We want it snapped in that amount of time to keep the defense from resetting in their alignments. The defense may move, but it will be on the fly because we will snap the ball.

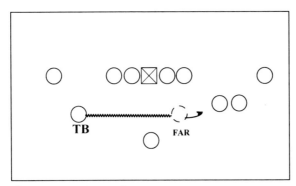

Figure 16-4. Far motion

I am not talking about plays, because you can design the offense you want to run. This is what we do from this offense. We use what we call "near motion" to go from a three-by-two set to a three-by-one set (Figure 16-5). It is the same type of motion, except we snap the ball in three seconds. That means we snap the ball with the tailback in his one-back position. We can run the zone play from this type of motion. The defense tries to make all kind of adjustments to the defense. That means they have to communicate a change of responsibility, which could work in our favor.

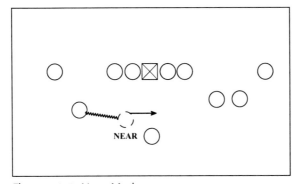

Figure 16-5. Near Motion

I am not going to spend time talking about the plays because I want to cover as much ground as I can. The center calls the snap. The quarterback gives the hand signal to the center. When the center snaps the ball, he yells, "Go." The offensive line reacts to the center's cadence. That helps the offensive line because it is so loud in most stadiums. The offensive line aligns in a two-point stance most of the time.

If we want to go from a one-back set to a two-back set, we use the same calls for the #2 receiver (Figure 16-6). If we align the tailback in the backfield, we call the slot receiver into the set with "near" or "far" motion. To designate the motion runner, we use our terminology, which gets into another lecture. The timing of the snap is the same as before. We snap the ball in five seconds for far motion and three seconds for near motion. We can run a load scheme with the extra blocker in the backfield.

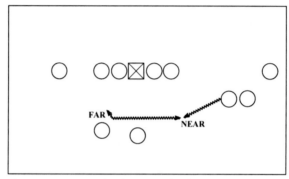

Figure 16-6. One-back to two-back set

We can motion from a two-by-two set into an empty set. We do not do that many times. We usually go from the three-by-two set into a three-by-one set. Every week, we create particular plays from unusual formations and alignments so the defense has additional planning to get ready for us. When we do some of these things, I have to change some of my thinking on the sidelines. However, it is one of the best things we do in expanding the offense and making it difficult for the defense.

Spread offenses are similar when the quarterback runs the ball. On defense, someone has to be responsible for the quarterback in everything we do. The defense has to hold a defender back to take the quarterback in the running game. That is the theory behind the spread offense. When our quarterback was Brad Smith, who now plays for the Jets, he could hurt the defense in a hurry. Our quarterback this year, Chase Daniel, is not as fast as Brad. Your quarterback does not have to run 4.4, but he has to be a 4.7 player with good quickness. They have to run the ball to put pressure on the defense.

We do not want the quarterback running the ball as a steady staple. If the defense does not hold an extra defender to take the quarterback, they are putting an extra defender into the running game. We do not want that to happen, so the quarterback has to be a threat to run the ball. We do not run many plays for the quarterback, but we do have some. We run him on the inside zone play, counter, and speed option. We also run the zone play with an option principle and a load scheme on the option. We always have some special plays that we use from week to week. It is simple, but it is effective and it works because it is designed with our passing game.

On the zone play, we let the quarterback read the backside defensive end. If the defensive end crashes to the inside, the quarterback keeps the football and runs out the backside (Figure 16-7). We can use motion and load the quarterback's run on the zone option. Sometimes, we hold our backside tackle back to make sure the tailback carries the ball. The backside tackle is responsible for the backside tackle or linebacker. However, we slow him down to make it harder on the defensive end to get inside.

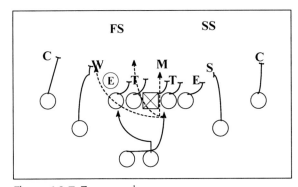

Figure 16-7. Zone read

We want the running back—not the quarterback—carrying the football. If we had Brad Smith, we turned him loose on the zone play. The defensive end on this play is the defender the defense holds back to take the quarterback, which is the principle of the spread we want. If we let the defensive end come down the line and make the play on the running back, that is not the offense we want at Missouri.

The bubble screen is another example of the defense having to be responsible for the quarterback. We package the bubble screen with the zone play and read the defense (Figure 16-8). What we want to do is run the bubble screen. If the defender responsible for the inside receiver aligns wide, we run the zone play. In this case, the quarterback is looking at the outside linebacker.

If he leaves the box and widens with the #3 receiver, the quarterback runs the inside zone play. The quarterback reads the defensive end. If he comes down on the tailback, the quarterback keeps the ball. If the outside linebacker stays in the box, we run the bubble screen. We do not worry about the outside linebacker because he is too far to the inside to make a play on the receiver. If the defense plays the bubble screen to that side, they have one less defender on the quarterback.

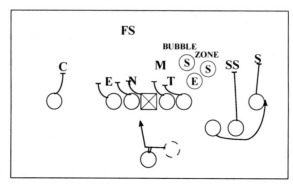

Figure 16-8. Bubble screen

Before he snaps the ball, the quarterback knows which play he will run. If the defense brings the extra defender into the box, he runs the bubble screen. If they play wide with the defender, he runs the inside zone and reads the defensive end. It is a good concept because it stretches the defense. The offensive line runs the inside zone play, and the three receivers run the bubble screen. We run many bubble screens. If we run the zone play when we call the bubble, it puts all the pressure on the backside flow defender.

When we run the speed option (Figure 16-9), the quarterback runs the option off the end man on the line of scrimmage. We try to get a hat on a hat and make five or six yards on the play. We run this play about five times a game just to keep the defense honest and make them scheme for the quarterback. If they do not plan for the option, the quarterback can make the big runs.

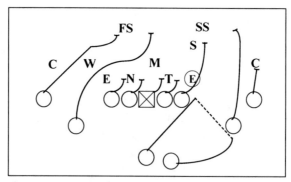

Figure 16-9. Speed option

We teach the quarterback to work the ball to the sidelines when he runs the ball. That way, the quarterback does not take any direct hits. We do some subtle things to help the play. We tighten our playside tackle to make the distance shorter for the quarterback to the option key. That allows him to get rid of the ball quicker. If we have a quarterback we want to carry the ball, the tackle widens to give the quarterback more room.

I hope you see that the concepts we teach all fit together. We do not just run plays; they fit together within the principles of the offense. We stay on our wide receivers and emphasize their blocking on these plays. We want them to be great blockers. The previous season, if our perimeter players had held their blocks a second longer, the plays would have gone for 15 additional yards. We sat our perimeter players down and showed them the films. We showed them that giving more effort on those plays would have meant huge gains.

Tempos are important for our no-huddle offense. Our offense would not be what it is today without the no-huddle aspect. Last year, we were fourth in the nation at 79.8 plays per game. In one game, we ran 112 plays, which was second in the nation for number of plays run. This fatigues the defense and causes them to substitute more. When we create the tempo, it allows us to get an advantage. The defense has to substitute players; they get tired, do not get set, and make mental errors. In practice, we signal plays all the time. There are many different ways to do it. If you saw us on television, you saw four coaches signaling at times. At other times, we had one coach doing it or two coaches doing it.

The first tempo is "fast ball." When we call this, we get into a formation and snap the ball. The perimeter people, tight end, and tailback look to the sidelines and get the formation and play from one of the four people signaling the play. The quarterback tells the linemen the play or protection. When we started doing this with signals, we thought we might have trouble. However, the players took great pride in it, and we had zero problems.

The next tempo is "look." When we signal the look tempo, the players get the formation, but not the play. We align just like fast ball, except we do not snap the ball. Everyone looks to the sideline. We game plan for a formation, and whatever alignment the defense gives us, we run the play we planned against that alignment. If the defense changes, we can change to play.

The "hold" tempo is the one that makes the entire thing work. This takes into account that the defense will change defenses when the quarterback looks to the sidelines. They assume there is a play coming from the sidelines based on their alignment. When the quarterback looks to the sideline, the defense changes their alignment.

On hold, the offense gets the formation and play. However, we know the quarterback is not going to snap the ball right away. He looks to the sideline and is told to run the play called. He turns and snaps the ball immediately. In most cases, we catch the defense in the mist of moving their front or secondary, which complicates their execution. If we do not like the defense alignment, we change the play. During the entire year, we did not have one team try to change the defense on the look. They want to get their defense aligned correctly and do not want to risk being in the wrong position.

If we call a play when we run fast ball and it does not work, that is a coaching error. We have to able to run a fast-ball play against anything we see; that includes a blitz. Selecting the plays you run in a fast-ball situation is all coaching. We can run the motion game from the hold or fast-ball tempo.

"Super" tempo is for our two-minute offense. We align in a three-by-two formation, and the receivers stay on their side of the field. This is "super fast ball." We run the plays as fast as we can. Generally, we take the running back out of the game and put in another receiver. It is an uptempo scheme in an intense part of the game. The play still comes off the sideline, although we have select plays we run in the two-minute situation. In this situation, we can end up with the three-receiver side into the boundary. That sometimes works to the advantage of the offense. It screws up the secondary as to their responsibilities.

The last tempo is "sugar." This is a situational tempo that comes at the end of the game. The quarterback is five yards off the line of scrimmage with the offensive line in a little huddle around him. I will not call it a huddle because I told you we never huddle. It is a little gathering. We do not want the offensive line in their stance forever. We give them the play at 15 seconds, and they go to the line of scrimmage. We want to run the clock. The receivers understand what we are doing. That prevents the offensive line from setting in a stance for 30 seconds waiting for the ball to be snapped.

There are three principles that are important when we spread our offense. We call the first principle "uncovered." The recognition of this principle falls to the quarterback and the uncovered receiver. With the down-and-distance in our favor, we throw the ball to any receiver left uncovered. If it is third down and 16 yards to go for the first down, we do not throw to an uncovered receiver. You have to make sure the defense covers everyone on the football field. This situation occurs numerous times with outside motion by a tailback.

The second principle is the "hitch" scheme. In 60 percent of our dropback or quick-passing game, we have a hitch pattern somewhere on the field. Generally, it is to the wideside of the field. In the spread offense, you have to get the ball into the wideside of the field. If you do not, it allows the defense to cheat back to the inside. The hitch rule is purely the responsibility of the quarterback. On the hitch rule, the quarterback can go away from his read and take the hitch anytime he wants. That gives the quarterback a chance to get away from his read and take the hitch because it is open. That spreads the field.

The next principle is the "bubble." The responsibility of the bubble falls with the coaching staff. The bubble screen puts a great amount of pressure on the defense. We call the bubble six to seven times a game. It is like a sweep play for us. We want a minimum of four yards from the play. It usually gets 10 to 15 yards. This play stretches the defense without using play action. The bubble puts true pressure on the perimeter of the defense.

To run this offense, you must be able to deal with the blitz. With the tempos we run, we have many ways to handle the blitz. However, you want to limit what you give the quarterback. Since we call the plays from the sideline, we have in our game plan plays we can run and those we cannot run. In the running game, we have to be able to get our five offensive linemen with a hat-on-hat scheme with the defense. In the passing game, you must be able to block five and six defenders. In our game plan, we do not let the defense dictate what we do. We run our entire offense, but we have a plan to do it.

The NFL says if you can be 40 percent efficient against the blitz, that is great. Last year against the blitz, we had 52 percent efficiency. We are successful because that is the way we practice. We work hard on it in practice. We bring at least five rushers 50 percent of the time in practice. Teams do not blitz us much, because we are good at picking it up. When we block the zone play against the blitz, we get a hat on a hat with the first five defenders to the side we are running.

If we game plan for a fast-ball play and it does not go, it is a coaching error. When we get in the red zone, we "look" almost every play. Defenses do not bring three defenders down and back them all out. Against the blitz, we game plan to get a block on the five most dangerous people on the defense. That could leave two defenders running free on the outside of the play.

In quick-game passing, the quarterback cannot hold the ball. He sets and throws. We throw the slant pattern against the blitz. By throwing a slant pattern, it is a good way to advance the ball down the field. We block the blitz from the inside out. Any defender coming free will be from the outside. If the defense brings an unblocked defender from the outside, he should not get to the quarterback before he throws the ball.

If the quarterback holds the ball and gets knocked down, that is his fault. When we see no defender in the middle of the field, it is like an alarm going off. The quarterback knows he has to get rid of the ball, but it is a great opportunity to go down the middle. In our dropback passing game, the quarterback has the same rules. He is in the shotgun set, takes three steps back, and delivers the ball. He cannot hold the ball.

We use a number of different personnel groups in this offense. We try to get mismatches with personnel groups. We make sure our playmakers get the ball. We find ways to get the ball to the players who can make big plays for us. I want to show you some of the things we do weekly that make it difficult for the defense to prepare for us. This is the fun stuff we do. We run five to seven of these special plays weekly. We put a wide receiver in the backfield at tailback and work the backside against a linebacker playing cover 2 on the slot receiver. We sneak him into the game and throw to him.

We align a tackle wide with the wide receiver and align a tight end in his position away from the wide set. The wide receiver to the tight-end side backs off the line of scrimmage. We look like a three-by-one set; however, the tackle is ineligible, and the tight end is the inside receiver into the boundary. If the defense does not see the tight end, it is a good play.

The next thing we do is put the tight end in the shotgun at the quarterback position and put the quarterback into a wideout position. I told the quarterback he is not allowed to block anyone. The tight end can run the zone play, or we have run a reverse from this set. When we run the reverse, the tight end hands the ball to the quarterback. He runs for three steps and throws the ball back to the tight end, who continues out the backside. We put five wide receivers to one side and run the quarterback zone play away from them. We put the tailback to the three-receiver side and watch the adjustment of the middle linebacker. He is responsible for the tailback in his pass coverage. If he adjusts to the tailback, we work 1-on-1 to the single-receiver side.

Our players love doing this stuff. I had to mature some before I could run these types of plays. I have never done anything like this, but it is what makes our base offense go. It keeps the defense in a guessing mode and makes them spend time in practice preparing for these kinds of plays. This is not our base, and we have fun doing it.

Columbia, Missouri, is right in the middle of the state. We are an hour and 45 minutes west of St. Louis and an hour and 45 minutes east of Kansas City. We have brand-new facilities and have no excuse for not being successful. I appreciate your attention. I want you to remember that all the X's and O's are fine, but the influence you have on your players is the important thing. Do not ever sell the influence you have on young men short. Thank you very much.

17

Shotgun Wide Open Spread Offense

Rich Rodriguez
West Virginia University
2005

My topic tonight is "Running Out of the Spread Offense" which I have been doing for 15 years. I heard Urban Meyer talk about the things he has done at Utah. Everyone has some version of the spread offense running game in his package.

I started running this offense when I was the head coach at Glenville State College, a Division II school in West Virginia. I want to give you some of the background as to why I went to this type of offense. The offense is a shotgun wide-open spread offense and a zone-read scheme.

I stayed there seven years and then went to Tulane University to have some fun down there. When I started running this offense, I had a six-foot quarterback. We started running the zone play out of the shotgun. I was not smart enough to think about the read option from the play. My quarterback was smarter than I was. This kid scored about 1600 on his SAT test.

We practiced the zone play all practice and the defensive end kept making the play on the ballcarrier. After practice, my quarterback told me he would take care of the defensive end tomorrow. I asked him what he planned on doing. He told me he would "read" him and pull the ball if he came down the line after the ballcarrier. That was in 1990, and we stumble onto the read on the zone play by accident.

We had some good years at Tulane when Sean King was the quarterback there. When we went to Clemson, we developed another diminution. We had a quarterback in our offense that ran the ball like a tailback. That added a diminution because of the faking and the ability to run a quarterback trap and other companion plays.

The biggest coaching point I can give you about offensive football is to find something you can hang your hat on. You have to be flexible but simple and fit your offensive schemes to the personnel. I know you cannot recruit in high school, but if you have a big, strong athlete, build the offense around him.

If we can recruit a great athlete that can run and throw, we emphasize those parts of our offense. Our offense is flexible enough to take the things he does well and build the offense around those skills. Your offense has to be simple enough for everyone to understand.

If you have eleven dumb players and can only run one formation, make sure you can execute that formation. It is not what the players know; it is what they can execute. If you cannot execute the zone-read plays, do not run them.

The more people run a particular scheme the faster the defense catches up with what the offense does. Defenses are finding ways to get more defenders into the box. We still run the ball, but we found it goes much better if you can be versatile with your formations.

We hang our hat on the zone scheme. Rick Trickett tells his offensive line we will run the zone play each game as a major part of our offense regardless of what the defense does. If the defense gives us what we want, the play gains 10 or 15 yards. If the defense does a good job, we still gain something positive. Our players believe in the zone play. If the numbers are in your favor, the four- or five-yard runs become 10- or 15-yard runs.

I am going to get into my clinic talk and I go fast. If you have a cell phone, turn it off or put it in your pocket. I do not like the phone ringing because it interrupts me. Besides, having the cell phone in your pocket on vibrate is fun sometimes.

The offense has certain advantages. They know where they are going and when they are going. That means they know the play and the snap count. The offense can establish the tempo of a football game. In our no-huddle offense, we have three tempos that we use. Our regular tempo is a quick tempo as compared to other teams. We have a tempo called indy. The indy tempo is fast but we sometimes change the play we have called. The last tempo is get tempo. The get tempo is a tempo that says, "As soon as the umpire spots the ball, get the hell out of the way. We are running the ball." We practice all three tempos and they are part of the game plan. If the offense knew the defensive alignments before the snap, they could call a play that would go

100 percent of the time. When you control the tempo of the game, that is the situation you get into. We snap the ball so fast that the defense we saw on the last down is the one we see on the upcoming down. If we do not huddle, the defense cannot huddle. I can call the right play for the defense, but we may not execute it or we might be whipped.

Another reason we change tempos is to prevent the defense from stemming from on defense to another. When they align, it is hard from them to communicate a change before we snap the ball. What you see is what you get. On occasion, we have to wait for the defense to align because we are ready to go before they line up. In that case, the quarterback is not sure what the defense is.

Even if I were a huddle team, I would still use tempo to make it hard on the defense. On one down, I would sprint to the line out of the huddle and snap it quickly. On the next down, I would use the regular tempo and try to draw the defense off sides. I would keep them off balance and make them stem early or not at all. When I talk to our defensive staff, they tell me the change in tempo screws them up as much as anything.

I prefer to have fewer schemes and more formations. It is easy to teach formations. I would rather take one run and run it from a multitude of formations than add another run. The first thing the defensive coordinator does on Sunday night as he puts the game plan together is list the formations the opponent runs. He lists all the formations, all plays run from each formation, and how he will line up against them.

We use the no huddle because we can control the tempo. The no huddle eliminates disguises and stem by the defensive line. If you ever watch the classic games of the past on ESPN, the teams that played in those games ran one front, one formation, and only one pass coverage the entire game. They ran power and isolation and had one play-action pass. In present times, nobody does anything like that. Every one is in multiple fronts and formations. They run all kinds of coverages and blitzes. By going to a no-huddle scheme, we eliminate many those types of things.

Running the no-huddle scheme gives the coaches time to change a play. The quarterback does not make an audible and change a play. Although a quarterback is a junior or senior in our program, he uses the checks we call. He knows what are good plays and bad plays, but the coaches make the audible. I trust our coaches more than I trust the quarterback. Some quarterbacks can handle the audible, but most of the quarterbacks I coach watch cartoons on Saturday mornings. They are not watching film of the opponent. Therefore, I trust my judgement and the decisions of my coaches in the press box before those of the quarterbacks.

If you are a no-huddle team, you have more practice repetitions. In a five-minute period, most teams run seven or eight plays. We run 13 plays in a five-minute period. We go fast and get more repetitions for our time on the practice field.

The last reason is important in running the no-huddle offense. It makes conditioning a factor earlier in the game. The most compelling factor in determining the outcome of a game is conditioning. That holds true for professional, college, or high school football. You run your team during pre-season and two-a-days, but after the games start there is that doubt of running them too much. Coaches talk all the time about making conditioning a factor in the fourth quarter. It may be too late by the time we get to the fourth quarter. We have to make conditioning a factor in the first quarter. Our team prides themselves on running the no-huddle offense.

In West Virginia, we have about 50 signs with our slogan posted all over the complex. It is a simple message: spot the ball. That is not just an offensive slogan; it applies to defense and special teams. When the referee spots the ball and gets out of the way, we are ready to play. We take a lot of pride in it and conditioning is a big part of it.

We are a shotgun team and there are advantages of being in the gun. Being in the shotgun gives the quarterback time when a defender comes free on a missed block. It gives the quarterback vision. If you have a short quarterback and put him under the center, he cannot see peripherally the way he can in the shotgun. If we back him away from the center five yards, he sees the outside so much better.

When a quarterback throws an interception, the reason is because he did not see the defender. That is his excuse when he comes back to the sideline after the pick. More times than not, the quarterback is right about the play. I do not expect him to say I saw the defender and threw the ball to him.

I had a 6'5", 245-pound quarterback that could throw the ball a mile. The first game he played, he threw three interceptions. I noticed when he looked to the sideline for the signal he squinted all the time. I sent him to the eye doctor after the game for an examination. The eye doctor called me after the examination and told me he should not be driving a car. The doctor fitted him with contacts and the next game he was 35 out of 45 in the passing game. Vision is important in the mechanics of the quarterback.

What I want to talk about before I get into the zone play is the game plan. When you decide what you are going to emphasize in your offensive scheme, you must have the answers to all the defensive adjustment the opponents will throw at you. We put together what we refer to as an answer sheet. The thing we look at between series, halftime, and during TV time-outs is the answer sheet. It has the adjustments we go to if the defense plays a certain defense. If a team is playing a Bear defense, the answer sheet tells us the adjustments we need to make. We have a series of plays that provide the answers to the questions.

We establish the answer sheet at the end of spring practice or at the end of two-a-day practice. We sit down as a coaching staff and decide what we should do against different defensive looks. The answer sheet does not change during the season. You must have more than one answer for each situation. The answer sheet helps our coach in the press box when thing go fast and we need answers.

An example from the sheet is a change in cadence. We are in the shotgun and the center has control of the snap. The defense watches film of the center snap. If they find the center is in rhythm from the time he looks to the time he snaps, we must have an answer for that problem. To keep the defense from timing up the shotgun snap, the center has to change up his rhythm to keep the defense onsides.

We have to do the same thing with the quarterback. He signals the center when he is ready and the center snaps the ball when he is ready. If you have 15,000 fans in the stands, you can say, "Go." If you have 60,000, it makes a difference with communication. The quarterback has an indicator to let the center know he is ready. At times, the quarterback uses a leg lift, a clap, or a finger signal as the indicator. We give false signals to keep the defense confused.

On the answer sheet, there are solutions for coverages, fronts, and stunts. All our coaches understand what how to use the sheet and what to look for. On the main page of the answer sheet is the down and distance situations. It lists calls for third and long yardage, third and short yardage, third and medium yardage, and every different situation you could possibly have.

There is a special section for a great player. If you have a great athlete, you want the ball in his hands. We list ways to get the ball to the star and beat special defenses designed for him.

One of the biggest advantages of going to a no-huddle offense is the NCAA rules that govern it. There are no NCAA rules that govern the number of players you can have on the field. If you huddle, you can only have eleven players in that huddle. If you break the huddle with 12 players, that is a five-yard penalty. If you are a no-huddle scheme, you can have the whole team on the field before the snap of the ball.

That reminds me of a story. In my early years of coaching, we were struggling with finances. I had a big booster that wanted to donate $10,000 to the football program. He had a nephew playing in our program. This boy was the worst football player I had ever seen. The booster wanted to know if he could see his nephew on the field. I told him he would be on the field for about half the snaps in our game. I told the player I wanted him to check the numbers on the field. I told him to go out on the field, run to the number, stand for three or four seconds and run right back off the field. He was on the field for 35 plays and did not interrupt anything.

I want to get into the zone play. A rip formation for us is a four-wide receiver formation. There are three principles for running the football. The principles are numbers, angles, and grass. That sound simple and it is. When we run to the numbers, it means the number of defenders to each side of the center. If there are four defenders to the right of the center and three to the left, I want to run to the left.

The grass principle relates to the wideside of the field. We want to run the play to the area that has the most room or most grass. The hash marks in the college game are 20 yards off the sideline.

The angles refer to the blocking angle we get with our offensive line. I would rather run at a 1 technique than a 3 technique. It is easier for a guard to block down on a 1 technique than it is to reach block the 3 technique. If the numbers are the same, we run at the 1 technique.

The reason we like the zone play is the fact that the 1 technique does not stay a 1 technique after the snap of the ball. Generally, the 1 technique is slanting somewhere else. The zone play allows us to zone block on moving linemen.

We run the ball to the grass. That means if your numbers and angles are the same, we run to the wideside of the field. If the defense is head up on their techniques and evenly defended on both sides of the ball, we run to the wideside of the field. That gives us more room to run the ball.

The most important thing is the numbers. We want to run and throw to the numbers of the defense. If the defense is in a cover zero, you should be throwing the football one hundred percent of the time. If there is one safety deep, you have numbers to run the ball.

It is still a numbers game because if we run the football, we have four defenders coming to the weakside. The defense shows you three defenders weak and brings the four players from outside the box to balance their scheme. Even with the safety aligned on the hash mark, we expect to get a safety rolled into the box from somewhere. When we design the offense, we must be able to block four defenders to the weakside.

The split between the guard and center depends on the alignment of the defense. If the center has a shade technique on him, the guard is almost toe-to-toe with the center. He has to be in a position to cut off the shade in the zone play.

In our formation scheme, we play with three wide receivers on the field most of the time, and sometimes with four. We name our receivers with letters. We have an X-, Y-, Z-, and H-receiver in our offense. The quarterback is in the shotgun set with the tailback to his right or left depending on the play or blocking scheme. The zone play in the first diagram comes from a "rip Max" formation with the outside zone play going to the left. In the formation, rip means right and Max gives a two backs in a split set in the backfield. We have Y- and Z-receivers in a wide slot right, and the X-receiver in a split position left (Figure 17-1). We tell our wide receivers to stalk the defensive backs unless they can run them off. It is easier to run off defensive backs than to stalk them. We tell our receivers to get in front of the defensive back and allow him to run over him slowly.

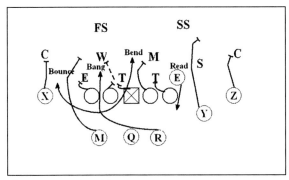
Figure 17-1. Outside zone

We pick up the extra blocking on this play because the quarterback is reading the backside defensive end. If he chases the ball down the line of scrimmage, the quarterback keeps the ball and runs out the backside. That is one reason we run the shotgun.

To run the zone play, the offensive line needs to give a little ground to gain a little ground. We do not give as much ground as traditional zone teams because penetration kills you. We take a quick-set step, turn, and put the hat on the outside of the breastplate of the defender. We would like to knock the defender down the field, but many times it is not going to happen. If the offensive lineman is good enough to get in front of the defender and get run over slowly, that is good enough for us.

That theory is the same with pass blocking. In the pros, you might see an offensive lineman lock up a defensive man, but at the college level that does not happen often. We coach our players to get in front of the defensive lineman, get a good hold on him, and allow him to run over the blockers slowly. The coaching point is to make sure he comes over the top so the lineman can pull him down as he falls backward.

If the nose guard stays in a 1 technique, the offensive center gets help from the guard. The guard stays on the nose tackle until the center can come to take him over. When the center takes the nose tackle over, the guard climbs up for the Will linebacker. The coaching point for the guard is not getting in a hurry to get to the linebacker. He stays on the 1 technique as long as he can. The faster the guard gets to the linebacker, the faster the linebacker steps up.

As long as the linebacker stays deep, the guard can stay on the 1 technique. The backside guard zone steps to the inside and climbs to the next level to cut off the Mike linebacker. The backside tackle zones steps and tries to reach the 3 technique. If there is movement in the 3 technique, the tackle cannot reach him. In that case, he pushes him down past the hole and the back runs on the backside cut back lane. That is a hard thing for a back to do initially.

The way the back runs this play is the whole key to the play. He is toe-to-toe with the tackle in his width. He opens, cross steps, and on the third step he is parallel with the quarterback. The biggest mistake a tailback can make in the zone play from the shotgun is to start immediately downhill after he receives the ball. When the back starts downhill, the Will linebacker starts downhill. When the linebacker starts downhill the guard cannot block him.

The aiming point for the back is the outside hip of the offensive tackle. After he receives the ball, he goes two more steps parallel before he starts to press his aiming point. I do not care how wide open the play looks; he must take those two additional steps. He reads both down defensive linemen to playside. He reads the end first and the tackle second. If we reach the defensive end, he bounces the ball outside.

If the defensive end beats the reach block, the running back's cut depends on where the defensive tackle is. If the center has taken over the shade tackle, he cuts the ball into the hole. If a shade tackle slides down the line of scrimmage, the tailback bends the play behind him. The tailback has three paths to run the ball. He bounces it outside, bangs it into the crease, or bends it back. If the defensive front is an even front, we generally get a bounce or bang path for the tailback. If the front is an odd front, the play is usually a bang or bend path.

It has been our experience, that we will not get a bounce on an odd-front defense. The odd front has a nose tackle, a 5 technique, and a linebacker outside of him. You cannot get outside on that type of alignment.

If we have a split backfield where we have a second back in backfield, it is a Max set. He aligns toe-to-toe behind the offensive tackle. He reads the defensive end for his blocking key. If we reach the defensive end, he goes outside and blocks on the run force player.

The left tackle splits about two feet. The split of the right tackle may be tighter because he has to cut off the 3 technique to his side. If we get the backside tackle cut off, we have a play.

The companion play to the outside zone play is the naked bootleg by the quarterback (Figure 17-2). The offensive line blocks the outside zone play and stay on the line of scrimmage. They cannot get downfield. The outside receiver runs a hitch at five yards. The inside receiver runs the smash route. The smash route is a short corner route. This is a good play because both plays look alike.

The difference between the naked bootleg and the outside zone for the quarterback is the mesh. On the zone play, the quarterback does not put the ball into the pocket of the tailback and ride him. In the zone play, the quarterback does not ride the tailback and decide to pull the ball. By the time the tailback gets to the mesh area, the quarterback has decided what to do with the ball. It is not like a veer play. He gives the ball to the tailback or he keeps it around the end.

On the naked bootleg, the quarterback puts the ball into the pocket of the back and rides him. He pulls the ball after the ride and runs the pattern.

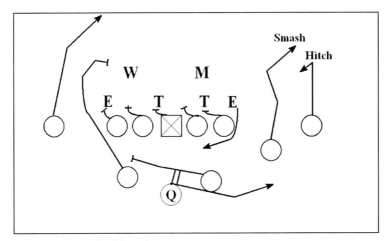

Figure 17-2. Naked bootleg

Once the backside defensive end begins to play the naked bootleg, we run the quarterback trap play from the same set (Figure 17-3). The Max back comes across and kicks out on the defensive end. The quarterback rides the tailback, keeps the ball, and runs inside the Max's block. That is a nice adjustment to that series of plays. That is an answer for the defensive end playing the bootleg.

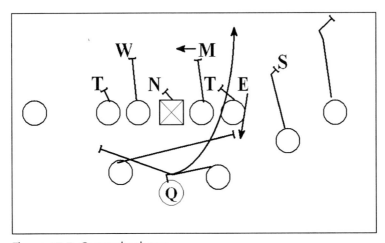

Figure 17-3. Quarterback trap

When we run play-action pass, our linemen do a good job of keeping their pads down. They do not sit with a high hat to tip the defensive linemen. They go through their run blocking and assignments and try to stay down on their blocks. We tell them to go at the family jewels. We do not tell them to go at the knees. Defensive players will protect their knees, but if they are any men at all, they will protect the family jewels first and stay down.

This is different from the naked because we pull the backside guard to protect the quarterback (Figure 17-4). To the twin receiver side, we run a take-off for the outside receiver and a snag route by the inside receiver. The X-receiver comes across the middle on a deep cross. The quarterback rides the tailback and brings the ball to the outside.

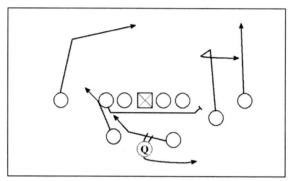

Figure 17-4. Play-action pass

On this pattern, we go further down the field with our routes because we have some protection on this pattern. The play we like to run takes some time (Figure 17-5). Against a cover-3 secondary, we want to get four verticals down the field. We use the same type of action in the backfield. To the twin side, the outside receiver runs his vertical up the numbers of the field. The inside receiver comes into the hash marks to that side. To the backside, we bring the X-receiver into the hash marks to threaten the safety right away. The Max back comes out of the backfield and runs a wheel-up route down the numbers to the backside.

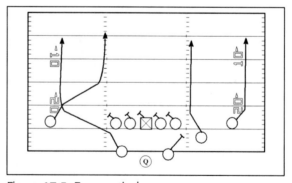

Figure 17-5. Four verticals

The protection for these types of plays is gap protection. Gap protection gives you a zone type of blocking scheme for your protection. We block both backs one way and the line blocks the other. We do not have many man-blocking schemes. When you set up your blocking schemes, you have to consider your personnel.

Your blocking scheme depends on the ability of your offensive linemen. Remember you should always play to your strengths and never your weaknesses. If your linemen are athletic, you can do more man schemes. If your linemen are short, fat, dumpy players, use zone schemes.

I had one player play for me that was two inches from being a complete circle. He was 61 inches tall and 59 inches around. We tried to get him to be a complete circle. We bought him a bunch of cheeseburgers and French fries to help him make it.

I played defense at West Virginia University. When I first started coaching, I was a defensive coach. My first full-time coaching job was as a defensive coach at Salem College in West Virginia. At Salem College, if you could spell Salem they would let you enroll. If you could not spell it, they gave you the S, A, and L, and hoped you could come up with the E and M.

Corky Griffith, a coach from the state of West Virginia, was the head coach at Glenville State. I was 22 years old and this was my first full-time coaching job. I ran the defense at Glenville State. At our first coaches meeting, Coach Griffith comes in the office. He was a good ole' hillbilly and he called everyone "Jack." He told me he wanted me to run the "Cat" defense. Since he was the head coach and I was a company man, I was going to do what he wanted me to do. He told me he coached the Cat defense and one year his team got 16 sacks in one quarter using it.

I told him I had to see that defense. I asked him how to run the Cat defense. He said, "After the offensive linemen get in their stance, you flex the defensive linemen off the ball and back them up five yards." I thought he was talking about the flex defense that Dallas ran at that time. He told me, "You flex all the defensive linemen five yards off the ball. You have all the fat offensive linemen up on the line of scrimmage. We have our defensive linemen five yards off the ball.

"You get your fastest and quickest defensive back and he is the 'Cat.' You put him at the end of the line of scrimmage in front of the end man on the line. Remember, you have the defensive line backed off the ball five yards. As the quarterback starts calling out the cadence, the Cat starts walking up and down the line of scrimmage. He walks up and down the line of scrimmage mocking the quarterback. He points to one of the offensive linemen and tells him, 'I am the Cat and I am going to get you now! I am the Cat and you cannot block me.'"

Coach Griffith went on to describe the Cat defense. The idea is for the Cat to make something happen. He wants to disrupt the offense and get them to jump offsides. He goes from one gap to the next gap yelling, "Here comes the Cat! Here comes the Cat!"

Those offensive linemen start thinking, "What is he going to do next?" You know how those fat offensive linemen hate blocking those small skinny defenders. You can imagine what they are thinking. They get in their stance and then they start yelling. "Watch out, here comes that Cat. Man, I hope that Cat does not come through my gap."

The Cat is trying to get the offense to make a false start to draw a penalty. The Cat goes from one gap to the next gap screaming, "Woo-e, woo-e!" Coach Griffith is serious as a heart attack. He told me to run the Cat defense in practice. He said, "As a matter of fact, I want you to run the Double Cat too." I asked him what the Double Cat was. He said, "You get one Cat on the left side of the line and one Cat on the right side of the line. They both start yelling and screaming at the same time. When the Cat strikes, there will be a hole in the line for him to run through."

I was not going to tell Corky I was not going to use the defense so I made some notes on it. Two weeks later, we started spring practice. I got the practice schedule and saw that I had a 10-minute period to work on the Cat defense. At the end of practice, we had a scrimmage set up. I was to run the Cat defense in the scrimmage.

I had a set of twins on the defense and they were perfect Cats. They were about 5'10' and 190 pounds and they could run all day. So I worked on the Cat defense to get ready for the scrimmage. That first scrimmage we were only running the Single Cat, not the Double Cat.

At the end of practice, we came together to scrimmage. On the first play from scrimmage, the offensive right guard jumped offsides. Coach Griffith came sprinting up to me screaming, "I told you it would work, I told you it would work."

Coach Griffith told the offense to run the play again. The offense wore one of the twins out. The offensive line knocked his butt 20 yards down the field. They ran up and down the field with ease for about five plays. Coach Griffith started yelling at the defense, "You guys are doing it all wrong, damn it." I asked him what he meant by that. He said, "The Cat can't just walk up and down the line of scrimmage like that. It is all rhythmic, Jack, all rhythmic."

When I first went to West Virginia University as head coach, I was about ready to run it. I wanted to be creative, but I was not brave enough to run the Cat defense. We did have a lot of fun with the defense. If I see the Cat defense show up in Florida, I will know where it came from.

Now, most teams are going to some form of the spread offense. People think when you get in the shotgun that you lose the timing of your throws to the receivers. Our timing from the shotgun is just as efficient as it was from under the center. When we throw from the shotgun, we want the timing to be the same as it is from the three-step drop or the five-step drop. If the snap is good, we can get the ball off in the same amount of time as in the drop scheme, and sometimes we can get it off faster.

If the snap is bad, the quarterback's eyes come off the coverage to catch the ball. After he catches the ball, he has to refocus and throw the ball. If the snap is away from his face the timing is good. The timing is the same in the shotgun or under center for the five-step pass. In the shotgun on a five-step pass, we throw it with the same reaction as we do on a three-step drop. That makes the timing the same or betters from the shotgun.

If the quarterback runs a play fake from the shotgun, he has to speed up his throw to keep the timing the same. He play-fakes, sets his feet, and throws to keep the timing the same.

18

Option from the Spread Offense

Clint Satterfield
Trousdale County High School (Tennessee)
2006

Thank you. Many coaches begin by giving some background about their schools, particularly if they are fortunate enough to have a large, impressive facility. In our situation, we are not blessed with a lot of resources in Trousdale County. We are in a very rural community with not a lot of money. Unemployment is high, and people are leaving the county rather than moving in. We lose good athletes instead of gaining them.

Our staffing over the years has been really thin, but I am lucky now to have the best staff we have ever had. With regard to our facilities, we have had to raise money for everything we have (or build it ourselves), and we have had to do it over a long period of time.

We do not have an athletic period within the school's curriculum. All of our athletics happen after school, including the weight program, and that makes it difficult for us.

National Signing Day is this week and I hear coaches talking about which of their best players are signing with which major schools. I did not have one player sign with even a Division III school this year, and yet we won the state championship. My quarterback is a 4.9 guy and the running back beside him is a 4.8 guy, and they busted their tails for six years to get their speed down to that. If any of you are in similar situations, then we can all relate to each other.

Our players and coaches work awfully hard, we have good discipline, and we expect our kids to do things right. Everyone does a good job with that, but the big thing is that we have to be master teachers and master motivators. For us to win, that is what we've got to do.

I have to talk to our coaches and players about our shotgun offense. A lot of people think that this shotgun stuff is a gimmick. Some see it being done on TV and think they have to do it. Others think it looks like it's fun, and it gets the basketball players out for football. Everyone has his own situation to deal with though, and coaches do what they feel they have to do.

On the other hand, some coaches say that they want their team to be physical and they don't want to get away from what has been good to them, and we are the same way. We are not in the shotgun to try to become something that we're not, and I'll talk about that in just a minute.

Another big thing that I talk to our players about all the time, which is essential to our shotgun offense, is that we cannot have fumbles, interceptions, or busted assignments. I constantly stress this throughout practice, and our kids understand it. And then, we are going to keep penalties to a minimum. These are our points of emphasis.

The shotgun doesn't win for us and neither does the no-huddle scheme. Winning is a combination of a lot of things. We are a no-huddle football team and we use multiple tempos. We use three different tempos.

The first tempo that we use is really, really fast. We're going to call it, snap it, and run it like a two-minute offense run out of one formation. We may try to use two different formations in it next year, but we now go two-by-two, and that is our fastest tempo.

The second tempo is a fast tempo in which we get up on the line really quick, line up, get a play called, and then run the play that is called.

The third tempo that we run is a "check-off" tempo. We will do as we did in the second one, in that we are going to run to the line really quick and get our hands on the ground. After we call a play, we will give an indicator. If we like the play called, then we will give a thumbs up and go with what's called. If we don't, we'll dump it, give them another call, and go with it.

Now that's a big thing. I don't think you can run no-huddle with just one tempo. There are teams that run four or five tempos, but we run three.

Why do we run the no-huddle? We hear defensive coaches saying that they want to dictate pace, but with the no-huddle offense, we dictate the pace of the game. We will determine when the ball is snapped. We will snap it at once or we will make the defensive players line up, put their hands on the ground, sit there, and wonder what's coming next, or have to adjust if we move around on them. We are going to be proactive as opposed to being reactive.

I do not like going to the huddle to get the play, coming from the huddle expecting a front, then not getting that front. Then what? Are you going to run a bad play? Are you going to check it off and take a chance on your players getting the new call? Are you going to take too much time off the clock? I do not like all of that.

Instead, we are going to get to the line of scrimmage, get our hands on the ground, and we're going to make you show your hand really quick. If you don't show your hand, then we're going to go faster and we'll make you show your hand. Or we'll make you show your hand and let you stew around, and then we will get the play called that we want, and then we'll go. But in any event, we're going to be proactive as opposed to being reactive.

The next thing that is really big is our conditioning. We don't do a lot of conditioning anymore because practice is so fast. I mean it is really fast and we want to make it fast. We want to make them learn on the run. We will drive kids crazy demanding that they concentrate and listen on the run. We make them do up-downs on the sideline if they fail to get the signals, and we will run everything we do at a very fast pace. Because of the pace of our work, we don't have to spend a lot of time conditioning at the end of practice, so I like that. It fits my personality.

We get a lot more repetitions in practice. I think we can get three plays off in one minute of practice. I remember in the old scheme, when we used to huddle, I would have a script of about 30 to 35 plays and it would take forever, walking in and out of that huddle. When we go no-huddle, all of that walking is over with, and we get a lot of reps.

The next thing about our offense is that we don't make our quarterback do any checking off. No check offs. I don't want kids making decisions for me. So when we make decisions, I have a coach up in the box, and all he does is look at the line. At home games, he is in an end-zone tower and can see every technique across the front. I have another coach who watches the secondary, and he is like a passing-game coordinator. This way, when we go to the line, we are going to get the best call in the secondary with our passing game, or in our run game with our line coach. What I do is call a play and if we are going to go on that third tempo, when we said we don't know exactly what we are getting, then I will just hurry up and get a play called. The team will go to the line and they're going to give a "leg kick," and I'm talking on the phone the whole time. I check with my coaches in the box to see if the play called is what we want against that particular defense. They will give me the okay or they will tell me that the call isn't a good fit for the defense and suggest a better choice. I will signal the play in myself, but I am talking to the coaches all of the time. So that play selection is a collective effort, but everything goes through me. It has worked real well for us.

I am real big on clarity. I want to see it because I am a visual learner. You can't tell me about it. Instead, I want you to show me a picture of it and you have to draw it up. When I go no-huddle and I line up, then you have got to line up. When you line up, I can see what you are going to do and we'll get a good play called.

Another thing that is big with me, and I have to argue this with our coaches sometimes, has to do with wristbands. I know that you have all seen teams utilize wristbands in running the no-huddle offense and that's fine, but I personally despise them. I don't like lining up and looking down at a wristband. Somehow, in or out of the classroom, you have to make kids responsible for learning, so everybody has to see the hand signal, and there is no wristband.

Another advantage of the no-huddle offense is that the two-minute offense is already built in and we don't really have to practice it. We do spend 10 or 15 minutes on Thursday with a clock drill when we talk about spiking the ball, when do they stop the clock, when do they start it back, or when not to flip a formation. That's all we do on the clock drill.

Now, let's talk about why we run the shotgun. Let me explain it by using an example of an offensive lecture we heard the other day. They were under the center in a one-back set, running the zone play and faking the reverse to hold the 5 technique. For us, I can put the quarterback in the shotgun, hand the ball off, and the quarterback himself will hold the 5 technique so that I don't have to use another player to do that.

Every defensive coach knows that if the quarterback is under center in a one-back set, they won't worry about the quarterback running the ball. He is not a threat. There are 11 men on the field, but if you stay in the same perimeter formation with a running back and a quarterback in the gun, it is now a two-back running game. So now I feel like I am playing offense with 12 men. Furthermore, if I'm playing with 12 men, and your 5 technique is no longer a factor, it is almost like I'm playing with 13 men. I hope you can appreciate the math I use in my counting.

I grew up as a wishbone quarterback running the triple option, and I remember being taught that if defenders are hard to block, then they are easy to read. If you have trouble scheming them to block them, or if they are so tough that you cannot block them, then don't try to block them and just read them. It makes things easier. You know, the guys that are hard to read are the ones that just stand there, like our scout teams do sometimes.

I really believe it was easier when my daddy coached because they didn't see as many games on television every day and then come into staff meetings on Sundays wanting to try to run all the things they saw Oklahoma or Florida do on TV. I am tempted just like everyone else is, so the thing that we are going to do is to have a toolbox. We talk all the time about the toolbox. The toolbox is this:

We are going to run the inside zone, the outside zone, the trap, the counter, the dart, and the power O, and that's it. If it doesn't fit into those blocking schemes, then we aren't going to do it.

Our passing game consists of the quick game, the dropback, the sprint-out, the play-action bootleg, and a screen package or two. That's it, and that's pretty simple.

Now, our coaches don't always like to hear this, and I don't like saying it about myself, but what you see on the film is a result of your coaching. You either taught it that way or allowed it to happen. That is a fact and you have to take responsibility for that—bottom line.

I tell our players all the time, all the time, and it gets really personal sometimes. "What I am seeing on film ain't good. I know there is one of two things going on. Either I can't teach, or you can't learn, and I know dang well that I can teach. So you better start learning!" We put the responsibility on them. We are going to keep it in that toolbox, but we are going to tell them those things right there.

Now, let's talk about our option drill (Figure 18-1). In our option drill we put one quarterback in as a snapper, and another in the gun. If you practice the shotgun, the quarterback cannot be standing there and assume that he will get a good snap, and just start with the ball in his hands. The other quarterback will give an underhand shovel, and he has to catch that ball, find the laces, and proceed with the drill.

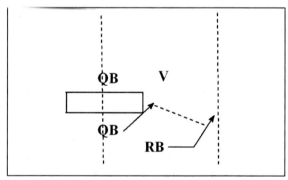

Figure 18-1. Lead option drill

We take every person we have, every running back and receiver (we only have 27 players in all), and everybody is going to be a runner, so there is a big line of players right there. We will put a coach in place as a pitch read, and we will put a cone on the other hash. We will teach the running back that he will run like a bat out of Hades, parallel to the line of scrimmage, and he is going to run to that hash mark flying. He will open up, cross over, and his eyes will be on the quarterback, and he is going to run to the field as fast as he can run. When he catches the pitch he will come downhill.

To the field, we tell the quarterback to attack the outside shoulder and pitch the ball unless he widens. If he widens and creates a running gap inside, then we will just take it inside, but we want the ball pitched. We are coming downhill, we are attacking the outside shoulder, and we are going to pitch the football.

The big thing here is that I think you have to go to the basketball pitch. When I played, it was all "thumb under." But a coach convinced me a long time ago that it's the basketball pitch, that's the pitch. The reason is that the basketball pitch can be pushed down the line, while the thumb-under pitch is always pitched behind.

We tell our running back to stay on that line, on the "ceiling," running towards the sideline. As soon as that quarterback looks at you and makes eye contact, then you break down, come off of that "ceiling," come down at 45 degrees, and go for the corner pylon. That is the angle, and the pitch will be a good pitch. As you will see on the tape, the pitch could be as much as 10 to 12 yards. It is wide, it's downhill, and it is really good. That's the first thing we are going to do. We are going to teach that pitch.

The next thing we are going to do is have a dive read key right there, the next defender out will be the pitch read key, and we are going to split our running backs to here and here (Figure 18-2). We use the word "phase" to tell our back to get into phase with the quarterback. We put a cone three yards behind the quarterback and we tell that back that as soon as the ball is snapped to run and try to get right behind that cone. His inside foot is up and he is going to drop and he is running for three yards right behind the quarterback.

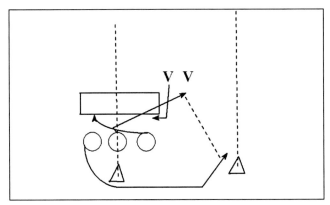

Figure 18-2. Triple option drill

When he sees the disconnect between the quarterback and running back on the zone play, he will spin, keep his eyes on the quarterback, and get right on the ceiling that he worked to get on when he was in the backfield in the lead option drill.

He has got to learn to get on the ceiling, and he has to learn to stay on that ceiling until the quarterback makes eye contact with him. Then he will break down at 45 degrees and aim at the corner pylon.

Now, the quarterback is working on reading that thing. When the handoff key comes down inside, and I'm going to say more about that in a minute, then he is going to disconnect, attack the outside shoulder of the pitch key, and we are running the triple option.

When we read that 5 technique on the handoff phase of the play, we tell the quarterback to give the ball to the player on or outside the offensive tackle whom we do not block, unless he turns his shoulders and comes down inside. Number one, if he turns his shoulders and just stands there, we are going to give the ball. If he stays square and he just shuffles a little bit, we are going to give the ball. We are going to give the ball *unless* he both turns his shoulders *and* comes down inside, because we want to run the football. We do not want to be pulling it and pitching it out on the ground, but if the 5 technique is going to make the hit on the back, we are certainly going to execute the triple option out of it. That's going to happen.

So we are just going to drill that over and over. We will start with the lead option and then we are going to go to the triple option, and then we are going to do two more things.

We are going to teach the quarterback what to do when he is going into the boundary (Figure 18-3). When we go into the boundary, we want the back to run to the bottom of the numbers just flying, and when the quarterback looks at him, he will break down and go for the corner pylon as before. The difference is, when running lead option into the boundary, the quarterback will attack the inside shoulder to force the pitch key to make his decision real quick. If his shoulders turn, then we are going to pitch the football.

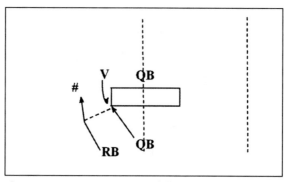

Figure 18-3. Bounty option drill

If he widens, then we are going to run that gap, but we have got to tell the quarterback that it isn't like running it to the field. When running it to the field, he has a lot of time. He runs it to the outside shoulder, and everybody knows that it is: hash – numbers – sideline. For example, if the quarterback runs to the outside shoulder, going to the field, and the end man on the line of scrimmage widens, then he gets under that. The next place he's going is to the hash, then to the numbers, then to the sideline. If we pitch the ball, then it's hash, numbers, and sideline for the running back to get away from the free safety.

Now, when we go into the boundary, we don't want to go hash because we are already there. We don't want to be on the numbers. We want the quarterback to come downhill, attack the inside shoulder, and force the issue really, really fast. The quarterback has to make a quick decision when we run the lead option into the boundary.

From there, we get into what we call rocket (Figure 18-4). We put a running back by the quarterback and another in the slot and we run what we call a bounce technique. We run the zone play against a dive-read key and a pitch-read key. The slot gets on the ceiling going down, and we're running the triple option.

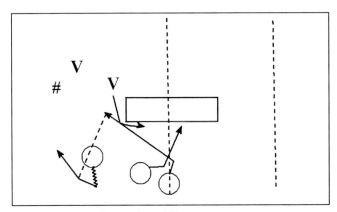

Figure 18-4. Rocker option drill

We have two-foot spacing across the line, and our back starts out directly behind the tackle. We may fudge him some on certain plays, but when he bounces, his heels will be on the quarterback's toes and our quarterback's heels are five yards from the front point of the football. That way the back is just a little bit ahead of the quarterback, where we get that good across parallel mesh. So we will do this out of rocket.

Then, we'll get in here with our quarterback, and we'll have a runner here, and another runner here, and we'll run the Utah play (Figure 18-5). We have a dive read and a pitch read, and we're going to run him on the ceiling, just as he has been taught. We tell the running back to come down to the cheek of the tackle and get with the guard who is pulling. We are going to power O it, and we are going to tell the quarterback to replace the feet of the other back, and execute the thumb-under read, or shovel read on the dive read, and the next defender is the pitch read.

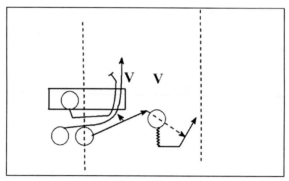

Figure 18-5. Utah option drill

If the dive read comes up, we will shovel it using the thumb-under pitch, and if he squeezes with the down block, we will execute the pitch read off of the next man outside. If the shovel pitch goes on the ground, it is just an incomplete pass, and we remind the referees of this before each game.

This is our option game, and that is how we teach it. We did not invent it ourselves of course, but we think it is pretty good.

Now I want to talk about how we teach our zone read (Figure 18-6). This is an important drill for our running backs. We put a quarterback and a running back in their regular positions here, and we take a bag and lay it right across where the center would be. We have a coach who will snap the ball to the quarterback and then he's going to move that bag. He has to hold the light bag in one hand and the football in the other at the start of the drill. He snaps the ball, and then either holds the bag where it is, or he will move it.

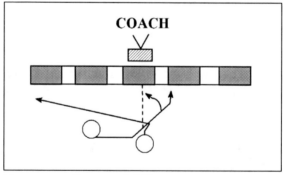

Figure 18-6. Zone read drill

We tell our back when he runs the zone to read the first down lineman on or past the football. If it is an odd front, that would be the noseguard; if it is an even front, it's the man around the guard area to the playside. We tell the back to be "slow to, fast through." That means we want him slow to the line, and when he makes his decision we want him to be fast through the line. We tell him that the best cut is no cut, so that if our linemen have gotten on that down lineman and he hasn't moved playside, we want to "cram him," and it is nothing more than a dive play. Now, if we get movement, then you want him to get to heel level. You've got one "jump cut" back inside. It is A gap to A gap, and there's your play.

The beauty of the zone play, and it took a while for our linemen to understand this, is that everyone is a frontside blocker. There is not a backside blocker, because that play can go anywhere from callside to all the way back.

In teaching this play, we run the back right across there, and if he can, take two little steps past the handoff. Out of the gun, we press the outside leg of the guard and we want him up in there square. If we happen to be under center for some reason, we would press the outside leg of the tackle, but we are in the gun most of the time. So he presses the outside leg of the guard and reads the first down lineman past the ball. If that guy goes, he's got one jump cut and he's going back behind that dummy and getting north. That's the drill we use to teach the zone.

Another drill that I think you have to have to teach the running back is the jump cut drill (Figure 18-7). This is a great drill. These square bags are about two or three feet apart. The back will start in there at the first bag, jump cut it, and then he is going to explode to the next bag. Then, he will jump cut that bag and explode to the next one, and continue past the last bag. Then he will do the drill coming back, developing good habits and switching the ball in his arms.

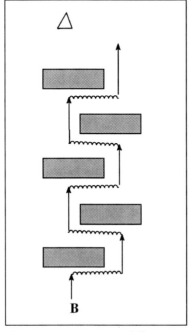

Figure 18-7. Jump cut drill

He's got to explode, and then he's got to jump, and then he's got to explode. As simple as that sounds, again, it isn't the plays, but it's the techniques that win for you.

Now, let's talk about blocking the zone. The first thing that we've seen this year, most of the time, is the odd-man front. We run a lot of traps and they've gotten those people in 4i alignments, and we do not know where their 9 techniques are going to be (Figure 18-8). They are on the line, they're off the line, and they move them around. We have some rules that we use for our lineman that we have to center up the defense. We count the box and number the defense, so theoretically, tackle has number two, guard has number one, and center has zero. But we know that we have to pick up the combinations that we see, so our linemen always talk.

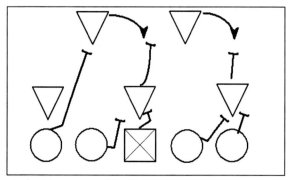

Figure 18-8. Zone-blocking scheme

The onside guard and tackle make a call and work together, and so do the offside guard and center. The covered guy will take a jab step and go through the outside breastplate, while the uncovered guy will take a drop-step and be vertical by the third step also going through the outside breastplate. They will see how the lineman and linebacker are playing their gaps and they each block the man who plays their gap.

On the backside, we make a sift call. That tells our tackle to take a "subtle" step to the inside and lets the defensive tackle go where he wants to go. If he wants to run around, that's okay, and if he wants to go across our face, we'll just help him. The key for our tackle is that he will sift up to the linebacker and block his backside breastplate, because the defense wants to chase with the linebacker and nest with the tackle. Then, if we get his outside breastplate and the ball is disconnected, there's our dive read. Our pitch read is outside, and we have the linebacker blocked. We really think that is important.

We use a similar counting system on other fronts that we see, and we number the defense to set up our combinations. We will still sift the backside tackle, dive read the 5 technique, and run the option outside, while the running back is reading the first lineman on or past the football. There are a lot of things going on in there.

We tell our quarterback that if they have three-over-two outside, then we want to hand the ball off. Now if the safety is very deep, we may go on and run the option and see if he can tackle in open space.

We can also use the word "load" in our scheme. When we say load, we are going to read the 5 technique and load the pitch-read key. If the 5 technique chases the play, the quarterback just keeps the ball.

Let me add that, on anything we call, we can put the word "option" on it and read the backside 5. We can do that off of counter, dart, trap, or any of our plays.

This concludes my presentation. Thank you.

19

The Spread Passing Game

Philip Shadowens
Smyrna High School (Tennessee)
2007

Thank you. It is a pleasure to be here today. We are a team that wants to run the ball first, but we do it from multiple formations. This year, we had two running backs in our offense who ran for 1,400 and 1,100 yards. We did that from the spread look. People think we are going to spread the entire field and throw the ball. This year, we averaged 16 throws a game. We do not throw it all over the field, but we do a lot of things from different formations.

I want to say something about the opportunity that we have as coaches and the obligation we have to our young men. Six years ago in Smyrna, Tennessee, I did a survey about our football teams. I wanted to see how many players came from one-parent families. I wanted to know how many lived with one parent as opposed to living with two parents. I found in our middle-class city of Smyrna, we had 60 percent of our players that came from one-parent families. Most of those players lived with their mothers.

As a coach, I truly believe our first obligation is to set a great example, be a great leader, and be a great molder of men. I think that is more important than anything we will ever teach our players about football. We have to teach them how to be men. We have to teach them how to be good daddies and husbands. We have to teach them how to be good workers one day. I think that is our first responsibility when we deal with those kids. Every year, each senior class gives me a plaque or something like that. Usually it always says the same thing. I do not display them because I do not want them to know what the previous class gave me. My goal is to teach my players a lot about life and a little about football. I think that is our responsibility.

What I am going to talk about today is the spread passing game. Since we were able to win a state championship, people want to know what we did differently. In the quarterfinals, we played a team that we had never beaten. We were 0–18 against them. In the eighth week of the regular season, they beat us 49-0. Because we had a lot of dedicated coaches and players, we played that same team in the quarterfinals and won 9-7. To have a chance to win in the playoffs, we had to convince our players they were a good football team.

We knew we were a good football team. We knew the night we got beat 49-0, everything went wrong. The newspapers in our town wrote all the stories about never beating this team. I guess the players read all those papers. Something bad happened early in the game, and the wheels fell off the wagon. Somehow, going into the quarterfinal game, we had to convince our players that we had an opportunity to win.

We did not lie to them. I told them the night we got beat 49-0 that we were a good football team. They looked at me in disbelief. They thought you could not be any good and lose 49-0. Our coaches stood up and tried to take the blame. We told them we did a poor job of preparing them and a poor job of coaching. We tried to take the loss off our players. Most of the time when you get beat like that, they never believe you. Our players believed we still had a good team and could come back and win the game.

In the finals, we played a team that had beaten us in the regular season. We came back in the finals and beat them. We won that game 35-14. We had a great group of players who believed in what we were doing and were extremely dedicated. I had a great coaching staff that worked very hard.

I think there are three keys to success. This is not anything that you have not heard before.

- Convince the players that they are good.
- Players must believe in what you are doing, and the team must buy what you are selling.
- The longer the season, the more you focus on fundamentals.

We are high school football coaches. We have to play a player sometimes who is not worth a darn, but they are the best we have. When I talk about having good players, I do not mean you must have good players who are going to college on scholarship. We have to convince those players they are good. We know that sometimes our players are not very good athletes and not very good players. It is our job as coaches to convince those kids they can play football. It would be easy to coach a bunch of great athletes. I guess. At Smyrna, we have never been in that situation.

I am not trying to say we do not have any big-time athletes, because we do. I have a receiver this year who is a big-time player. However, my outside linebacker is 5'6" and 150 pounds. He has a 4.0 grade point average. He runs about as slow as I do. He will knock your teeth out. He understands what he is going to face every game, every play, and still makes plays. We have players like that who are not good football players, but it our job to convince them they are.

Players have gotten so street smart, you cannot lie to them because they see right through you. You have got to find a way, and it has to be your way, to make them think they are players.

When I hire coaches, I hire ex-players and guys I have known. You have to be yourself when you coach. I am a screamer. I yell a lot. That is my personality. When things are good, I am going to yell and act stupid. That is fine, if that is your personality. However, you cannot only yell when things are bad. If you do, the players will turn you off. If you are going to yell and jump up and down when things are going bad, you better do the same thing when it is good.

So many times when you come to clinics, you hear about schemes and philosophy. There are 50 different ways to play defenses and at least that many ways to play an offense that can be effective. Whatever you are teaching, you have to believe in it and know it. When I first became a head coach, we had a great quarterback. He was a great athlete and good student. He went to Stanford and became an All-American as a kick returner.

That year, we ran the veer offense with him because that was our best chance to win. The player who followed him was not a runner. He could throw the ball and spent two years at Notre Dame backing up Brady Quinn. We had no running back, but we did have wide receivers. We installed the spread offense. That was our best chance to win, and we made it to the playoffs. We made it to the quarterfinals with him as a freshman quarterback. We matched the offense to what he was able to do. Whatever you know, coach that.

You have to make sure your team believes what you are selling. There are a lot of ways to do things to be successful. I cannot stand a team that is so street smart that they think you are trying to fool them. We are smarter than the players we coach. We have lived longer and had more experiences. We have to find ways to make them believe in themselves and their coaches.

Game eight in our season was an eye-opener for us. There is tendency to change something as the season goes on. When we arrived at week eight in our season, we were 6-2. We played poorly in that game, but we did not think about changing anything we did on offense or defense. We went back to basic fundamentals. From that week until the end of the championship, we focused on fundamentals. We had periods on Monday and Tuesday during which we did nothing but focus on fundamentals. That made a gigantic difference in our players.

The longer the season lasts, you do not need to add more things into the game. The thing coaches have to focus on is going back to the fundamentals. We never wavered and stayed with what we knew. Because of that, we were able to win a state championship.

I have been a coach at Smyrna High School for 13 years. I was raised there and played football there. I was not particularly good and became a volunteer coach there while I was still in college. I have been there all my life. For 12 years, I was a dumbass. In coaching, it is amazing; if you lose your last game of the season, you are a dumbass. People in Smyrna do not mind telling me that because I grew up with them. The greatest thing about coaching at your alma mater is it is your alma mater. The worst thing about coaching at your alma mater is it is your alma mater.

Smyrna, when I was in high school, had 8,000 people. Today, Smyrna is 38,000 people. I was truly blessed to be able to be a part of the state championship. If you do not get anything from this spread offense lecture, remember to stay true to what you believe in and stay focused on fundamentals.

I want to start with three basic formations we run. Everything I talk about today will be versus a one-high safety look. Everyone has different ways of doing things. We call personnel groups by color. After we call the color, we call a formation side. The twins open set is "purple" (Figure 19-1). That is a three-wide-receiver formation with a twins set one way and a split receiver to the other side. There are two backs in the backfield with the quarterback in a shotgun alignment. This formation is purple right.

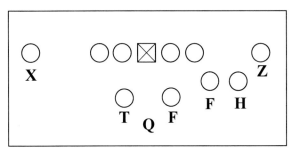

Figure 19-1. Purple right

The X receiver is always away from the call, and the Z receiver and H receiver are to the callside. The tailback sets to the split-end side, and the fullback sets toward the twin side. The quarterback can be under the center or in the shotgun. We can tag the formation and get a different look. If we call F-8, the fullback aligns in a wing set outside the offensive tackle. We have a running strength to the right and a trips passing set that way also.

If I want to get into a double-slot look without changing personnel, I can call T-9 or T-11. That sets the tailback to the split-end side. The T-9 puts him in a wing set outside the tackle. If we want him in the slot, we call T-11. If I want the tailback to the twin side of the formation, I call T-8. That sets him to the two-receiver side outside the tackle. That makes it simple for our players.

We do not want to spend a ton of time learning formations. We want to spend our time learning routes and fundamentals.

The next formation is "black" (Figure 19-2). The black formation is our double-slot formation. The fullback comes out of the game and is replaced by a wide receiver. I do not give a direction to the formation unless two of the receivers are much better than the other two. From this set, we can go to the empty set. We did that 15 to 20 times this year. To get to the no-back set, we tag the tailback. We add T-8, T-9, T-11 or T-12. That moves the tailback right or left and tight or wide. The even numbers go to the right and the odd numbers go left. The 8 and 9 positions are outside the tackle. The 10 and 11 are slot positions.

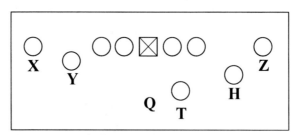

Figure 19-2. Black

Our "white" personnel group is three receivers, one tight end, and one back (Figure 19-3). We have a right and left call with this formation. The tight end goes away from the call. The Z receiver and H receiver go to the direction side, and the X receiver goes opposite the call. To get the tight end to the twin-receiver side, we call R or L. If we call "white right R," the tight end aligns right with the twin receiver set. The X receiver moves up on the line, and the Z receiver backs off the line.

We have many more sets. We have two-tight-end sets, regular pro, and numerous adjustment sets. We create additional formations by moving the backfield personnel around in our regular sets. In our championship game, we ran the pro set, which is our gold personnel, with a fullback set strong or weak. We also ran our purple personnel. Those were the sets we ran for that particular game.

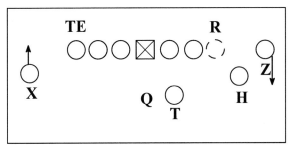

Figure 19-3. White

The field for the receivers is divided into zones (Figure 19-4). We teach our players what zone we are trying to attack. The out/flat zone goes from the wide-receiver alignment to the sidelines. The curl zone is from the ghost tight end's outside shoulder to the wide receiver's alignment. Between the tight end's alignment is the hook zone. We also explain to our players that the zones will change and widen, based on the hash marks. We want our players to the wideside of the field to expand what the defenders have to play.

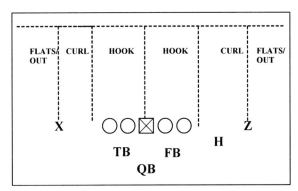

Figure 19-4. Pass zones

The first play in this offense comes from the purple set. That is the twins open set. I am going to talk about four routes we run and how we go about doing it. Our X receiver is an outstanding player; therefore, to the single-receiver side, we get many different looks. Our three-step game is 400 and 500 series numbers.

In our pre-snap read, we look at the weakside flat player. If he is wide, we run the ball. If he is in the box, we want to throw the ball to the X receiver. The release of the receivers is important. We are blessed enough that we do not get press coverage too much. The X receiver is 6'2", 205 pounds, and he can fly. He is hard to press. We have an excellent receiver in our Z receiver also.

Our five-step patterns are the 600 series. In our five-step game, we want the receivers on their release to press the corners on the outside. The first pattern is the 1 route. In the 601 route, the outside receivers run a five-step stop at 12 yards (Figure 19-5). They run the pattern to five steps, plant, and come back down the stem of the pattern. In 12 yards, the receiver needs to get the corner going backwards. If he cannot do that, he cannot play in this part of the offense.

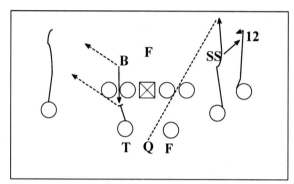

Figure 19-5. Purple 601

In a 12-yard pattern, if the corner is not bailing out going deep, there are one or two things that have happened. Either the receiver is not very good, or we have called the wrong plays. We have not run enough deep patterns to make the corner feel threatened. He does not back up because he does not feel the receiver will go deep. He sits on our short patterns. We must throw the ball deep to take away his comfort zone.

Both wide receivers run the 12-yard stop pattern. It is a mirrored route for us. With each of our routes, we have corresponding routes for the inside receivers. If we do not tag the 601 pass, the H receiver's corresponding route is a takeoff. If the H receiver releases straight up the field, the strong safety widens to the outside. That takes away any angle our quarterback has to make any read. He has to throw through a defender to get to the receiver.

The H receiver stems his route to the inside three to four yards. That depends on the position of the strong safety. He stems inside on the outside half of the strong safety's body. Once he reaches that position, he takes the route down the seam. The route can change depending on the drop of the strong safety. If the strong safety works wide, the H receiver idles down, and we hit him with the ball. If the strong safety runs with the H receiver, he runs deep, and we throw the football to the outside stop pattern.

To the weakside, we have one-on-one coverage. Anytime we can get that coverage, we love it. The X receiver is so good; we get the flat defender running under him almost immediately. If the backer works wide quickly, we have a corresponding flat route run by the tailback. It is tied into his pass-blocking responsibility. This keeps the linebacker from jumping on the wide receiver.

The next pattern in this series is 607, which is a curl route (Figure 19-6). The curl route for us is like the stop pattern. It is run at a depth of 12 yards. When the receiver plants on his fifth step, he does not work down the stem of the route. He works straight back to the quarterback. If we get a 4-3 look, with the linebackers in the box, we throw the ball weak. We read the hole player, but the outside receiver is our target. If the weakside linebacker blitzes, the tailback blocks him, and there is no one under the curl.

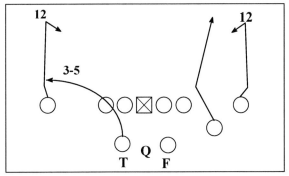

Figure 19-6. Purple 607

If the linebacker does not come, the tailback releases into the flat at a depth of three-to-five yards. We want the wide receiver first; however, the tailback on the linebacker is a good match-up for us. Our quarterback can do that type of read and throw. To the strongside, we run the curl/take-off combination. It is a simple pattern. But, against one high safety, that is all you need to do. They cannot not stop the stop or the curl in that coverage. If the quarterback can throw and the receiver can catch, you do not need to do anything else.

We can get complicated and develop a bunch of terms, but that is not my goal. My goal is to make it as easy as possible for my players. It is not about how much we know as coaches; it is what our players know how to do. We can look complicated and should look complicated to the defensive coordinator, but it has to be easy for your players.

One of our favorite patterns is a tag pattern to the 608 call (Figure 19-7). The 8 route for us is a takeoff route. When we run a 608 pattern, the outside receivers run a takeoff pattern. We have two backs in the backfield and are in a shotgun alignment for the quarterback. We can run all of our running game from this formation.

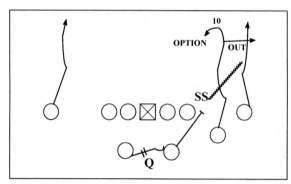

Figure 19-7. Purple 608 H out

We like to run this play from a play-action pass. We call the strong safety a cheater in our scheme of teaching. If they move him up to play the run, we take advantage of that adjustment. If you run this play with play-action and you have a quarterback who can throw, this play is unstoppable. We call this play 648 H out. If the safety plays straight and does not cheat to the line, we run the football. We release the H back on an inside stem. If the strong safety makes a false step or stands still, he cannot cover this pattern.

If the play-action does not make him move inside, we obviously cannot run the ball very well. The H receiver inside releases, gets vertical, and runs the out pattern at 10 yards.

When we throw the route and are successful, the defender has to do something different. He starts to undercut the route. If he does that, the quarterback has to make the perfect throw to complete the pass. To counter that action, we adjust the pattern and call 646 H option. If the strong safety sprints out to cover the out, at 10 yards the H receiver plants and turns inside. The strong safety is wrong every time. It is a simple throw, and it is simple to run. To me, this is the best set in football. You can protect the passer and run the ball equally well. By tagging the tailback, we can get doubles on both sides without any trouble.

We call the double set "black." Our favorite pattern from the black formation is either the three-step stop or the five-step stop. If we run the 601, we run five-step-stop patterns for the wide receivers (Figure 19-8). If we do not tag any routes, the inside receivers run takeoffs. With one high safety, we know as soon as the corners turn and start to run, they are out of the coverage. The wide receiver has to make the corner retreat into the deep third.

The teaching has to be done with the slot receivers. They will be covered by a nickel player or linebacker. They cannot allow the defender to make them widen in their pattern. If the defender makes the slot receivers widen, there is nowhere for the quarterback to throw the ball. We want the slots to attack the outside half of the defender and get deep. If we get a heavy ride by the linebacker pushing the receiver outside, the receiver rips inside and gets up the field.

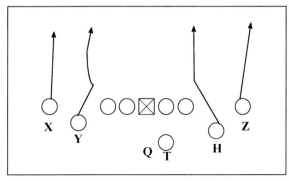

Figure 19-8. Black 601

Should the linebacker leave the receiver, he has to idle his route down and look for the ball. We do not stop the route, but he comes under control up the seam. The throw is made between 12 and 15 yards. The quarterback has to look the free safety off one of the receivers.

We can run the 608 H Y out pattern from the black formation (Figure 19-9). It is the same read for the quarterback as in the purple set, except he has two out patterns. If we tag the play with the option call, the slot receivers turn inside. The quarterback can throw the ball to either side, depending on the match-ups or scouting report.

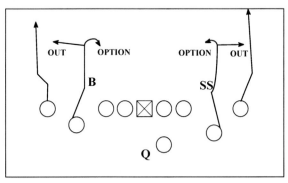

Figure 19-9. Black 608 H-Y option

I want to talk a bit about what we do against two-high safeties out of the double set. If there are five defenders in the box, I like to run the ball. Our favorite route against the cover-2 shell is 601 copy (Figure 19-10). The term copy means all four receivers run the same route. On this pattern, the outside receivers are in the "out" zones, and the inside receivers are in the "curl" zones. They understand it is their job to beat the defender in that zone.

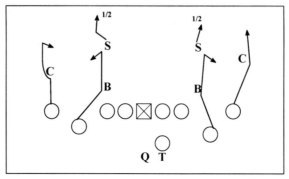

Figure 19-10. Black 601 copy

The slot receivers run their pattern off the curl defenders. In a cover 2, the slot defenders are coached to not let the receivers into the middle of the football field. Their job is to wall off the receiver and run with them deep. The slot receivers inside release, stem inside, and get up the field. The receiver reacts off the defender. If the defender tries to wall the receiver out of the middle, the receiver comes back to the outside and not down the stem. The receiver sticks the defender with a dig cut inside and works to the outside.

It is the receiver's job to get open. If they let a linebacker cover them, they need to be a fullback and not a receiver. We expect the slot receiver to get open. What we teach our quarterbacks against this coverage is that the throw always goes to the inside slots.

As we progress through the season, we tag the pattern with an option tag. That gives the outside receivers an option on their route (Figure 19-11). If the corner retreats, the receiver runs the stop route. If the corner rolls into the flat, the receiver runs a fade to the hole on the sidelines at 15 to 18 yards. When we first install the play, the quarterback does not have the option to throw the ball outside. It is only after the receiver and quarterback learn the concept of the pattern that we allow the outside throws.

The last route I want to show you is a high-low pattern on the safety. It is 601 copy X post (Figure 19-12). The X receiver in our offense is our featured receiver and the one we want with the ball in his hands. This pattern happens as a result of the success you have with the 601-copy pattern. The linebacker cannot cover the slotback in the middle of the field. The safety starts to creep up and stick his nose into that pattern. If he is knocking the ball down or making the tackle immediately, we know he is cheating on his coverage. When that happens, we send the X receiver over the top behind the half safety.

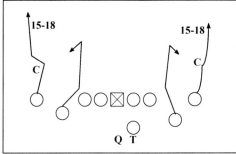

Figure 19-11. 601 Copy option

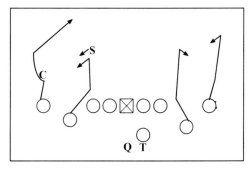

Figure 19-12. 601 Copy X-post

I believe high school safeties are susceptible to this pattern. That is particularly true if the coach is getting into his stuff for not reacting quickly enough on the copy pattern.

Before I stop, I want to show you some things we do on a video. You can see some of the fades, digs, and stop patterns I talked about. You will also see our big receiver in the film. You will understand how simple the scheme is and how easy it is to complete these patterns. If you have any questions about anything I talked about, please ask, and I will try to answer.

We got into the trips set in the film by calling "black over." Black is the double formation, and the term "over" moves the Y receiver from the slot over to the other side as the inside slot receiver. It is another way to get into a different look with very little communication. It is not a new personnel grouping or a new formation. It is an adjustment to black personnel.

We run the slant pattern, but I do not particular like to run it. Too many times, the ball gets tipped by the receiver or the defender and ends up in the hands of the defensive back. For some reason, our receivers do not like to extend their arms coming inside into the linebackers.

If there is anything I can do for you, please call on me. I appreciate your attention, and thank you very much.

20

Spread Formation Pass Offense

Robert Weiner
Plant High School (Florida)
2009

When you come to clinics, you hope to learn some things that will help you. You know the only reason I am here speaking to you today is because of the personnel I had and the success we enjoyed this year. I had an All-American quarterback. At the tight end, I had a 6'3" 230-pound tight end who ran a 4.5 and refused to be tackled. I had three other wide receivers, and two of them ran 4.4s. We had an offensive line that in nine games allowed only three sacks. I am up here talking about offense because I had some tremendous players. It is not because I reinvented the wheel or had some special magic dust that we poured over us.

You can trace the success in the program right back to the assistant coaches. I have a tremendous staff of coaches. Everything in football has different parts. I watched an NFL program the other day, and they were interviewing Herman Edwards. They were talking about the computer and all the advancements made in pro football. When they asked Herman Edwards about his slant on that viewpoint, he said, "All I know is somebody has to draw the cards." He was referring to the computer generated play cards used at so many NFL team practices.

You can put that stuff on a computer, and it comes out professionally done, but somebody had to put that material into the computer. That somebody is the assistant coach. We still draw them manually. When the week starts, we have 50 cards ready to go with the opponent's offense and defense, and they are all in the right order. The key to winning football games is the scout teams. You win football games because of what your scout teams do Monday through Thursday. The scout-team offense is the main reason you win.

The approach to our practice is based on what we see in films on the opponent. We practice whatever is in films. We do not try to guess what the other team will try to do to us. We feel, after four or five weeks, we have put together a volume of work. Should we see something they did not show us on film, we probably saw it two weeks ago.

In our first game of the season, we practiced against the 3-5-3 defense. In week four of the season, we will see another 3-5-3 defense. If sometime in between that time someone plays the 3-5-3 as a surprise defense, we have already practiced against it. We do not try to chase myths. We practice against things we think they will do to us. We practice what we see on film, and we know it will help us. It may not help that week, but somewhere down the road that practice will help. That is our offensive philosophy and approach about practice.

We won the championships in 2006 and 2008. There were big differences in the way we won in 2006 and 2008. In 2006, nobody knew much about us, and we felt we were always behind the eight ball, which made us play with a purpose and gave us an edge. I had players who had a chip on their shoulder every day. Every single day became a challenge to them.

In 2008, they were the greatest group of players I have been around. However, being great players does not win you football games. If you have players with good character but they are passive, that does not win you football games. Somewhere along the line, each team has to find their identity. My quarterback was setting records week after week. He set records for most touchdowns and yards in a half of football in the state of Florida.

We were going along and winning, but I did not feel we were getting where we need to get. We had no edge. We could not find an identity in eight touchdown passes in a half. In week six, our quarterback, Aaron Murray, broke his leg and was out for the season. In the second quarterback, when our starting quarterback got hurt, this team found its identity. It happened on that play. As coaches, we did not know it. All we were doing was coaching the next play. We had a sophomore quarterback, Bill Neely, step in to play. He won seven-and-a-half games for us. Aaron Murray played seven-and-a-half games and won six-and-a-half of them.

Bill Neely had never been in a varsity game except for some mop duty at the end of a game. That night, in the second half of the football game, he threw for

173 yards. In seven-and-a-half games, he threw for 19 touchdowns and 1,900 yards. I think the fact that we were close in the locker room was what won us that state championship. We pulled together after the injury to Aaron, and found resolve in ourselves. Bill Neely was not the only one who stepped up. Orson Charles, our tight end, said to Bill, "I've got you." That meant: "Do not worry, and lean on me. I have your back." Our defense started swarming all over the place. At the beginning of the year, our offensive line had given up six sacks, and Aaron Murray was hit 24 times. The last nine games, we got sacked three times. Those five linemen who were playing football were no longer playing football. They were protecting the sophomore. They were protecting their friend.

Our team came together that day in the second quarter. From that day on, there was never a game they thought they were going to lose. We knew we were talented, but we did not think we had a chance to win the state championship. There was never a doubt in those players' minds that they were going to win.

There was a moment in the championship game that tested our character and won the game for us. On a punt in the first quarter, we snapped the ball over the punter's head, and they recovered at our five-yard line. One of my players got in my face and at the top of his lungs he said, "We got you, coach. They will not score!" He made the first tackle for a loss, and sacked the quarterback on the second down. The third down was an incomplete pass, and we blocked the field attempt on the fourth down. They did not score, and the game was over. We lead 28-0 at halftime and won the game 34-14.

You must be committed to whatever you do. That does not mean we are a team that runs the ball, and that is all we are going to do. Coming down the stretch in our season, we won some games because we ran the football. In the championship, we had an 11-play, 80-yard drive for a touchdown. The touchdown that put the game away came on a 13-play 63-yard drive. Some people do not think we run the ball at all. We throw the football a lot, but we use the passing game as part of our running game. We look at those passes as long handoffs. In our passing game, we want to use the entire field. We teach our quarterback to make full-field reads on certain plays. We are one of a few teams that do that. We want to keep it simple for our quarterbacks. I may give Aaron a full-field read, but with Bill, I gave him one read.

Philosophically, we want to play the game fast. We talk in terms of 10-yard explosions. We want to do everything fast, and that goes for practice also. When we do our conditioning drills, we do them in 10-yard explosions. That goes back to the old adage of "You play like you practice." We want our receivers to be 10 yards fast, but we want the linebackers to be that fast, too. We want to dictate the game's tempo and pace.

VARYING SPEEDS OF OFFENSE

- Green
- Yellow
- Red

The yellow speed is the sugar huddle. When we go to the sugar huddle, I am calling the plays. If we play teams that show late on their defensive schemes, we have a series of plays for them. We develop a number of plays that go against a cover-2, cover-3, or man defense. We use the yellow tempo for teams that change up on us. If we have a team that declares the defense and sits, I read the defense and signal the play to the quarterback. The quarterback and receiver have their own vocabulary to communicate the play. An example would be "Orson, Orson." Orson is our tight end, and he wears number seven as a jersey number. The play would be number seven. The red tempo is the regular huddle call. When you want to run the clock, you use the red tempo.

The green speed is the no-huddle offense. The quarterback calls the plays at the line of scrimmage. We do not necessarily use the green tempo as a hurry-up offense. We have two different modes of offense in the green tempo. We have green and green go. The green go is the hurry-up, two-minute offense. We practice the two-minute offense every day. We practice all the speeds and tempos every day.

We throw the ball 200 times a day in practice. The wide receivers have to catch 200-plus balls in practice every day. I have three wideout coaches. I have 23 coaches on my staff. All our coaches are great coaches. Our quarterbacks look terrific because the four wide receivers make them look great.

We want the defense to play as fast as the offense. In practice, we run a double whistle all the time in drills and scrimmages. The first whistle is to stop the play, and the second whistle is to get everyone to the tackle. Everyone keeps coming after the first whistle. They have to be around the ball by the time the second whistle blows.

PHILOSOPHY

- Dictate pace and style of the game. Make opponent adjust to us.
- Timing
- Spacing and separation
- Protection

We want to dictate the pace of play to the defense. We are going to dictate where the defense aligns and dictate what defense you play. We have plays in our offense that will beat everything the defense can play. We make teams adjust to formations/motions/different looks and run the same plays.

TAKING FREEBIES

- Quick screen
- Bubble screen
- Scats
- Hots

VARYING LEVELS (PROGRESSIONS) OF THE PASSING GAME

- High (deep passes): Must take shots down the field (particularly early)
- Intermediate (middle range passes): Particularly against zones
- Low (short passes): Acts as this offense's version of a running game

Every defense gives the offense certain areas as a no-cover zone. We want to take advantage of what the defense will give. We want to take the easy completions and freebies the defense gives us. To keep the defense from setting on a certain pattern, you have to vary the levels at which you throw the ball. The key notes are to throw the ball deep, and do it early in the game.

I want to show you a couple of things that worked for us. Each year, the personnel are different and you have to change. We changed our offense a lot as the season went along this year. We had the receivers with the ability to do that. Orson Charles could play tight end or fullback, and get down the field. We had another player who was 6'3", 205 pounds, and ran 4.5. We used him at the tight end also. This season, we used a lot of tight end sets in our offense. That let us create a new protection scheme.

At the end of the season, we had one of the greatest defensive lines I have ever seen assembled in high school football. When we worked against them, I wanted to make sure we showed them something different every time we faced them. We had to create different protection packages against them.

In the spread offense, it is a new day. Football is an adjustment game. The defenses are starting to adjust to the spread offenses. We talk about dictating the pace of the game and dictating the defense played against us.

When teams play us, they feel that they must change their defense to cover what we are doing. We prepare for the defense we saw, and they change the game plan. Our main goal is to dictate to them what defense they have to play. We have not snapped the ball, and we have told them they are not going to play a 4-3 cover-2 defense against us.

This is not like Peyton Manning in the early part of his career. The defenses felt they could blitz him. They could not, and he threw for a tremendous amount of touchdowns. They thought he was too smart and they could not blitz him, so the next year, they rushed three and dropped eight into coverage. That coverage might be all right because those players are professionals.

We have played teams that were a 4-4 front and cover-3 in the secondary on film. When we came out in our set, they rushed three and dropped eight into the secondary. This is a high school team. They have dropped eight defenders, but they do not have eight defenders. We are extremely safe with that because we know they have eight in the secondary, but they do not know how to cover. To compound the problem, they have no pressure on the quarterback. I know the defensive coaches in this room will disagree with some of what I am saying.

We teach our quarterbacks against cover 2. We feel like there are certain spot to attack against cover 2. When we have experienced quarterbacks, we teach them eight different cover-2 situations they may face. I start with the basic cover 2. There are three hot spots in the basic cover 2.

In the summertime, I take my players around to different colleges to passing camps. I know what I will probably see in the upcoming season in coverages from our opponents. This was our second year in the spread offense, so I wanted to know about cover 2 or cover-2 man. I ask all the college coaches what their best play is against that defense. This play is called "gamecock" because we picked it up in South Carolina (Figure 20-1). The formation is a trips set to the right side. The X-receiver runs what we call a "show corner." The receiver starts on a slant to the inside, breaks straight up the field, and runs the corner route.

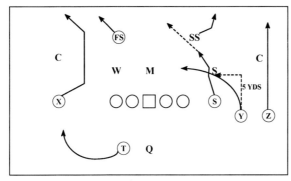

Figure 20-1. Gamecock

The slot receiver, who is the inside slot, runs the post into the middle of the field. The Y-end runs a shallow route into the middle. The Z-receiver runs the go pattern, and the T-back runs the swing.

We teach high principles the first day of practice. Some people will think that puts you in a five-man protection scheme. I do not look at it that way. I look at it as the wide receiver being in the protection scheme. The objective of spread protection is to have fewer defenders in the rush area. If you bring another blocker into the box area, you also bring another defender into the box to block. By spreading the formation, there are fewer defenders to protect against. With five receivers in the pattern, there are more places to put the ball. That is our approach to pass protection.

The responsibilities of the underneath coverage in a cover 2 is standard. The corners roll into the flat areas. The outside linebackers are seam/curl players. The Mike linebacker has the middle hook. The safeties are half players. The pattern we want to beat this coverage with is the seam-post route. That is a skinny post into the middle. In the gamecock, the skinny post is run by the inside slot receiver in the formation. The wideout base their reads on the safeties in the half-field.

The wideouts and quarterback always reads the safety opposite the seam-post pattern. We drive the X-receiver inside into the view of the free safety. He wants the free safety to see him as he drives up the field and into the corner. That is why we call the route a "show corner." The harder the free safety goes to the corner route, the deeper the slot receiver runs the skinny post into the middle of the field. The further the safety gets from the middle, the more to the post the receiver runs.

The slot and quarterback are reading the free safety and feeling the strong safety. We swing the tailback to the weakside. If the Will linebacker goes with the swing, the quarterback knows he has man coverage on the swing pattern. If he stays, we have a chance to get a fast running back in space against the defense.

The Y-end has the hot route if the Will and Mike linebacker blitz. If they blitz, the Y-end gets to the hot pattern immediately. He dives to the inside at five yards, looking for the ball. If they fly out into coverage, he runs his hot pattern five yards up the field and into the inside on a shallow cross. The quarterback reads the free safety and feels the linebackers. The Y-end wants to break up the field to get the Sam linebacker's attention so the slot can wiggle inside of him up the seam. The Z-receiver runs the go route and holds the strong safety with his route. He wants the strong safety to take a step toward his pattern.

We give our quarterback free rein to check the play at the line of scrimmage. We grade our quarterbacks as to their checks. There is more than one right answer to a checked play. In 2006, our quarterback graded 97 percent on his checks. So many times, the quarterback has a much better view of the defense than we do on the sidelines. When you teach the quarterback to play in the spread offense, he is the triggerman and the key to the offense.

You must have a catalog knowledge of the offensive playbook:

- Automatics
  - ✓ Based on defense
  - ✓ Keep them simple
  - ✓ Based upon game plan
- Audibles
  - ✓ Number system and language tied in to two-minute/green offense.
  - ✓ Let the kids (led by the quarterback) create additional code words and signals.
- Knowledge of every player for every play
  - ✓ Formations
  - ✓ Responsibility: Know all positions.
  - ✓ Nuances: Draw up every running and passing play with full explanation.

On Saturday and Sunday, we sit down with the quarterbacks and go over the game plan and checks. We show him what we have seen on the film and give him a list of the checks we like. We give him three or four checks against the cover-2 secondary. We also give him three or four checks against man, cover 3, and anything else we might see. We give him a list of automatic calls against something the defense may do. I do not want to sound cocky, but I want the players to know those plays are going to work.

We do these things daily in practice. We call them "things we do every day without fail."

DAILY PRACTICE: THINGS WE DO EVERY DAY WITHOUT FAIL

1-on-1

- Go to combos, 2-on-2s, and such.
- Play it as a game.
  - ✓ Make everything competitive; the players love it.
  - ✓ One point for a catch, six points for touchdown, two points for defense for incomplete, six points for interception, 12 points for intercepted touchdown.
  - ✓ Usually play to 30 with penalty for losing.
- Run some reps where the quarterback does not know what the wide receiver is going to run (no tells).

Scramble Drill

- High comes low.
- Low comes high.
- Shadow parallel.

7-on-7 Period: Play It as a Game

- 7-on-0: Dummy reps with no-huddle, two groups, 20 reps in a 10-minute period
- 7-on-7: High tempo, enthusiasm, trash talk

Two-Minute Offense: Bingo

- Dummy it in every day.
- Play it live on Wednesday nights (best-on-best).

We run a number of 1-on-1 drills. We work it down to 2-on-2 combination routes against two defenders. They can use zone techniques or man techniques. Every time we do the drill, we want to make it competitive. We want to put something on the line. The loser has to do some penalty. It does not matter whether it is a push-up or an up-down, but someone has to do a penalty exercise.

We work a 1-on-1 drill called "no tells." No one knows the pattern except the receiver who is running it. We do not tell him what to run, and he does not tell the quarterback what he is running. The quarterback takes the three-step drop and has to read the body language of the receiver. This builds the unspoken ties between the receiver and the quarterback. He reads his moves without knowing his pattern.

We run the scramble drill with the quarterbacks and receivers. We have some simple rules. If we run a slam pattern and the quarterback scrambles out of the pocket, the receiver running the corner or high route breaks his pattern and comes back to the quarterback. The receiver running the hitch route or low pattern breaks his pattern and goes long. The shallow pattern runs parallel to the quarterback.

We do a drill called "9-on-4" as a scramble drill. There are nine defenders and four wideouts in the drill. It is a free-for-all drill. All the defenders are defensive backs. There are no linebackers in the drill. We put four defensive backs man-to-man on the four wide receivers and the other five defenders are in a defensive shell, reacting to receivers coming into their zone. The defenders can grab the receivers. They can knock them down. If they get him down, they can jump on him. They can grab the jersey. The receiver runs a pattern, the quarterback scrambles, and he has to find a receiver.

The 7-on-7-period is a high-intensity period. We dummy the drill for 10 minutes with two groups. After that, we go 7-on-7 with the receivers against the defensive backs and linebackers. We want it competitive and enthusiastic. We want the offense and defense to get after one another.

Every day, we work our two-minute offense. We dummy it every day. The real deal comes on Wednesday night. We practice under the lights and at 8:00, we have a live two-minute drill. We play two-minute offense against two-minute defense. We go the best against the best. It is a battle. We do it every Wednesday night.

In our pass-protection schemes, the center is responsible for making the calls at the line of scrimmage. We want to keep the protection scheme simple. If the front is a four-man front, the offensive line blocks big-on-big (Figure 20-2). The offensive line is responsible for the four down lineman and the Mike linebacker. The center designates the Mike linebacker that fits the protection. He may designate the Will linebacker as the linebacker the five offensive linemen are responsible.

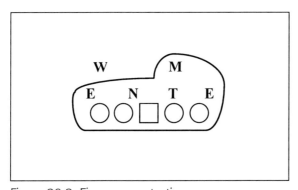

Figure 20-2. Five-man protections

If we release everyone on a pattern and the defense brings six rushers, the quarterback reads the hot receiver on the play. We have a number of special protections. We can unbalance the set by bringing the X-receiver to the trips side and moving the quarterback into the trips side. The single back blocks to that side, and we slide toward the sprint-out. We release the backside defensive end since we are sprinting away from him. We can deliver the ball before he can get to the quarterback.

On play-action pass, we use turnback protection with the offensive line. The back blocks the edge to play-action side. The big thing in a protection scheme is to make sure we are all on the same page. The center is in charge of all offensive line calls, but there must be communication down the line of scrimmage.

The rule of thumb to follow in the protection scheme is to protect the weakside. Any pressure release has to come in the face of the quarterback and not to his backside. If the one-back is included in the protection scheme, the quarterback is in charge of that adjustment. The quarterback's mobility can always help the offensive line. Being able to avoid rushers is a plus in any protection scheme. If the quarterback has to vacate the pocket, the receivers know they are to help him find a receiver.

A drill we use with our pass-protection techniques is a 3-on-3 drill (Figure 20-3). We have a center, two offensive linemen, a wideout, and the quarterback. There are three defensive linemen and a defensive back. We do eight reps of all-out pass rush. It is man-on-man blocking for the offensive linemen. The quarterback has to work on his techniques and keep his head and eyes downfield. The receiver works 1-on-1 with the defensive back. This drill exhausts the offensive linemen. The actual plays we run in practice will be 50-50 run to pass plays.

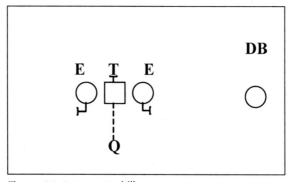

Figure 20-3. 3-on-3 drill

Question: How do you protect against the 3-3 stack?

The 3-3 stack defense is a man-protection scheme (Figure 20-4). With a three-man front, we use a two-man rule. There are five offensive linemen and six defenders in the box. If they all come, the quarterback has to throw hot. The hot receivers are aware of who they are responsible for in the protection scheme. We assign two offensive linemen to two defenders. If we are going to read hot to the outside linebacker on the right, the tackle to that side blocks the defender who is the greatest threat. He cannot block both of them and takes the most immediate threat. If both the linebacker and down lineman rush, the B-gap rusher is the man he blocks.

The playside guard and center block the middle stack. The backside guard and tackle block the outside stack. If we want to secure the pocket, we keep the one-back in to block the playside linebacker.

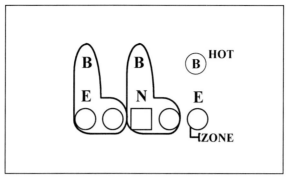

Figure 20-4. 3-3 stack

In the off-season, we work on our protection packages. You cannot pass the ball if you cannot protect the quarterback.

I have enjoyed my time, and I appreciate your attention.

About the Editor

Earl Browning is a native of Logan, West Virginia. He currently serves as president of Telecoach, Inc.—an organization that conducts football clinics and produces the *Coach of the Year Clinics Football Manuals*. A 1958 graduate of Marshall University, he earned his M.Ed. and Rank I education certification from the University of Louisville. From 1958 to 1975, he coached football at various Louisville-area high schools. Among the honors he has been accorded are his appointments to the National Football Foundation and to the College Hall of Fame Advisory Committee on moving the museum to South Bend, Indiana. He was named to the Greater Louisville Football Coaches Association Hall of Legends in 1998. From 1992 to the present, he has served as a radio and television color analyst for Kentucky high school football games, including the Kentucky High School Athletic Association State Championship games.